THE
BABY
BOOMER'S
GUIDE
TO GETTING IT RIGHT
THE SECOND TIME
AROUND

GARY NULL, PH.D.

with Vicki Riba Koestler

THE
BABY
BOOMER'S
GUIDE
TO GETTING IT RIGHT
THE SECOND TIME
AROUND

CARROLL & GRAF PUBLISHERS, INC.
NEW YORK

First Carroll & Graf edition 2001

Carroll & Graf Publishers, Inc.
A Division of Avalon Publishing Group
19 West 21st Street
New York, NY 10010-6805

Library of Congress Cataloging-in-Publication Data is available.
ISBN: 0-7867-0851-4

Manufactured in the United States of America

CONTENTS

Introduction   vii

PART I:
TEN MISTAKES BABY BOOMERS MAY HAVE MADE   1

Mistake Number One:
   Letting Others Control Your Life   3
   Worksheet   25
Mistake Number Two:
   Attaching Too Much Importance to Things   27
   Worksheet   52
Mistake Number Three:
   Planning for the Future   53
   Worksheet   79
Mistake Number Four:
   Avoiding Risk   80
   Worksheet   99
Mistake Number Five:
   Believing Our Culture Is the Best   101
   Worksheet   131
Mistake Number Six:
   Looking for "Magic Bullets" to Solve Problems 132
   Worksheet   147

Mistake Number Seven:
  Trying to Do Too Much 148
  Worksheet 173
Mistake Number Eight:
  Neglecting the Power of Silence 175
  Worksheet 198
Mistake Number Nine:
  Thinking We Have to Age "On Schedule" 200
  Worksheet 225
Mistake Number Ten:
  Forgetting We've Reached a New Millennium 227
  Worksheet 259

PART II: EIGHT LESSONS
EVERY BABY BOOMER SHOULD LEARN 261

Lesson 1. Connect! 263
Lesson 2. Live Consciously 284
Lesson 3. Honor Your Life 294
Lesson 4. Determine Your Focus 307
Lesson 5. Stop Blaming Others 317
Lesson 6. Forget the Excuses 326
Lesson 7. Empower Yourself 336
Lesson 8. Don't Be Afraid to Create
  Who You Really Are 349

FROM THE 1960s to the 1980s a generation of people came of age who wanted to have it all. Indeed, the baby boomers were the first generation that had been led to expect that they could have it all—a superb education; a fulfilling career; a home, complete with the full complement of consumer goods; enjoyable relationships; a family. While, theoretically, the boomers could have everything, practically, many could not. And many, although they attained all the prizes in the game plan, found that they could not achieve the happiness they'd assumed would go with these prizes. They had worked too intensely, made—and in some cases lost—a lot of money, and in the process burnt themselves out. Now, in the new millennium, we have millions of people who, if not completely demoralized, are walking around with a pervasive sense of unease. They have no energy. They feel used up. They wish they could start over.

They can, if they're willing to begin a process of change. One of the things I enjoy most is getting people to a point in their lives where they're willing to make some changes. That's why I wrote *Change Your Life Now* and *Be Kind to Yourself*, and, to a lesser extent, *Who Are You, Really?* The conviction that everything exciting happens at the window of change was an impelling spirit behind these books, and I've been gratified to hear from some readers that that spirit came through and motivated them to make some personal changes. It's wonderful to hear from people of all ages—from teenagers to octogenarians and beyond—that my writing has made a difference in their lives.

But in talking to people of the baby boom generation I've been struck by the fact that so many are dissatisfied or burnt out. These are some of the most well-educated, privileged, and savvy people around. Why, in many cases, haven't they been able to use these assets to make necessary changes and find a measure of contentment? Some have understood, intellectually, the need to look within and reprioritize their lives, but they've been unable to translate that understanding into meaningful change. They've conscientiously tried such exercises as meditating or going on health or spiritual retreats, but their outlooks have not changed at all. Now, as members of this generation leave youth and advance into middle age, many have a feeling of emptiness, or of searching for something they haven't found.

So what?, you might say. It's been this way for every generation; all people have difficulty finding contentment and all have midlife crises. Only I don't think that's true; I've visited places in other countries—rural Italian villages, for example—where that doesn't seem to be the case. And if it's been true for Americans throughout the years, I still think that this generation is having a particularly rough time of it.

The question is why, and here's how I answer it. The baby boom generation grew up in a unique time. They may have reached adulthood in the socially tumultuous late 1960s and in the 1970s, but people actually absorb their values in childhood, and for many boomers that means the 1950s and early 1960s, a time when conventional values, seemingly reinforced by our recent victory in World War II, by the advent of television, and by a growing economy, were stronger than ever. Some conventional values were—and are—good, but some assumptions and attitudes prevalent in those days were counterproductive to human fulfillment. My idea is that many boomers are carrying around, unquestioningly and even unknowingly, attitudes and assumptions picked up during those years that are now causing them to make repeated mistakes in their personal choices.

In this book I've concentrated on ten mistakes that I see baby boomers commonly make. I look at why people may be making them, how they can stop, and how they can go on from there to enrich the second half, or more, of their lives. As in my other books, I ask a lot of questions. I use the question format because, even though I come up with my own answers, I want readers to come up with their own. The implied message to readers is, "Don't agree with me—please." Of course, if you do agree with me, that's fine, but if you don't, the important thing is the investigatory process and coming up with answers that are right for you.

To extend this idea, you may not even think that everything I call a mistake *is* one. For instance, I call planning for the future a mistake. I explain why, but many readers may not agree with me on this one, and I have to respect that. Conversely, readers may come up with some mistakes that I don't see as such, or that I haven't thought of. Basically, I want to start a dialogue, not pronounce and prescribe.

By the way, one of the mistakes I see—and that I'll discuss—is looking for "magic bullets" to solve problems, an approach that was ascendant in the 1950s with the advent of antibiotics, new vaccines, and television advertising. This approach is still very much with us, but the more I see of life the more I'm convinced that it's a mistake. That's why I have to stress that if you want to remake the second half of your life, it's not going to be simple or easy. Achieving insight and change require hard work, and I can't guarantee that simply reading this book is going to revolutionize your life. It's up to you, the reader, to take what is in this volume and use it in whatever large or small ways you can.

To aid readers in breaking out of habitual patterns, after discussion of each of the ten mistakes, I've included a worksheet tailored to that particular mistake. The worksheets describe exercises people can do to begin the process of change. Some of these are things I've suggested to people in my workshops. Some are new. While a number of these exercises require considerable effort, a number are very easy to implement; never let the fact that something is easy, or free of charge, lead you to think it's not of value. That assumption is yet another mistake that people commonly make, and it leads them to miss out on a lot in life.

A note on the exercises: You don't have to do all of them. Read through them all, but as for doing them, I recommend choosing just one exercise from one worksheet that you feel is particularly relevant to you. Then implement that one, giving it your all. Whenever you feel you're ready, choose another one. There are a couple of reasons this approach is better. First, rather than having someone else—me—prescribe what's right for you, you'll be choosing your own way. That's always preferable. Second, experience with thousands of people has shown me that small, incremental change is the most lasting kind. Larger, grandiose regimens usually get dropped.

Finally, this book includes a section on eight lessons every baby boomer should learn. This section was born out of a series of talks that I gave recently, spearheaded by one on connecting with your essential self that elicited an enormously positive response. Lesson 1, "Connect!" is a further development of this talk, and Lessons 2–8 grew out of other talks. My idea is that, after finishing the mistakes section, readers will want to go through this section at their leisure and perhaps refer to it from time to time in the future. These lessons are not, like the worksheets, keyed to the mistakes, but they do expand in a general way on all the themes discussed in the first part of the book. Anyone who knows me knows that I like to get as many perspectives as I can on an issue, and that's what I've done here.

So join me as we look at life. Let's take a journey exploring mistakes made, lessons learned, and the wonder of new beginnings. And whatever mistakes you choose to tackle or changes you choose to make along the way—here's to you—and to a joyous second half of your life!

PART I

Ten Mistakes
Baby Boomers
May Have
Made

Letting Others Control Your Life

CONSIDER the following situation. Today, in what's arguably the most successful civilization in the world, millions of our most prosperous citizens are experiencing a surprising deprivation: they never get to sleep late in the morning. Now, those who know me know that I personally wouldn't consider this a deprivation; I require little sleep and genuinely enjoy getting up with the birds after going to bed a couple of hours previously. But that's just me, and I understand that the vast majority of the adult world considers getting up late once in awhile to be one of life's delicious pleasures. Yet this is becoming an unobtainable privilege to a vast group of Americans—middle class baby boomer parents.

They're just too busy doing important things. Of course they've got to get up early every weekday morning to go to work and/or take the children to school. But then they've got to get up early every weekend morning to go to organized activities with the kids. A morning of rest or idleness is simply not part of the successful American parent's calendar, not nearly as often as it used to be, anyway. Even our phraseology for such a phenomenon has changed: What used to be called "sleeping late" is now referred to as "sleeping in," as if "late," with its connotation of ten or eleven o'clock, or of having missed the boat, is too blatantly graphic a word. Replacing "late" with "in" makes the phrase a little less descriptive, and thus less awful.

Why is sleeping late an obsolete pleasure for many? I'd say it's because they're letting others control their lives. And by others I don't mean their children. Young children don't organize, schedule, and enroll themselves in the myriad of organized sports teams, lessons, and play groups that families are busying themselves with today. Adults do, and other adults are the ones telling them that today's unprecedented level of organized busywork is good for kids and is, in fact, what the good life is all about. These other adults are parents' peers, as well as the "experts" who contribute to the print and broadcast media and paint a picture of what's "normal" and of what is expected of the good parent today. From that picture parents derive a series of messages about what they should be doing as part of the job of raising their children.

Granted, no one has to listen to these messages, or let them guide their life, but millions of parents do. And it's not just parents who let others control their lives. Think of all the consumers who receive an advertising message about a product they didn't even know existed, and then have to run out and buy it. Think about all the workers who are made to believe that working late every day at the expense of their personal lives is necessary for survival. Think of all the people on a working-shopping-consuming treadmill who aren't getting any joy out of the process, but who have become involved in it because someone expected it of them. Note that this someone wasn't necessarily nefarious advertisers—it could have been their parents. My point is not that there is a conspiracy forcing people to behave in certain ways, but rather that people too often cede control of their lives to others.

I think the baby boom generation is particularly prone to this problem. They've been set up for it, because the 1950s, when many grew up, were a time when father, the authorities, the experts, and the government, knew best. At first glance the rebellions of the late 1960s—against the Vietnam War and against the materialism of "the establishment"—might lead you to think that I'm talking about the wrong generation here. After all, wasn't it largely the baby boom generation that led these rebellions? Yes it was, but one has to remember that it was only a small percentage

4

of this generation who demonstrated against the war or became "flower children." As is the case with many movements, the powerful influence of these rebellions was disproportionate to the small numbers of people who actually marched, or danced, in the streets.

One could argue that there were a lot of boomers who, while they didn't fully embrace the counterculture, identified with it somewhat. There were people like this on college campuses all over the country. But it's my feeling that these people had been so primed, in the 1950s, to respect the powers that be, that while they may have undertaken some token rebellion when it was the thing to do, later in life they fell back into the earlier mindset of letting others call the shots. Besides, on many campuses striking a hippie pose was the "in" thing to do, so that for many people whose hearts weren't fully into it, looking like a hippie was no more than an extension of the conformity of the 1950s.

How did the world of the 1950s prime children to let others control their lives? History has always been full of people telling other people what to do, but part of what made America in the 1950s unique is that we as a nation were at the apex of our feeling good about ourselves. We had reason to be. We had recently won World War II; the economy (for most people) was doing well; exciting new products, from frozen foods to plastics to vaccines, were being developed; and exciting new places to live—the suburbs—were being opened up. For these successes we had the military, the government, the business establishment, and the scientific establishment to thank, and obviously, the implied conclusion was, these authorities must know what they were doing.

What's more, television, with its authoritative advertisers and newscasters, came on the scene, and the baby boomer generation was the first to have these awe-inspiring and at times scary gentlemen making pronouncements in their living rooms during their formative years. And while it's true that today's TV ads are slicker and more colorful than those of yesteryear, the tone of those earlier messages was more earnest, more forceful, and less tongue-in-cheek than the tone of today's. Advertisers then were allowed to make more claims about products, and there were more hosts of shows, particularly children's shows, hawking products than there are today. Important too is the fact that there was no consumer movement, and no environmental movement, to counter the claims of advertisers. Today, although we still have powerful corporations trying to control our minds and pocketbooks, we hear and read more questioning voices, even within the mass media.

In general, the whole tenor of the times was authority-fearing. For those who don't remember the time, it's hard to imagine the fear-inspiring power—for people who were quite influential—of the McCarthy hearings. More readers may remember the many years when the white-coated physician was practically a god and when the term "doctor's orders" connoted something akin to a heavenly commandment. The psychiatrist was another highly respected figure. Psychoanalysis was becoming fashionable in the 1950s and all the pronouncements that psychiatry made—for example, that homosexuals were sick or that schizophrenics got that way because of their mothers—were accepted as gospel truth. Public school teachers were still allowed to strike children in the 1950s, and state governments could still segregate the races and enforce their authority in doing so with fire hoses and vicious dogs.

(By the way, many of these situations existed in the late 1940s and continued into the 1960s, covering the period when the baby boomers—born between 1946 and 1964—received their important early impressions of life.)

WHERE WE ARE NOW

But that was then and this is now, you might say. If the 1950s were the era of the gray flannel suit, our wardrobes are more varied now. We're less conformist and less easily manipulated.

Or are we? How many suburbanites have bought sport utility vehicles recently because they are the vehicle du jour, even though they're top-heavy gas guzzlers and the only canyons these people drive down are the ones between big city buildings? How many have gone into tremendous debt buying houses with twice the living space they really need, and rooms they never use? How many are running themselves and their families ragged with schedules, as I've mentioned, that are unnecessarily tight? How many are workaholics, not out of passion, but out of insecurity and a sense of obligation?

If you're one of the people who are letting others' expectations control your life, you're in good company. And you'll probably know you're in this cohort by virtue of having had the question "Why am I doing this?" pop into your head at a variety of times. To get back to a place in life where *you* are actually in charge, I think you have to start with this question, and then ask more. Following are some questions relevant to the issue of regaining control of your own life.

THINK BACK TO THE IMPORTANT DECISIONS YOU'VE MADE. WERE THEY TRULY YOURS?

Yes, I'm suggesting that it may have been someone else's choice to put you in the school you went to, to get you married, to get you a job, even to tell you how many children to have, and where to live. I'm suggesting that there may have been someone else meddling in your life, or a whole lot of someone elses. Now this may or may not be true, but you owe it to yourself to go back in time and try to remember all the conversations you had about these important choices. Whose advice did you listen to? And whom were you trying to emulate? Sometimes it's not a matter of being explicitly told what to do, but of having examples you feel you must live up to.

Can you imagine what your life would have been like if you had been in control? Would you have gone to that college? Would you have chosen that career? Would you have put that much money into a house? Would you have taken on a work-heavy lifestyle to the detriment of your children? And think: Would you have changed things knowing what you now know?

You are not irrevocably restricted by your early decisions, not all of them, anyway. This is an important issue to deal with, because you may assume that you can't change now because you have too much to lose. Wrong. Just lose whatever you have to, and go on. I frequently find that the more you lose, give up, give away, and change, the more free you become. After all, what's the whole point of the exercise of life? What do you want from it? Once you know what you want from life, then you've got to take a look to see if what you've got is going to get you there. If it's superfluous or burdensome, lose it.

ARE YOU LIVING ACCORDING TO YOUR BELIEFS?

Take a moment to review your beliefs, and to see whether or not you are living accordingly. Then ask yourself if your beliefs honor life.

On my radio program's Hidden Agenda series, I asked a simple question. Should a company make a land mine knowing that it is going to hurt innocent people, and that no one is going to be responsible for digging it up once it's been buried? That company has a board of directors, mechanics, technicians, secretaries, and a whole lot of other workers, all responsible for that product being produced, sold, marketed, shipped, and distributed. Those people can say they are religious, and peace-loving, and doing this to protect our country, but look at the results of their actions.

Look at everything that you do. Does it honor your beliefs or not? More importantly, do your beliefs honor life or depreciate life?

WHO CONTROLS OUR COUNTRY?

To understand issues of control in our own lives, it can help to understand the big picture. Think about who controls our country. I took the time to look at who really runs America. It is not about Democrats and Republicans; those artificial categories are irrelevant. People in control are part of multinational groups. There are only about thirty-five international corporations that control 90 percent of all the major business in America. Shortly, they will control the world. These are companies that collectively do nearly $10 trillion in business.

These interests do not recognize boundaries. National sovereignty is not an issue and they have no loyalty to any one group. Rather, they see everything and everyone as a commodity. Every action is based upon its return—that is—profit. Economic interests supersede all other standards.

We allow multinational interests to control us because we believe that they have special and unique gifts and skills. They try to make us feel that we are not as educated, and not as bright, as they are. We therefore need their control and advice.

The people who control America act in ways that are not necessarily representative of what America's people would want. For example, I wouldn't give a five-billion-dollar loan to Brazil to build a hydroelectric plant in the middle of the Amazon that displaces natives and destroys 2000 endangered species. There is no need for it. Nor would I give two billion dollars to a California-based construction company working internationally that has no oversight from anyone.

How does this affect you and me in a practical sense? Here is what happens when you do not realize who is controlling what, and why they are controlling it. From the time you graduate from high school, or even before, you are led to believe that you have to achieve a certain status as an adult. You need financial success. That is measured by the amount of money you earn, the house and furnishings you buy, the entertainment devices in your house, the car in your driveway. You're lulled into thinking that you and your family actually need these material things. But most people in this country need only a fraction of what they have to live comfortably. In reality, you're buying many of these things not for yourself or your family, but for the companies that produce them. You've got to keep these companies going—that's your job. Providing for your family is, in an underlying sense, only a "cover" job.

If you think about it, what do you really need to own a house for? After all, you don't need to own something to live in it. Do you really want to be tied down to one place? If you didn't have to be in one place permanently, wouldn't you enjoy seeing a lot of different places? If you tie yourself down to something you can't afford, you'll have to work beyond normal limits, and you'll be living an imbalanced life.

The people in control of the economy want you to spend what you don't have on what you don't need. So they get you to believe you have to maintain an image, and this becomes part of the American dream. But the part of the American dream they don't tell you about is the nightmare of the payments that you can't meet, and the imbalance in your own life as you devote more time to work and less to family, friends, community, and outside interests. One morning you wake up thinking, "We have everything we're supposed to have. Why are we so dysfunctional?"

Imagine how devastating it would be for the people in power if you stopped buying. They wouldn't like it, but you would have the freedom to do more. If you wanted to go on a long trip with your family, or alone, you could. If you wanted to see what it was like to be a Native American, you could live on a reservation and learn about their history and way of life. If you wanted to go to other countries and enjoy different cultures, that would be an option. If you wanted more quiet time for meditation, you could work that into your life. You'd be able to build your life around what is essential to you.

Letting go of the American dream involves a new mindset. It means that we have to be without many of the toys we are used to having. It also means learning to feel good about yourself in the face of judgments from others. If you are a thirty-eight-year-old college graduate who gives up a job and house and moves to a remote area to start a new life, you are going to be considered irresponsible by most people. You must realize within yourself that you are being responsive to your own needs, and that that is more important than living just for others. After all, you can't live this day over. Then why not give it some value? Until you make your time valuable, it is used only for spending. You are merely a tool of the multinational corporations. Once you change your direction, you do not belong to anyone else's belief system and you are free to go wherever you want to go and do what you want to do. Honor your time from your standards, not someone else's.

WHO INTERPRETS YOUR REALITY?

Most of us think we interpret our reality ourselves when in fact we don't. We are strongly influenced by our parents' or other guardians' understanding of reality, and if their beliefs are flawed, ours are likely to be just as faulty. So you may believe, for instance, that you shouldn't trust men, or women, because of a parent's beliefs. Or you may "know" that people with money don't ever deserve it. Or that recipients of welfare are always lazy. Or that teenagers can never be trusted. Or that older people can't be athletes. The list goes on and on, but the point is that your perception is based not upon actual observation, but upon someone else's generalization.

It's exciting to replace others' beliefs with a new perception of your own. The person who decides to do a marathon when they're fifty, sixty, or seventy years of age goes against everyone else's perception of reality. That person has created his or her own, new perception, which takes courage. It means that person has to be positive and focused, and has to repeat over and over again the positive messages about being able to do it, while everyone else is calling him (or her) old, sick, and incapable. But proving others wrong is part of the joy of creating your own perception, as many people in my running and walking group have shown.

ARE YOUR LIMITATIONS AND CONSTRAINTS BASED ON FALSE PERCEPTIONS?

Have you ever seen how elephants are trained in Indonesia for logging? Early in life, they cross-chain them with large chains that make it impossible for the elephants to move or break free. Later they take all this off and place a simple little reed onto the elephant and tether it to a tree. The elephant could break that with one yank, but doesn't. Early conditioning has created what seems a real constraint, but isn't.

Similarly, many people go through life limited not by real constraints but by illusions based on early conditioning. Like the elephants of Indonesia, they're being controlled not by real chains, but by the ghosts of earlier chains.

IN WHAT AREAS HAVE YOU CEDED CONTROL OF YOUR LIFE TO OTHERS?

Some people have conscientiously remained in control of their own lives in certain areas, but not in others. For instance, I know health-conscious individuals who have designed their own fitness programs and wouldn't dream of letting anyone talk them into eating junk food. Nevertheless, they are completely without satisfaction or autonomy—or a plan to get either—in their work lives. Then there are those who are innovative leaders at work, but who don't have a clue about what's going on with their children.

They've ceded their role as their children's guides to hired help, teachers, and "the experts."

A friend told me the following story. She used to wait outside an elementary school every day for her two children at dismissal time. Often, many of the children coming out of the building, and their parents, would be talking about a class that these children had to be shuttled to right after school called CCD. It seemed to be some kind of religious training, and parents were always talking about car-pooling to CCD and the necessity of not missing CCD. Sometimes kids would want to go to one another's houses, but were told, "Not today, you have to go to CCD."

One day, curious, my friend asked another mother who was sending her child to this activity, "What does CCD stand for?"

The woman didn't know. Here she was, reported my friend, repeatedly carting her child off to some activity whose name she didn't even understand. She'd never even been curious about it. Someone in authority must have said that you had to send your child to CCD (which stands for Confraternity of Christian Doctrine), and so she was sending him.

I'm not saying that religious classes are bad. The point is, rather, that some people are awfully willing to let others control their lives, and the possibility of asking questions doesn't even enter their minds.

DO YOU ACT DIFFERENTLY AROUND DIFFERENT GROUPS OR INDIVIDUALS?

It's interesting to see how most of us act differently around different people because we're tailoring our actions to their response. Even more limited are the many people who stay in the same types of groups with people similar to themselves, because they know in advance how people will respond to them and they want to maintain a consistency in the roles they play. They feel they can't just be who they are in any circumstance, so they stick to one circumstance only.

Imagine if you felt free to go anywhere in the world and inter-act with any part of society, and just be yourself. Only a few adults I know can do this (to children it comes much more naturally). It might be something to strive toward.

WHAT MASKS DO YOU WEAR?

Here are three important questions to ask yourself: "What masks do I wear?" "How do they benefit me?" "From what am I hiding?"

My old friend Tom was a football player. One day I went over to see him. He said, "Gary, I have some writing to show you." He pulled out a box from his closet filled with wonderful poetry. I said, "Tom, this is great stuff. I didn't know you wrote poetry." He said, "Don't ever tell anyone." I asked him why. He said, "They've got an image of me as a quarterback. They'll start to think some-thing is weird about me."

He was right. My reaction was, "You need to move out of this town. You're not going to change them, and they're not going to accept you. You're going to be hiding who you are. You're going to have to pretend to be this one-dimensional super-jock. You're going to spend the rest of your life hanging around beer joints talking about long-gone victories or defeats. They're never going to know that you're a multidimensional person. Why don't you go someplace where you don't have to hide?"

Today he's back in the same West Virginia town, hidden behind a mask that keeps people from seeing a more sensitive part of him, and that keeps him from interacting honestly with the world.

Did you ever wear a real mask as a child, at Halloween perhaps, or in a school play? Remember how hard it was to see, to breathe, and to connect with the outside world? That's the way it is with the figurative masks we wear as adults as well.

Remember how freeing it felt when you finally took off your Halloween mask? Imagine if you dropped your adult masks now.

DO YOU LIVE AN INTEGRAL LIFE?

Here in New York, there is an organization called Integral Yoga Institute that tries to integrate body, mind, and spirit through the foods they sell in their health food store and their classes in yoga. It's a valuable concept that should be standard, but it's not, because most people live fragmented lives. Whatever is fragmented is going to be a source of conflict.

You need to take a look at your life by stepping back and seeing whether or not it is integrated. If it is not, ask yourself why. What's missing? How does the lack of integration impact on how you feel? The answers to these questions will probably be right in front of you.

DO YOU DO THINGS FOR THE SAKE OF APPRECIATION ONLY?

Many of the things we do in life we do to elicit a positive response from others, not for the sake of the activity itself. Frequently, though, we won't admit this to ourselves.

John works late every night. He got into the habit because something needed to be done in a hurry and he reasoned, "If I don't stay late to do it, who will?" His co-workers went home thinking that John was a great guy, and his employers thought they would be a lot worse off without him. But after awhile John is not staying late for the work. He is doing it so that other people will know he is doing it. He needs their positive feedback.

A pattern develops and John forgets that life outside of work exists. He loses a sense of balance. He becomes afraid to reduce his workload and leave on time. Doing so begins to feel wrong. Besides, people might not value him anymore.

It's one thing to work late when a real need arises; it becomes counterproductive when you take on extra responsibilities so that people will think of you in a certain way.

WHEN IS APPRECIATION WARRANTED?

I've noticed that honest people who do good work don't need others to reaffirm their accomplishments. Of course when they do something exceptional, then they generally like someone to pay attention to what they have done, and they should. But playing the martyr day after day does not qualify, in my book. In fact, I'd suggest we start raising our standards and letting people know that we appreciate them only when they have done something exceptional. John, in the scenario described above, may have deserved others' appreciation when he took up the slack in a crisis situation. But by becoming an unbalanced work addict, he's probably short-changing his family, and why should we appreciate that?

On the other hand, much of what we do that's exceptional is never publicized, applauded, or even known about by others. That's why I also believe we need to take a closer look at our lives and ask ourselves, what do we do that's out of the ordinary? What might be worthy of someone else's appreciation, even if it never comes to light? Scrutinizing our own behavior is a part of character development, and developing character is part of the reason we're alive.

It's vitally important to acknowledge yourself for your accomplishments. One way to do that is to keep a journal or make a list of what the day meant to you each night a half hour before going to bed. In it, you can explore what you did that day that was worthy of appreciation. How did you use your special abilities and talents? What did you share with other people? Analyzing your own accomplishments in this way can spur you to continue growing, and can shift your perspective dramatically. It puts you in control of your own life because now you, and not others, are "writing the report card" on your activities. Journalizing or list writing is easy to do, and people have told me that this activity has made a real difference in their lives.

WHAT IF WE DIDN'T NEED RECOGNITION FROM OTHERS?

What would we do differently? We'd lighten up and free ourselves. We'd be more open and spontaneous and able to remember what it was like to be a child. We'd be able to experience things and explore again. That's what I loved about the late 1960s—there was an atmosphere that promoted our being open to experiencing life. Some of us used it to free up our minds, bodies, and spirits. And I'm not talking about drugs here, because some of the freest spirits at that time eschewed drugs and yet reveled in the atmosphere of personal liberation. These were people who felt free to question the prevailing dogmas. They tended to make humor a part of their personal coping strategy, to have no tolerance for hypocrisy, and to refrain from engaging in false dialogue (i.e., they usually said what they thought, which was sometimes jarring, but a refreshing departure from the old norm, especially for women). Interestingly, some of the freest spirits of that time did not look terribly "hippie-ish," and, again, were not involved with drugs.

WHAT HAPPENS WHEN YOU STOP ENGAGING IN FALSE DIALOGUE?

Some people won't like you. In fact, you may be short of friends for awhile.

Stop the false dialogue anyway. Stop disguising who and what you are. Let people see the real you. If someone doesn't accept you for it, then that's not a person you need in your life. If twenty people don't accept you for it, then those are twenty people you don't need in your life. If this means you'll have a much shorter Christmas card list, so be it. With the time you save not writing or opening cards from false friends, you can go out and make real ones.

I've always felt that if people can't accept who I am—and many can't—that's not my problem. I refuse to waste energy trying to fix that. Once you realize that you don't have to disguise or hide anything about yourself—that you can say what you feel and be who you are—you'll be saving more personal energy than you can probably imagine.

A while ago, someone called me who was writing a book on America's most eligible bachelors. This person wanted to write about me, but I told her, "No thanks." When she asked why, I told her I wasn't eligible. She seemed confused and asked, "What do you mean?" I proceeded to explain that I didn't want to get married. I was very happy with the relationship I was having with myself and I wasn't particularly interested in developing a relationship with someone else. She replied, "That's kind of sick, isn't it?" Maybe it is by her standards, but it isn't by mine. So I refused to say the accepted thing, to engage in false dialogue.

Think of what you would be doing if you didn't have to hide your real thoughts and feelings. Would you be working where you are? Would you be living where you're living? Not engaging in false dialogue is the first step in not making wrong choices.

HOW DO YOU PERCEIVE REJECTION?

Rejection can affect your self-esteem. But what if you didn't accept rejection?

When I first started out in New York City, I tried to publish a book about settling in the city and surviving on a shoestring. I didn't have any contacts. I had friends who were authors and if they got one or two rejections, they'd be upset for a week. I had 131 rejections on my first book, and some of them were really nasty. The publishers would send me letters saying that I couldn't write. And they'd ask me not to send them any more unsolicited manuscripts. I was wasting their time, they said.

I'd stop and think, okay, I know I can write. That person doesn't know me. And they're not looking at me for what I've done because I'm not a money-maker for them. Agents wouldn't look at my work because I wasn't a known commodity. They could only make money off something that's known. But I didn't get angry about it. Instead I said, as long as I continue to believe in myself I will never reject myself. So no matter how many times I was rejected—and I've been rejected a million times in my life, it seems—I didn't reject myself. The 132nd time I got that book published.

Actualize your intentions. Don't look at temporary solutions. Seek to develop a pattern of behavior that allows you to feel good all the time no matter what's happening around you. I was as poor as you can be poor. I was under the welfare level, yet I chose never to feel helpless. I never disliked myself for what I didn't have. Learn never to accept rejection on a personal level because the people out there who have rejected you have not thought about the consequences of what they're saying or doing. So don't engage in their insensitive reaction to you. Remember, no matter what happens, you're still a good person. Don't forget that.

WHO'S RESPONSIBLE FOR YOUR FEELINGS?

Whom do you hold responsible for your feelings? Have you ever been stuck in a traffic jam and started to beat on the steering wheel and curse? Who created that anger? The other drivers? The car that broke down in your lane? The highway designer?

You created it. Stop blaming other people for how you feel. You have a choice about how to react to a less than ideal situation. I'm not saying that anger is never called for, but in many situations, such as a traffic jam, it's useless. A person in control of his or her life will realize this, try to drop the anger, and use the time he's stuck in traffic to listen to the radio, or to plan the next day's activities.

Your choices in reacting to situations are not always immediately apparent, but you should be open to them. Above all, always be open to your choices in reacting to what people say. When I hear politicians advocating policies that make no sense, I don't get angry with them. I know friends who do. They get on the phone: "Did you hear that?" I simply say, "Okay, that's their point of view." You don't have to accept that point of view. Let it go through you—it's there and it's gone. Now you're not upset. This is important because you could make a career getting upset about politicians who don't make sense! Some people do. Every time they pick up a newspaper or turn on the TV news, they're livid. They're letting others—the newsmakers—take control of their emotional equilibrium, and it's not healthy.

Only when you react does someone else have power over you. Think about this: There's always yelling before there's fighting. My point is that a fight won't develop if you say, "How's it going?" "Feeling okay?" "You look alright." "Do you mind if I hit you?" "Not hard. You wouldn't mind. You're a nice guy. Thank you." No, it's not going to happen. Instead we say, "You looking at me? You talking to me? Now I've got to kill you." It's the ego talking.

There's a certain way people are conditioned to put their ego out in front. You have to be very careful of how you talk or you could get yourself in big trouble.

Sometimes, with anger, it helps to ask, "Where could this emotion have evolved from?" Sometimes that's how you stop the pattern and break it. You suddenly realize, "This is exactly the way my father dealt with things! I must have learned this response in childhood." We act one way for so long that we forget that there's any other way of responding.

WHO CREATES YOUR EXPERIENCES?

Do you create your experiences? How many things do you do that you really initiate? How much of what you do is merely reaction? You could spend a whole life without making a creative decision for yourself, letting society, or relatives, or friends—or even mere acquaintances or the TV set—determine the course of your days and years.

There's no shortage of people in the world who are ready and willing to help you plan your life. And I understand that the ones who can best attest to this fact are pregnant women and women with young children. A friend with a toddler in a stroller report-ed to me: "Gary, every day when I take my afternoon walk, I get so much free advice I don't even need to subscribe to child care magazines. The crossing guard is telling me how to space my chil-dren! God forbid I should decide to have just one, I'm going to be branded a criminal, and I'll have to change my route!"

It sounds funny, but the sad fact is that many people do have children only because of social pressure. Likewise, many people get particular jobs, stay in them, and die in them, only because of social pressure.

When you create your life, you wake up and say, "Alright, here's my life. Certain parts of it I like, and certain parts I don't. I'm going to do something about changing what I don't like. I'm going to get rid of what's negative in my life, and create a plan of action to achieve the following positives: *a, b,* and *c.* I'm going to take steps *1, 2, 3,* and *4,* and I'm going to try to take them by such and such a date. . . ." Thus do you create your experience.

How do you deal with relatives who try to direct your life?

Blood is thicker than water, they say, the idea being that relatives are more likely to stick by you than friends. I don't know about that, but it sure seems like blood can be more annoying than water! I'm referring to the fact that your relatives often think they can tell you what to do.

The fact that someone is related to you does not entitle them to have influence over you. There are members of my family with whom I spend time and others I avoid. I'm willing to listen to the ones who want to share something positive, but I'm not willing to share the negativity expressed by other relatives. I can't disown them, and I wouldn't want to, but neither do I intend to honor negative attitudes or advice that runs counter to my own spirit.

What meaning do you want from your life?

Once you know what you don't want in life, you have to determine what you do want—not in terms of possessions, but in terms of meaning. You must create your meaning. Perhaps you've fantasized about a goal but didn't have the courage to go after it. You can start by writing it down and looking at it. Each day, you should take a step toward it. Start to picture who you want to be and what you want to look like. If you don't do that, it will never happen. So look forward instead of to the past. When you give too much attention to the old self, you will not give enough to the new self.

Decide to be unpredictable; in the process, you will become who you really are. And while you're involved in the sometimes taxing process of change, don't become defensive or hypercritical. Instead of paying attention to what doesn't work, look at what does. In your experimentation you must have felt things that gave you pleasure or peace of mind. You must have the confidence to recreate those every day. Remember that the healthy self finds pleasure and a sense of peace in life, and that you're entitled to them.

WILL YOU ALLOW YOURSELF TO BE REBORN?

We only hear of being reborn in the religious context, where people have been born again. I use the term to mean starting over, being reborn to the best that you can be, regaining the innocence and honesty of a child. Think of the jaded mainstream doctor who is reborn and becomes an honest holistic physician.

Sometimes we get stuck for five, ten, fifteen, or more years doing something that does not express our ideals. We can become reborn to something that does.

CAN YOU CONNECT WITH THE REBEL IN YOURSELF?

Break the rules. Be a rebel for a change! That's one of my favorite lecture themes because, frankly, I can't imagine a really fulfilling life without some element of rebellion in it. Being a rebel means taking control of your own life and letting your own convictions come to the fore when they conflict with those who would control you. People who know me, or who listen to my shows or lectures, know that the rebellious impulse is a large part of what makes me tick, and I understand that not everybody is cut out to be like this, nor should they be. But I believe everybody should be fired by the spark of rebellion at least once in awhile. It makes us more alive.

What do we admire about the young Marlon Brando and James Dean? We like their boldness and defiance, but there is something more. Defiance, per se, is not a virtue. We must be defiant with a purpose. Being a rebel means standing up to something bigger and stronger than ourselves. Look at Rachel Carson. She, by herself, started the environmental movement in America. No major media supported her. Rather, she was denigrated, and the pesticide industry was allowed to gang up on her. But consider her achievement. One woman, alone, without financial resources, with just truth on her side, waged a single-person war against an entire industry, and a government that supported that industry.

When we're children, defiance comes naturally. When pushed against our will, we pull all of our strength together, and shout, "No!" But as adults, we find this difficult. Too much is at stake. At work, for example, we frequently complain about what is not right, but we don't do anything about it. Being the rebel in an office situation often means the loss of a job.

In every phase of our lives, going with the flow has become the norm. But it was not always this way. Many of us who grew up as baby boomers saw a time when we could rebel. We met en masse in Washington to protest an unjust war, and influenced President Johnson not to run for a second term.

Then the rebellion stopped. More and more people started to adopt mainstream norms, a situation that continues to the present day. What I always seek to do is reintroduce people to the rebel in themselves, with the intent of waking them up to more of their potential.

Can you feel the rebel in yourself? The rebel is that part of you that grabs people's attention and says, "I don't like what I see," or "I can do better than this." In the process, you connect with your true feelings, and you express sentiments that others may share. This can open the way to change—not just for you, but for the world.

Mistake Number One:
Letting Others Control Your Life

1. Eliminate advertisements from your life for a month. To do this, think of ads as noxious fumes you must avoid inhaling or getting in your eyes. Tape all the TV shows you're interested in so that you can fast-forward through the commercials. Don't listen to commercial radio and don't read print ads.
After a month, is your outlook different? _____
Go back to the commercial world for a day. What do you think?

_____

_____

_____

2. Mentally write your own "commercials"—not for material things but for activities you believe are important. Example: "Jogging with the dog is great! It's good aerobic exercise, it helps you meet the neighbors, and Fido loves it. So do it today!"

3. List the important decisions that you've made so far in your life. Which ones were truly yours? Which were made mainly to please others? Which do you feel best about?

4. Look ahead to a decision you'll be making. On paper, list the pros and cons of each alternative. It's okay to consider others' feelings as factors, but the essential thing is to make the decision with a conscious mind and on your own.

5. Is there something you'd like to do but aren't doing because it goes against your image? Write it down._____

_____

Do it. For example, you'd like to learn to water ski, but have never been known as a sportswoman. Go ahead and water ski.

Attaching Too Much Importance to Things

YOU'VE PROBABLY HEARD of AA and OA, Alcoholics Anonymous and Overeaters Anonymous. But if you ask me, we could really use an additional self-help organization: TAA—Thing Addicts Anonymous. Millions of baby boomers need to join such a group badly. They're thing addicts.

Imagine what someone might say at a TAA meeting:

Hello, my name is John, and I'm addicted to things. I wasn't always. When I graduated from college I didn't have or need many things; in fact, then, I was kind of a hippie, and professed to wanting to live a simple life. I wasn't faking, either. For instance, back then, my idea of entertaining was placing a pot of spaghetti in front of my friends. And it was great!

But once I got out into the real world and began working, it was exciting to make money and finally be able to buy a house. I had to buy a few things for the house, of course. Then, when my wife and I started a family, we decided we needed a bigger house in a better neighborhood, and that's when I first noticed my thing addiction. I mean, I started to feel I needed a whole *lot* of things.

First, I needed more furnishings for the new house. Then, my wife and I needed two cars, and we had to keep trading them in for bigger ones, until one of the cars turned into a really huge van, and we actually needed furnishings for the car!

Soon we needed tons of stuff for our kids. There were the clothes and the baby paraphernalia to begin with; later on, we became toy consumers in a big way, buying not just one of each popular toy, but multiples of the same toy when they came in innumerable variations, as with Legos and Barbie dolls and Beanie Babies. We actually did try to control the toy buying, but it wasn't easy with all the TV advertising. Speaking of TV, we needed about five of those, and one of the big ones had to be part of an entertainment center housed in a specially designed wood cabinet with all the latest components in their proper compartments. I also needed a couple of computers in the house, with the latest games and gizmos for those—plus printers, of course. Our kitchen needed a makeover because, even though you could cook in it, it didn't have the right kind of countertops, the right color cabinets, or the particular brand-name appliances that would ensure that our family didn't look like losers to our neighbors. Also, the family needed to possess a snow-blower, a leaf-blower, and several hair-drying blowers because if we didn't, we'd be suspect.

Next, I needed to get several exercise machines—top brands (I always check consumer magazines)—to work off fat that was accumulating because I never did things like shovel snow, rake leaves, or even towel-dry my hair. I also needed to update our four baths and the laundry room—did I mention that when we bought the house our washing machine didn't match the dryer? So we needed a new washer. Another big item was a deluxe leather recliner, to help me relax, because life was getting hectic.

We got a dog, and the dog needed a lot of things, including a special bed with his name embroidered on it, and a couple of sets of really good chow and water dishes because we didn't want him to be seen eating out of the cheap dog dishes from the supermarket. (You need at least two sets of dog dishes, so that you have a clean one when the other's in the dishwasher. Which reminds me, we had to replace our dishwasher recently because of the extra wear and tear from the dog dishes.)

We needed a new dining table recently too. We had to get one made out of a high-grade wood, although we cover it with table pads and a cloth, and keep it in a dining room that's hardly ever used. At the same time, we got a more trendy set of china, and some crystal glasses, for entertaining. Not that we do much real entertaining anymore. Mostly it's just all of us collapsed in front of the entertainment center. We're too busy working—so that we can afford our massive collection of things—to have anyone over.

Nobody has time to come over anyway. They're also too busy and tired from working to afford *their* massive collections of things. I'm beginning to think this life is a little crazy, because even though we have at least five times more stuff than my parents did, we're not all that happy. We don't get to spend enough time with the kids, so they're not all that happy. Even the dog's not terribly happy, because he doesn't care if his dishes come from the supermarket. All he wants is a relaxed home environment where people have time to play.

Which brings me to why I'm here at TAA. I wish I could get back to a more relaxed time when I didn't 'need' so many things, a time, for instance, when a party could mean placing a pot of spaghetti in front of my friends. I wouldn't even have to call it pasta! Where did I go wrong exactly?

Granted, not all baby boomers went wrong like John did. This picture is a gross generalization, and as with all generalizations, it's inaccurate for a lot of people. Still, doesn't John's story ring a bell? I've implied in this vignette that the boomer generation as a whole has been the most materialistic ever, and I do see it that way.

Now don't get me wrong; I think this generation is wonderful in a lot of ways, and that they've accomplished much. They've relaxed our codes of dress, of age-appropriate behavior, and of sex-appropriate roles, all of which means that people are a lot freer to be who they want to be than they were a few decades ago. In the area of parenting, the boomers were the ones who pushed to include fathers in the experience of childbirth and in the daily care of young children. In the field of health, they're largely the ones who are beginning to embrace more natural healing modalities. People condemn this generation for being pleasure-seeking, but I think pleasure-seeking as a concept is good, and that Americans should be doing more of it. The only thing is that, for me, pleasure-seeking has to be experience-seeking, not thing-seeking. And here's where the problem comes in. The boomers often confuse the two.

Why they do this may have to do with the era in which baby boomers grew up. Their parents lived through World War II and all the deprivation and shortages that went with it. After the war, they felt they deserved a few pleasures, one of which was having a family; hence the baby boom itself. But people were also able to indulge in a variety of new possessions, such as houses, appliances, and cars, all of which went along with the new suburban way of life that many Americans were now adopting. A good economy, the growth of our highway system, and the development of cheap mass-building techniques, as in Levittown, were all factors that contributed to the rapid growth of suburbs after the war. People's sense of optimism and entitlement impelled them to move to these new suburbs and start experiencing the good life. We had won the war, after all; America was the greatest country on Earth, and there was no reason we shouldn't live like it. Children who grew up in the late 1940s, the 1950s, and the early 1960s were surrounded by these good feelings, and with the idea that material acquisitions were part and parcel of being an American in the middle of the twentieth century.

It is true that there was a shadow over all of this—the threat of Communism—but part of the proof of America's superiority over the Soviets was supposed to be that we capitalists could produce more and better goods, and that we didn't have to work as long, or wait in line as long, to buy them. So it was almost as if buying things was a patriotic act, because it demonstrated how well our system worked.

An important impetus driving the country's post-war materialism was television. TV raised the American preoccupation with keeping up with the Joneses to a new level, because now you could see not just how the Joneses across the street lived, but also how the Joneses across the country lived, and you might want to get some of what they had. Not just advertising, but the TV programs themselves made this possible; for instance, people in the city could admire the suburban lifestyle of Beaver Cleaver's family week after week. Even a cartoon like The Flintstones showcased a gadget-filled suburban way of life. Fred Flintstone's automatic can opener and hi-fi may have been powered by prehistoric animals, but they still represented the kind of appliances that viewers might want to acquire.

Another factor facilitating the acquisition of things was the development of plastics. One of the reasons baby boom children were able to have more toys than the previous generation did was that plastic was beginning to supplant metal and wood as a cheaper material for toy manufacture. In addition, as toys became cheaper and Americans richer, families could afford to toss toys out and get new ones in a way they never could before. We became more of a "throw-away culture" in the 1950s.

WHERE WE ARE NOW

One of the tenets that baby boomers grew up with is that every generation should enjoy a better standard of living than their parents did. Considering that, and considering the general affluence and material go-get-it-ism of the 1950s and early 1960s, is it any wonder that so many baby boomers today are awash in a sea of possessions?

But there is good news today and it's that some baby boomers, and people of all ages, are asking themselves another question: Why has "standard of living" always been equated with how much stuff you own? And people are concluding that possessions are not necessarily the most important part of the good life. There's a burgeoning trend called "voluntary simplicity." This involves cutting down on what one has in terms of things, but increasing what one has in terms of time spent with family and friends, in local activities embodying communitarian values, and in enjoying simple pleasures, such as gardening or walking. This movement started in the late 1970s as an outgrowth of environmentalism, but it has gathered momentum in the 1990s, and forecasts are that it will continue to do so.

The reasons people turn toward voluntary simplicity are several. First, many people are simplifying their lives to save money; they just can't afford the upper-middle-class suburban lifestyle that is still put forth as the American ideal. Second, there's the environmental aspect, with many advocates of voluntary simplicity feeling that America's high-living, throw-away lifestyle puts a big drain on the planet, one that is unfair to other, less developed, countries, and to future generations as well. Also, modern American life has gotten so complex and demanding that people get tense trying to fit everything they're supposed to do into a twenty-four-hour day; thus, it makes sense to try to simplify the demands and cut down on stress. Further, some are drawn to this movement for philosophical and spiritual reasons; they feel, for instance, that creating a unique child's toy out of materials they have at home is more what parenting is about than purchasing a ready-made toy clone at a toy superstore.

For these reasons, there are now a variety of books, magazines, speakers, and websites offering suggestions on such topics as: making your own toys, growing your own food or forming co-ops to purchase locally grown food, home baking, energy-spare heating systems, bicycling. People are finally beginning to see that we don't have to enter the new millennium amassing ever-larger collections of things in our quest for fulfillment. There's another way.

It's to help explore this other way that I pose the following questions. They have to do not just with our attachment to things, but with our relating to other people, because the issues are so often intertwined.

See if you agree with my answers.

DO YOUR COMFORTS LIMIT YOU?

We work toward making our lives comfortable. Comforts provide a sense of security. But they also prevent us from trying anything new. We become afraid to quit our jobs and find new work, change relationships, or even change the way we eat, dress, or comb our hair. New situations create discomfort. We have no way of predicting how we are going to feel and what is going to happen to us. Comfort also creates complacency. Complacency stops the growth process. It prevents us from asking questions that are critical to growth and improvement.

Look at what happens in the urban environment. People tend to find comfort in their little apartments and in the things they buy, but not with other people. They forget how to communicate with each other. I gave a lecture on making new friends during which I asked people to turn to the person next to them and say hello to someone new. Until I made that request, no one had asked anyone else a single thing. Imagine that—a lecture on friendship and they were afraid to say hello to someone next to them! They needed permission and encouragement; their comfort level wouldn't allow them to take the risk of talking to someone new on their own.

It is important to challenge yourself by pushing through discomfort, which helps you to expand and grow. Then what was once uncomfortable becomes completely comfortable. Now you can make decisions, make changes, let go of old notions that no longer serve you. As you get rid of the old you can allow in the new. You can meet new people and do things you never thought you could do. You are able to say things you wouldn't have said before, and eat foods you wouldn't have eaten. That is what happens when you get out of your comfort zone.

DOES BUYING A HOME FOR SECURITY MAKE SENSE?

Our culture tells us to go buy things, the biggest of which is a home. We're told to buy a house for security. However, that's when we can become really insecure about losing a job. That's when we lose sight of our other options, such as being free to travel. That's when we become anxious when the real estate market goes down. We get high blood pressure and other stress-related diseases because we worry about our investment.

Instead, we need to think about the ultimate investment in our lives: ourselves. When you think of it, all a house, literally, is is something that contains us. Perhaps what we really need is something to set us free.

CAN SEPARATING FROM OUR POSSESSIONS SET US FREE?

How much of your life is spent maintaining and guarding possessions? What do they mean to you? Can you see yourself without them? Picture yourself without one third of your possessions. Without half of them. Without three quarters of them. Mentally choose which ones you might jettison. How do these images make you feel?

When you were a young child, possessions weren't viewed as permanent but were used to explore, experience, and then let go. Your joy was in using and sharing more than in owning. Once we become adults, though, we don't want anyone else to touch our things. One floor is only for the president, the executive vice president, and the executive secretary. Everyone else is kept out. But the president, the executive vice president, and the executive secretary may not know who they really are. They may get their identities from their titles, and from the fact that they have their own floor.

What happens when you cease to take your identity from what you have? You find other things more meaningful, things you can't possess, such as a sunset, or the graceful movement of an animal. You're freer to experiment with new jobs, new activities, new environments for living, new people. I truly believe that unless you are able to separate yourself from your possessions, you will never find true pleasure nor see the beauty in this world.

DO YOU KNOW THE DIFFERENCE BETWEEN HAVING NEW EXPERIENCES AND GETTING NEW THINGS?

Having a new experience can enliven you for a long time afterwards, and can even provide you with a new perspective that lasts a lifetime. Simply getting something new, on the other hand, ceases to be exciting after about a week, at the most. Then you realize that the new thing isn't doing all that much for you, and that you'll now have to perpetually clean and maintain it. What's more, if you've been in the habit of getting new things, you may not even have a place to put it.

A lot of baby boomers have a dirty little secret—a dirty big secret, actually. While their houses may at first glance look uncluttered, like the occupants don't have a problem with thing addiction, if you go into their basements or garages, you see the material overflow of their lives, and it's astounding. There's a floor-to-ceiling collection of toys, appliances, clothing, kitchen equipment, knickknacks, games, and gadgets that makes Macy's basement look understocked by comparison. How much of this stuff was bought because the people really needed new experiences but went out and got new possessions instead?

WHAT ARE YOU WILLING TO GET RID OF?

Having too many things is not only a substitute for having new experiences, it can actually get in the way of having new experiences. You have to spend time and money acquiring, taking care of, and storing all your things. Then, you don't want to leave them to go somewhere else on an adventure. What if someone steals your stuff while you're away? Too much is at stake.

This is one of the reasons I advocate not having too many things, and why I think it's a good idea to periodically ask yourself, What can I get rid of? Do I really need the five TV sets in the house? Do I really need that fondue pot from a 1970s bridal shower? I haven't fondued anything in decades. Do I really need all these clothes? These shoes? These knickknacks that make my living room look like a gift shop about to have a fire sale? Am I dusting them all for a reason?

Do you know those bumper stickers that say, "I'd rather be golfing" or "I'd rather be dancing"? When you're dusting your knickknacks, ask yourself what you'd rather be doing.

MAKE A LIST OF THE NEW EXPERIENCES YOU'VE TRIED AS AN ADULT.

Childhood is loaded with new experiences, but they're not necessarily ones that you've chosen. As an adult, your new experiences are probably fewer and farther apart, but they're more likely to be ones that you've chosen—ones that are tailored to your interests and aptitudes. Doing new things can be harder for an adult than for a child, but the experiences are at least as rewarding.

A list of the new things you've undertaken as an adult might include your first trip to Africa, to Europe, or to a neighboring state. It might include learning to sky-dive, learning to swim or to drive, going rock-climbing, enrolling in a continuing education course, or getting your first dog. Your list might contain three items, or it might be so long as to be impossible to complete. The last thing on it might have occurred yesterday, or two decades ago.

The point is not how long your list is or how adventurous you've been. Rather, it's to get you thinking about the experience of trying something new. Remember how you felt, for instance, learning to swim. It was a little scary, but it was exciting too, because suddenly there was a whole new element you could get around in, a whole new way you could exercise and have fun. The experience probably energized you and made all of life livelier for awhile.

Perhaps it's time to try something new again.

WHAT ARE YOU WILLING TO DO THAT'S DIFFERENT?

How many times have you had an opportunity to do something, but decided not to do it because you prejudged that you wouldn't like it, or that you wouldn't fit in with the others there. Later, someone said, "You should have come. It was fun." And you made an excuse.

What are you willing to do that's different? Are you willing to spend a Saturday doing something totally different from what you usually do on Saturdays? Are you willing to wear your hair differently? To wear different types of clothes? How many things in your life are you willing to change? Or is your life just a routine, predictable pattern?

I have friends who have never done one single thing differently for years. I can tell you what they're going to say, what they'll eat, how they will treat people, what their apartment looks like, and what they will do when they go on vacation. To me, that's boring. When people are that boring, they get old real fast. And when they get old, they stop taking risks.

When people stop taking risks, they stagnate. Joy is no longer there, and they don't see the happy side of life. They are only bitter and cynical. Why? Because the only perspective they have is one of the ferment that is occurring around them. Who creates that ferment? They do. But who are they going to blame? Everybody else, or they blame circumstances.

When you are willing to act differently and take some risks, before long, you will begin to feel comfortable doing something else differently. Soon you will start looking forward to experiencing life and not being afraid. Suddenly, your tiny view of life expands and your life is all the richer for it.

DO YOU FULLY ENGAGE IN LIFE?

Either we give of ourselves completely or we do not. Don't try something half-heartedly. You won't get as much in return as you could if you gave yourself over to the experience completely.

Many people build escape mechanisms into what they try. Ted asks Bob to go camping, for example. "Bob, would you like to go camping?" "Sure, I'd love to." "Let's go next month." Next month arrives. Ted asks, "Bob, what have you got here? You've got a cellular telephone, a tent with a CD player in it, a security system for insects, and a heater with a thermostat. This isn't camping. This is merely trying to create a suburban environment in the woods."

IS YOUR THINKING "ON AUTOMATIC"?

Our thoughts are not truly our own. They have been passed on to us, not genetically, but through our conditioning. We have thousands of associations in our mind by the time we're ten years old. When we think of something, an image comes up to identify it. We think of the word "pretty" and up comes an image to tell us what pretty is. We don't create that image. We are taught how to respond to words. We are given different formulations that stay in the mind, and that can pop up automatically without our ever questioning them.

What if how we are taught to respond is flawed? Then we can form negative emotions around concepts that aren't necessarily negative. If we are conditioned to believe that being poor is terrible, and we don't have much money, then every day we will wake up thinking that we are rotten and miserable because we lack wealth. The whole day we will perpetuate those images as we compare ourselves to others. We'll see someone in a car that we don't have. We'll see someone in a dress or suit that we can't afford. We'll see someone who has a fancier apartment than we do. Our thoughts will probably be negative if we're on automatic, and they, in turn, will create other negative thoughts and emotions.

At some point we need to ask ourselves, where do these thoughts come from? Whose perceptions are they? What can I put in their place? Until we learn to replace them we'll continue to live by them. We need to be a little more choosy about our thoughts and to honor only those that create the most positive reactions. Those are the ones we need to focus on.

DO YOU NEED A LABEL?

We have an identity problem in this society, and we think we need labels to solve it. What's more, we all want to have the "right" label.

School starts the process. In school, there is one right answer, and we base our sense of self-worth on what other people identify as right. Then too, it's in school that we first learn whether we are "high achievers" or in "the slow group." And this labeling process is repeated ad nauseam every day of our life. Are we working class or middle class? Lower-middle class or upper-middle class? Are we black or white? Jewish or Christian? Catholic or Protestant? Perhaps we're Hispanic or Pacific Islander. We're supposed to know what boxes to check off in the questionnaire of life.

A friend of mine told me of an experience she had looking for an apartment in a New York suburb. A prospective landlady seemed ready to rent her a place, but she had a question first.

"What are you?" she asked.

Hoping that her status as a human and a female were obvious, my friend said, "I'm an American." But of course the landlady still looked puzzled, because what the woman really wanted to know was what religious or ethnic label she could attach to this person. To attach "person" to her just wasn't enough. My friend thought it was, and she didn't take the apartment.

"Person" isn't enough for a lot of people. Did you ever go to a Mets or Yankees game and see how some of the fans have to grasp at an identity that isn't really theirs? Some of them are fanatics who dress up like the athletes, and live through them. It's one thing to enjoy a sport or participate in one. But when we begin to identify with something that is totally outside of ourselves, we can lose part of our real selves in the process. It's alright to acknowledge that someone out there is doing something we appreciate, respect, and find unique. That can motivate us. Motivation, stimulation, and support are good. But taking on another identity is not. We are a culture that's learned that copying styles, copying language, copying slogans, and copying rituals can give us our identity.

Brand names are big deals in our society. People use them to identify themselves as having good taste, or as having money. They actually wear brand names emblazoned on their clothes in a way that would have been considered totally crass until relatively few years ago. Instead of wearing a nametag that says, "Hi! My name is John," people wear a company name or logo on their clothes that says, "Hey! I've got the sense and the bucks to buy such and such a brand. In fact, it's part of who I am. Admire me."

But is that shirt company really part of who you are? The *shirt* is, because it's on your skin and it's sort of an extension of your body. But once you've paid your money to the department store, the shirt *company* cares about as much about you as that athletic team whose hat you're wearing does once you've paid for game tickets. They don't identify with *you*; why identify with them? I'm sorry, but that's how I see it. We're looking for identity in all the wrong places.

WHERE DO YOU GET YOUR SENSE OF SELF?

From wealth? Some people get a sense of self from the money they have. Others assume they have got to have it together to be wealthy. But it's not necessarily so. Look at old wealth. How do people obtain it? No one living today has worked for any of the old wealth. At some point their ancestors were corrupt robber barons who exploited everyone they could to get rich. They didn't give a hoot about anyone but themselves. But no one says, "Hold on a minute. You're spending bad money that was initially made by exploiting people." Maybe we should.

From popularity? The popular person gets his or her sense of self from being charismatic and charming. But that doesn't mean he is necessarily entitled to good self-esteem. Think of all the charismatic people who have charmed people out of their life savings. Think of the charismatic politicians who have no integrity.

From others' fear? I know a lot of people who get their sense of self from the fear they generate in others. They call it respect, but there's often an element of fear there. It's not just the Mafia that I'm referring to. Look at military generals. Look at CEO's and politicians. Look, even, at some medical professionals. What we don't always keep in mind about powerful people is that they are often capable of inflicting pain with the power they have.

From winning? We consider winners to be people who are successful and have a good sense of self. But being a winner is not essential to anything. I know a lot of winners who are absolutely bad people. We've all heard of those winners in sports who are coke-heads or megalomaniacs.

I grew up before sports became such a powerful and profitable franchise. A lot of the athletes were nice people who loved the sport and respected their fans.

Things are different now, though. Today these people, with rare exceptions, do not respect anybody. If you don't give them $25 million, they are not going to play. How much love of the sport can they have?

As a result, I have lost interest in sports. I don't find today the Willie Mays and Mickey Mantles, the people who loved the sport and honored it. In all sports, money has undermined the value of what the sport is.

From what you've done that was meaningful, and what you hope to do? These things make more sense as ways of getting a sense of self.

Think back to something you've done that has affected who you are today. Also, ask yourself, What was the best year of my life? What was the worst? How did I react to the wonderful times and to the negative experiences, and how did all of this mold me?

Ask yourself what accomplishments you're proudest of. Sometimes the things a person is proudest of are not the stereotypical ones, like getting a college degree or being promoted at work. They're more private acts, or accomplishments that others don't necessarily know about. They could be something like seeing an opportunity and seizing it when the temptation was to stay comfortable and let it slide by. They could be something like befriending a person and then finding out many years later that

that person always remembered the kindness. It pays to pinpoint your greatest accomplishments, especially if they include "little" ones like these, because doing so will help you define who you are in ways that go beyond "Ph.D. in chemistry."

Ask yourself what you want to accomplish in the future too. Do you want to get a second Ph.D.? Do you want to become a skier? Scaling down, do you want to be able to dine alone in a good restaurant and actually enjoy it? Again, the small victories, as well as the large, define who you are.

DO YOU FOCUS ON YOUR WEAKNESSES OR YOUR STRENGTHS?

If you are like most people, you focus on your weaknesses. The only time you focus on your strengths is when you are challenged. It is only through challenge that you are forced to use your strengths. You train for a marathon, for example, going out in bad weather as well as good, because you know you have to run each and every day if you're going to be able to do twenty-six miles. By challenging yourself in this way, you really bring out your physical and mental strengths.

Challenge brings out the best in us. But how often is it a part of our lives? Why don't you bring challenge into your life every day? Make it a natural, integrated part of your daily routine. Live by challenge.

ARE YOU LOOKING FOR SOMEONE TO CHANGE THE CIRCUMSTANCES OF YOUR LIFE?

People go after gurus and other charismatic characters. They look for that ultimate relationship. We seek people who will guide us out of our problems or protect us.

When people look for love, they're often really looking for social acceptance, in that being part of a couple seems to be society's ideal. Half the single people in America hate being single because of how others perceive them. "You're thirty-five and single?" others ask, the implication being that there's something wrong with you. When I grew up in West Virginia, if you were over twenty-five and single, you were pronounced gay. That's how stupid it was. They never thought that you might not want to be married. We have very strict standards about what we will and will not accept.

Sometimes we are terrified of being alone. We immediately equate being alone with loneliness. We assume there's a void, one we have to fill with a warm body. So we try to match a resume with our resume, but it doesn't often work because resumes are not people. We are not matching energy.

What would happen if, instead of needing someone to love you, you took the time to respect all the reasons you were lovable? After all, if you can't love yourself, how in the world are you going to love others? And why should they love you?

WHAT IS LOVE?

People try to prove their love through devotion, obedience, commitment, obligation, and responsibilities, but none of that has anything to do with love. Love is not attached to expectation or performance. Love is simply the radiation of the eternal self.

Trying to measure love is like someone saying, "Come to my class and we'll improve the spirit." You can't improve the spirit. The spirit transcends time. It is immortal and perfect. You can't improve something that is perfect. All you can do is touch it.

• • •

HOW MUCH FUN IS ENOUGH?

Most of us don't allow ourselves to have fun. At work, we're not supposed to have fun; we're supposed to be serious. Why shouldn't we have fun at work? We generally try to have fun on weekends, but we go in search of it and we try too hard. We think fun is something out there that we've got to find and connect with. Why can't we have fun before the party?

DO YOU LIVE WITH PASSION?

I believe that as a culture we lack passion. We are afraid people will misinterpret it. But passion is the engine that drives life. If you have a sense of focus, you don't have fears that limit you, and you put your passion into play. Then anything can happen.

Sometimes, people who are around forty or fifty feel that the passion has gone out of their lives. Each day, when they open their eyes in the morning, there's a sense of déjà vu—they've done this all before, too many times. They've already established a career, raised a family, or set up a home, and now there's that nagging question, "What's it all for?" and the disturbing suspicion that the best part of life is behind them. The adventure, the search, the exultation, the wanderlust—all those exciting things that caused them to study hard in college, to make sacrifices, and to adhere to certain principles—now seem to be fading away. Now that they've achieved a whole series of goals, like trophies on a mantel, they think, "So what? And what's next? Isn't there one more thing I can do that will finally make me feel good about myself?" Often, there's a turning to some form of addictive behavior to quell the anxiety.

The problem is that these people's passion has been too connected to achievement. By contrast, consider people who do not need to establish their identity through trophies won or life points racked up. For them, waking up in the morning is not fraught with the same anxiety or depression or sense that the best is in the past as it is for their more goal-oriented counterparts. These people wake up each morning driven by a passion *for life*, not for any specific goal or achievement. They simply look forward to enjoying each day, with the knowledge that it could be their last. Or it could be their best; they know that too. These people want to connect with what the world has to offer. They're like children in that respect. They have the kind of passion that makes all things relevant to them and all people unique, or, as George Leonard would say, tied together by a silent thread.

When you look at these people you'll generally see a smile. They're not smiling because they won anything. They're simply smiling out of an acknowledgment that, "I'm happy—and I want to share some of that with you."

IS WHAT WE GAIN OR WHAT WE GIVE UP MORE ESSENTIAL?

What we give up helps us to be free to have something take its place. If we gain something, but still hold onto everything else from the past, we gain nothing. When you start giving things up, you automatically gain the ability to have a whole new reality. And of course I'm referring not just to possessions, but to attitudes, notions, and emotions.

You cannot have a whole new reality, and you cannot have a solution-oriented mind if you are not willing to give up the mind that was causing the problem. Then you would be looking at the problem with the same mind. You would be using the same old biases, fears, and limitations to create a solution for you. If these couldn't create a solution in the past, how are they going to create one now?

When you give up the old mind, the new mind takes over and everything is possible. You look at the problem from a new perspective, with new feelings, new sensations, new awareness, new dynamics, new ways of integrating thoughts and feelings. That's why when someone has a problem and says, "I think I'll sleep on it," it makes sense. In a dream state the mind is unfettered, fluid, able to take new perspectives and make new connections. In a dream, your mind can let go of what's not essential and hold onto what's really meaningful to you. Thus dreams can provide a new way of looking at problems and even real inspiration.

IS BEING GOOD ALWAYS A GOOD THING?

A lot of people assume that by doing good things they will feel better about themselves. The problem is, in the process, they deny their own needs. Think of the people in your life who are good to others, but not to themselves. They devote their entire life to doing good for others. These are the people who have no real sense of self-esteem. They get self-esteem from being good, but that's a false way of getting it. It doesn't work because it isn't balanced.

If you're balanced, you're going to feel good genuinely. There is no conflict between what you feel and what you share. You are completely authentic. When you extend yourself, you are sharing your true self. There's no map, no hidden agenda, no manipulation. What you see is what you get. What you share is what you feel. What you say is what you mean. There is no message behind the message, no duplicity.

If you are *trying* to be good then you don't really feel that you are. There is a conflict between what you want to be and who you are now. You do not accept yourself for where you are at this moment.

It's better to be honest about where you are in the moment. Then you acknowledge and empower yourself to change. Change is a process, one that begins with the thought, "If I know what I am in this moment, then I can change."

Being authentic is essential. Whatever you do is who you are. The moment you know that you are capable of doing anything, and you do not do negative things, you have a real sense of self. That's the authentic power of self.

HOW DO YOU KNOW THAT YOUR BELIEFS AND FEELINGS ARE AUTHENTIC?

When you know what is right, it resonates as being right. You feel inner peace and balance. When something does not feel right, but you want to make it so, you force yourself into believing it. You argue with yourself, try to convince yourself, talk to yourself, and sell ideas to yourself.

If after all your arguments and mind games, another idea still resonates, then that other idea is your truth. And that's what should be followed. Your intuition, your inner voice, is talking to you. That comes from the authentic self. Listen to it.

DO YOU ACKNOWLEDGE OTHERS?

How often in a day do you compliment people? How often do you acknowledge them? We forget to do these basic things. We forget that what's important is the bond between people. Acknowledgement is the basis of communication. It's the purpose of a relationship. It makes relationships intimate and personal.

If you've got a dog, did you ever notice how when you come home, your dog immediately runs over and starts licking you? Ten minutes later, if you come in again, it's the same thing. What if you had someone who gave you the same kind of love and attention? When they saw you they would warmly say, "Gee, it's good to see you."

We don't know how to acknowledge people's differences. If someone is very sick and in the hospital we don't know what to say when we visit. We just sit there thinking we've got to wait a few more minutes before leaving, to be proper. We don't know how to treat someone who is sick like a human being. Don't treat a person like they're sick when they're in the hospital. Treat them like they still count.

Learn to acknowledge others. Always look for something good you can say. Genuine compliments are important because they're a form of acknowledgement.

WHEN YOU WANT TO RELEASE TENSION, WHAT DO YOU DO?

There are positive ways to release tension. You can go for a walk, listen to music, laugh, take deep breaths, dance, have sex, exercise, meditate, or party. There are negative ways as well. You can drink, take drugs, overeat, oversleep, shop compulsively, hold feelings in, let out destructive anger, project your negative thoughts upon others, or break things. These are all outlets for dealing with the same feelings.

The moment you start feeling tense, a process occurs. By paying attention to the process, you are in control of your behavior. Tension happens slowly. Then you start to visualize a response. You have something in your mind that shows you what a resonse to tension looks like.

You can't stop the feelings, but you can control the way they manifest by changing the visualizations you create in your mind. Then you can change your outlet from alcohol to music, from bursts of negative energy to meditation, from hurting something to deep breathing. These are the types of things you can do that will change your whole energy flow. It's the energy that you feel and internalize that is going to manifest constructively or destructively.

ARE YOU HIGHLY ACTIVE, OR ARE YOU MAINLY SUPPORTIVE?

Both of these traits are important. We like to think we should all be dynamic. But this is wrong. We should be whatever our true natures dictate. Some people are best at supporting the energies of others. They are naturally caring. Others have a natural leadership ability.

Honoring the energy of what you inherently are will make all the difference in the way you feel about yourself. There's nothing more frustrating than feeling like you should be leading when you're always following. Or being forced into being the leader when it doesn't come naturally to you and doesn't feel comfortable. You're suppressing your natural energy and pretending to be someone you aren't. Of course, there are times when you can expand on your nature and change in the way you relate to people. Being in touch with who you are creates a sense of internal balance.

IF A SOCIETY IS NOT VITAL OR HEALTHY, THEN WHY STAY IN IT?

I don't do anything just because I'm supposed to do it. I go out and create my own social context, my own friends, my own life, my own career, my own day. Last night I worked all through the night. I didn't say, "Uh-oh, it's ten o'clock. Time to go to bed to get my eight hours of sleep." I felt there were other, more essential, things to do.

You've got to understand that what you embrace you become. Be very careful about what you have embraced. Be honest about what it means to you. If it is important, if it honors you, if it's healthy, that's fine. If it's not, then ask yourself, can you disengage and have a life beyond that? If you are honest, you can.

Take a look at everything that you are a part of. Ask yourself, is this essential to what I want to be if I'm going to be whole? I had friends who were essential to me at one point in my life, but who aren't now. I had things that I needed, but I don't now. It's not a matter of good and bad. It's a matter of what's essential now if you are going to go forward. You have to have courage to go forward and you can't take the old with you. You can't lug everything in the past with you because you're used to it. That's not healthy. Let some things go.

CAN YOU REAFFIRM YOUR LIFE?

Every morning, I wake up knowing that everything I am going to do that day will be life-affirming. Each day has meaning for me. Life is not about fame or fortune, but rather about the quality of the energy that is shared. You can make this world a better place if you choose because you are an essential ingredient in society. It doesn't matter whether you are rich or poor. You have something special to share.

No matter what your situation, if you are working on improving it, you will be happy with yourself. For instance, when you look in the mirror you can't lie about what you see. If you are overweight, you'll see it. Yet if you are overweight but working on a better body, you will be happy with what you see. You will appreciate yourself for working on the process of change.

Affirmations are an important ritual for helping you focus on the purpose of your life. They help you to keep centered on your vision. Affirm health and you will eat only foods that enhance health. Affirm love and you will approach everything you do and everyone you meet lovingly. Affirm beauty and you will see it everywhere. This is a daily process.

Mistake Number Two:
Attaching Too Much Importance to Things

1. For the next week, go on a "buying diet." That is, pare down your shopping so that you're buying only those things that are necessary for survival, such as a warm coat, or food.

2. During the next holiday season, don't buy any presents for the adults on your gift list. Instead, write personalized poems for them, give them home-baked goods, or give them vouchers for services or time together doing special things.

3. Clean out one room of your house, or part of a room, such as a closet. Get rid of everything you don't use, and then reorganize what remains.
   How do you feel afterwards? _____
If there's a positive effect, go on to clean out the rest of your house, one portion at a time.

4. Totally eliminate brand status as a factor in what you buy. Do this for as long a period as you can, but for at least two weeks.
   Then ask yourself: Did my self-esteem level go down, or did it go up? _____ Were there other negative or positive consequences?_____

5. Give away something that you like or use to someone who you know will like or use it more.

Planning for the Future

A NYONE WHO KNOWS me knows that I'm big on goal-set-ting. I've always set goals for myself—two-week, one-month, and six-month goals, year-long projects, and even longer-range ones. I'll often graph these plans, so that I can keep track of my progress.

What's more, readers of my other books know that I recommend the goal-setting approach to others, advocating, for instance, the elimination of one bad dietary habit a week, with the simultaneous addition of one new good food. A question arises, then, as to why I'm calling planning for the future a mistake. Since goal-setting is, by definition, looking ahead to a future time with a specific aim in mind, isn't this activity an aspect of planning for the future? Aren't I contradicting myself?

Not exactly. Let's say you're overweight and unhealthy and you set a long-range goal of losing fifty pounds in a year. Along the way, you set mini-goals of one-good-food-in, one-bad-food-out a week, as well as a weight-loss goal of about a pound a week. Or let's say you're an aspiring actor who has set a goal of landing a part in a Broadway play within five years, with sub-goals of auditioning within a certain time-frame whenever you are unemployed. Both of these examples are typical of the kind of goal-setting I advocate.

Let's look at what might happen. At the end of a year, you may have lost fifty pounds, or you may have lost only twenty or thirty, but if you've made a reasonable attempt at sticking to your goal, each day along the way has been a step toward weight loss and health, and that's the important point. Likewise, at the end of five years, you may be starring on Broadway, or singing in the back line of a Broadway chorus, or perhaps you may only be in the chorus of a local dinner theater, but again the point is that you've furthered your dramatic experience and talents along the way. In each case, what you did was related to the goal you envisioned, and in each case you had an enriching experience. So whether you hit your goal exactly on the mark or not is not all that important. It's your participation in the process that matters.

To understand this another way, think of Olympic athletes. They train rigorously for years, and they all have the same goal— a gold medal. Only most of them are not going to achieve this goal; in fact, most of them won't even win a medal of any sort at all. That doesn't mean that the process of pursuing that goal was a waste of time (despite what TV commentators would have you think). On the contrary, the process was one that will make a positive difference in the future of each Olympic athlete for years to come.

So what's the kind of planning for the future that I would condemn? It's the kind where the process doesn't really have anything to do with the eventual goal, so that you're messing up your life now for some future gain. Instead of saying "messing up your life" you can use the word "sacrificing," but it's the same thing.

Let's say you have children and your plan for the future is that they should be happy. So you sacrifice yourself now, working eighty hours a week to afford everything your child might need to be well-educated, get a good job, and thus be happy in the future. The only thing is, he's not very happy now because he's not getting the time with a parent that's so important to a young child. Plus your life is messed up because you're working too hard and missing irreplaceable hours with your child as he's growing.

Unnecessary overwork is the kind of planning for the future that is characteristic of the baby boom generation. Of course, not every baby boomer makes this mistake, but it's a common one. Also, I realize that some people have to work many hours just to keep their families fed and sheltered, and these are not the situations I'm referring to. I'm talking about people working like dervishes who don't have to. They're knocking themselves out to amass wealth for some imagined future good—at the expense of the present. While hard work is commendable, unnecessary work, work that pulls you away from the basic pleasures of life, is ridiculous. It's a mistake people can make without ever realizing it because everyone else in their circle is making it too.

The habit of doing superfluous work can carry over into leisure-time activities. Years ago, people took a week or two of vacation, and during that time they went someplace relaxing, and relaxed. Today, the time taken for each vacation has typically shortened. There may be more vacations per year, but on each one the schedule is tight and people feel they have a lot to accomplish. I know folks whose family vacations are scheduled as precisely as military campaigns. But keeping up the frenetic pace is not a problem for them: They've had so much practice every weekend, not to mention on weekdays.

This not-very-leisurely leisure lifestyle is quite future-oriented, and this is true in two senses. One, the underlying assumption is that you have to improve athletically or culturally so you'll be more of an accomplished or worthy person in the future. Secondly, during every "fun" activity you're thinking about the next, because it's coming up so soon. What's lost in this obsession with the future is, of course, the present. You can be surrounded by the most wonderful friends, family, and environment, but if you're too caught up in the work ethic, you're not going to notice much of it.

The work ethic has always been a part of American culture, although there was actually a brief time, during the 1960s, when the baby boom generation started to question it. Remember the "be-ins"? People were asking, in effect, "Why can't we sit around with flowers in our hair, and just *be*?" It may sound totally corny today, but I still think it was a darn good question. Unfortunately, it looks like most people have answered it, "Nope, it was a good idea at the time, but we *can't* just sit. Life's too complicated and demanding, so we've got to rush around like maniacs in our sport utility vehicles, and make phone calls while we're doing so. We've got to prepare for the next meeting, the next deal, the next activity, our children's future, our retirement. No time to just be. Sorry."

Why is this generation like that? Part of the reason is insecurity. The boomers were promised a golden future in the 1950s. Then, everyone knew that with some study and hard work, you could have all the basic components of the good life—the home, the car, and the family—most likely all financed by one salary from a company you could count on staying with for years. Two general assumptions were that most people would do better materially than their parents had, and that society was by and large a meritocracy, so that the smarter you were and the harder you worked, the better you would do. There was a sense of entitlement to the American dream, at least for the middle class.

This feeling that all would be provided for lasted through the 1960s, and some friends who married in the early 1970s recalled still having it at the time:

"We got married right after college. We had nothing—unless you count debt—no money, no apartment, no jobs. Our honeymoon was a camping trip with a borrowed tent, and our first residence was an apartment borrowed from a friend who was traveling. But were we worried? Not a bit. It seems awfully irresponsible now, but nobody worried about money then. People who grew up when we did just knew that with a college education you could get a job, get a place to live, and make a life. Nobody was worried sick about the future—yet."

That began to change in 1973, with the oil embargo. Suddenly there was a gasoline shortage, and talk about future severe energy shortages that would compromise our American way of life. As energy prices went up, so did general inflation. And as the economic situation worsened, there no longer seemed to be a guarantee of the good life for everyone who worked hard. Women gained more access to the working world in the 1970s, which in a real sense constituted progress; the down side was that, increasingly, both members of a married couple had to work full time just to keep the children fed. *If* both people could find jobs; the unemployment rate was rising, and by the mid-1970s it was at its highest level since World War II, before the baby boomers were even around.

In the 1980s, Reaganomics further eroded people's sense of security because the idea of a social safety net was questioned, and government programs were being weakened or dismantled. The prevailing ethos was that of "everyone out for himself," so that even if you were doing well during that time you knew deep down that should things fall apart for you, you'd be on your own—it was no longer government's place to step in and help.

Also, it was in the 1980s that our tax system was changed in a way that furthered the stratification of economic classes, so that the "haves" wound up having more and the "have nots," less. While there might have been enough of the pie to go around if it was evenly divided, that was not going to happen, so the idea was to become one of the "have" group, whatever it took. The boomers had been made an implicit promise by the world of the 1950s— that with a little effort one could have a golden future—and if later years seemed to rescind this promise, they'd just have to work harder to keep the promise alive.

That's why becoming a workaholic seemed a sensible option to many. An extension of this thinking was that one's children should become workaholics too, to ensure their futures. The 1980s were when it became common for middle-class children to be signed up for a different extracurricular activity every day of the week, lest they become less smart and well-rounded than other kids, and thus eventually lose out in the competition to get into a good college. The idea of competition was a spoken and unspoken undercurrent in many areas of life.

WHERE WE ARE NOW

I do think that competition is a wonderful thing when you're competing against yourself. For instance, most people who run the New York City marathon have no hope of beating the front-runners and would be silly to try, yet anyone can compete with his or her own performance of the previous year, and try for a personal best. That's a healthy kind of competition that helps people grow. But the kind of competition where you feel that you and your family have to grab yours before somebody else does is an unhealthy, mentally corrosive kind, and unfortunately, even though the 1980s are over, many people still have that competitive mindset. Today, while the country's economic situation has improved and people are feeling less financially threatened than they were a few years ago, a lot of individuals are still living the kind of pressurized, future-oriented lives that are based on the assumption that they're competing with the world.

I don't think we have to do this. I don't think we have to strategize, scheme, and sacrifice for the future in ways that cut down on our enjoyment of the present. The flip side of excessive future-orientation is enjoyment of the present, and our capacity to enjoy the present is what we are going to explore with some of the questions that follow. We'll also look at sensible, constructive ways of approaching the future, because of course you can't be blind to its existence. Changes are going to happen, and you can help mold them through intelligent goal-setting.

ARE YOU ABLE TO BE HAPPY?

I remember as a child sitting with a woman who was in her seventies on the block where we lived. She had a wonderful garden out back; and she would always have sassafras tea. I loved the way it smelled. We would sit there on the swing. She was always at peace. And I remember asking her (I was only about twelve): "Are you going to die soon? Are you afraid of that?"

The questions seem a little nervy, but I was curious, and my mother had told me to always say what I felt, never to edit it.

The lady said that she wasn't afraid. She explained that she was not afraid of death because she had never been afraid of life. She had always lived with a sense of purpose in life, and that was simply to be a happy person. This seemed true; I never saw her when she was not able to be happy. When you were around her, you felt joy, peace, and love. You saw it in how she tended her garden and how she would take flowers to all the neighbors. Those are simple things, and that's why when people say, "Oh, I don't have enough money for this, and I don't have that," I think of how simple life can be, and of the simple pleasures, like noticing new buds on plants, or watching birds at a feeder, or walking in fresh snow. We forget about the simple pleasures until we're given an environment where we can enjoy them. Then we remember again.

The lady lived about five more years. But she was never depressed. There was never a sense of fatalism or defeat. And yet now I see people who, by the age of thirty, are already developing this mindset. They feel that they haven't achieved enough. Where are they now? they ask, when they're forty or fifty years old. How many points have they racked up in the career game? What have they got to show for their lives?

You've got a lot to show if you're willing to acknowledge it. Of course if you're only willing to acknowledge what you don't have, in terms of the material things, you might have to call yourself a failure. But then that would be a false standard to measure a life by, as I learned from my neighbor on the swing.

• • •

DO YOU APPRECIATE THE MOMENT?

We are often so preoccupied about getting someplace else that we forget about where we are right at the moment. Sometimes the moment has to practically come up and shake us by the collar, demanding our attention and appreciation. I've talked to people about this phenomenon, and a colleague told me the following:

The other evening I had to do some errands. It was the most inopportune time—right before dinner on a very busy day—and it looked like it was going to rain. I had to do the most mundane things, like look for a particular pen cartridge at a stationery store near the local train station. I wasn't enthused.

Well, all of a sudden, outside that store, I happened to look up the street toward the railroad station and at the sky above it, and I was transfixed. It was indeed going to rain—it was about to storm, in fact—and the sky was the most striking combination of deep, deep blue, and black. The wind was whipping up the flag on a pole in front of the station—I don't know why the flag was still up—and a train had just pulled in. The warm lights in the train were such a contrast to the chilly scene outside, and the whole picture was so beautiful that I wished I could just photograph it in my mind and then paint it. Unfortunately, painting isn't my particular strength, but I did store that scene in my mind. And the experience made me realize: I should stop rushing and look around more. There are probably beautiful things like this going on all the time, and I'm just not noticing.

This story got me thinking. Did you ever see tourists on the streets of New York? They're constantly looking up and around in wonder, moving at a slower pace than everyone else and providing a chuckle for native New Yorkers. Well, never mind the superior attitude. I think if we all went through life like New York tourists it would be a good thing because we'd be appreciating what each moment had to offer.

DO YOU THINK YOU'LL BE ABLE TO APPRECIATE THE MOMENT—BUT ONLY AFTER YOU CHANGE?

Self-improvement is great, but focusing on change should not be an obsession. If it is, it robs you of your enjoyment of the present. So while I may have a desire to change, and focus on getting there, the end point does not preoccupy my thoughts. Getting to where I am going is a process, and every step of that process is essential and vital. I do not want to say, "I will not like my body until I have it the way I want it." No, I am going to like my body at every moment during the time it takes to change.

A lot of people beat up on themselves because they are not at their ideal, and that is wrong. We need to accept the moment. It is all we have. We do not know what will happen tomorrow. And I don't just mean this in the sense that we may die tomorrow, or that something really bad may happen. Something really good may happen tomorrow, but that still does not detract one iota from the value of today. Today is where your life is right now, and you own today the way you own a unique, perishable, and nonexchangeable gift. Enjoy it.

DO YOU THINK YOU'LL BE ABLE TO ENJOY THE MOMENT—BUT ONLY AFTER CIRCUMSTANCES CHANGE?

Some people plan on really being able to savor life only after a particular event. Then the event comes and goes, and another one replaces it. Life can become a waiting game, with enjoyment put on hold as one anticipates a constantly changing series of circumstances. For instance, some people plan on being happy after:

they graduate;
they find a mate;
they get a good job;
they get married;
they buy a house;
they have a baby;
the baby is out of diapers;
they have a second baby;
the second baby is out of diapers;
the children are both in preschool;
the children are both in elementary school;
the children are both out of the house;
they've amassed a certain level of assets;
the children both graduate;
they retire.

As these people's children have no doubt said many times (before they were out of the house)—"Are we there yet?"

IS THE PAST POLLUTING YOUR PRESENT?

People compare everyone and everything to someone or something from a previous time. That keeps them from being aware of the present moment. They go to the Grand Canyon thinking, "This is nice, but it's not Sedona. The rocks are not as red." Or right after a lecture that I give, people will say, "This is the best lecture, Gary." From my point of view, every lecture that has something that can help someone is a good lecture. But people are always comparing.

What would happen if you didn't compare people and places? What if you simply accepted your experience for what it is in the moment? Suddenly your mind would focus on what it is. Then, no matter what it was, you would get something from it.

Things are never going to be the same. Once something is done, it can never be done again. It's always going to be different. The problem is, we want to repeat experiences. We expect sameness. We expect people to act predictably. We expect pleasures to always be the same for us. Such expectations set us up for unnecessary disappointment.

WHAT HAPPENS WHEN YOU PROCRASTINATE?

Procrastination is planning to do in the future what you really should be doing now. You miss chances. You miss opportunities. You miss growth. You miss insight. You miss resolving problems. You miss the opportunity to be in the moment. When you procrastinate, you're hiding. You keep postponing what should be a natural flow in life.

People who succeed in life are in constant motion. Their life is never static. Yet we want to create little insulated islands of security where we can be who we want to be and not move. It doesn't work that way, though. Everything changes. Rules stop working. Neighborhoods are no longer there. Our friends are not going to be there forever either. Our faces are not always going to look the same. Change is part of life. The person who doesn't procrastinate is the person who's aware of how to accept changes and control them. You lose control when you procrastinate. You only have control when you come in and grab change by the reins and proclaim, "I'm going to control the direction of this thing!"

Procrastination is self-destruction in the sense that nobody ever gets better procrastinating. Your situation always gets worse. If you're overweight, how do you think you got that way? You had plans to start losing weight, but you constantly put them off till tomorrow, or next week, or next month.

Procrastination can be a factor in addictive behavior: "This year I'm definitely going to start reading more. I got some books for Christmas, and I'm going to read them. I'll become a more interesting person, and I'll definitely have more friends." Now it's March. Did you read those books? "No, I just laid in front of the TV and ate and ate. I figured if I'm procrastinating, I might as well go ahead and self-destruct. I mean, I don't have any self-esteem. If I did I'd be doing something."

You always hurt yourself when you procrastinate. There is always some negative outcome. On the other hand, if you stop procrastinating, you will actualize. If you actualize you've got a real chance at health, growth, and happiness. It's your choice.

ARE ALL YOUR EFFORTS TO CHANGE ACCOMPANIED BY RESISTANCE?

I'll bet many readers have experienced this. You want to change. The desire is there. You're ready to change. You go to workshops. You read books. You write journal entries. You say, "Now is the time I'm going to do it." But then you take a few steps and you think, "I'm not so sure. I really want to be healthy and happy. I want to be more open-minded and free. I don't want to be constrained. But every time I take a step, I feel a corresponding need to stay put."

You know staying put isn't working for you. You don't have fulfillment; you don't feel whole and complete. That's why you're undertaking a program of change. However, at least where you were there was certainty; you knew what you had. With changes, you don't know what you will find. You're going into uncharted territory and you don't know what's going to happen. You're not sure you have the confidence to go through that period of uncertainty to get to where you feel comfortable and confident in what you do.

So, in effect, what you're saying is that the first part of change is the most intense and the most difficult because there are no certainties. There's no certainty that you're going to experience change in a positive way or grow from it. That means you have to have some courage. In order to forge on and resist the urge to go back to the old way, the comfortable way, the predictable way, you have to exercise strength—strength of character, strength of purpose, strength of ideals. You have to focus.

The fact is that you will focus, because you're committed. And soon comes the mastery of the change process. It will happen.

ARE WE BORN GIFTED,
OR DO WE DEVELOP OUR GIFTS?

I have never seen a prodigy remain a prodigy without continually mastering his or her gifts. It's a lot of work. It's not a matter of doing it, getting it right, and taking it easy. It's doing it, getting it right, and then committing yourself to continuing to maintain getting it right. Many people in my running and walking club have trained for the marathon for a year. The hardest part of that training is the first three months. What allows people to do the marathon after that three months' training is their commitment to maintaining standards and a sense of excellence in training. They go through a highly intense anabolic breakthrough stage. Then they get to a plateau. They feel some confidence. Many didn't think they could do it. Now they've done it. They feel good.

I myself have been training for over thirty years as a competitive athlete. For twelve years I was a top runner, and more recently I've been power walking. I've excelled. But when I did not keep to my standards, when I pulled back and didn't do my speed work, I could see it in my races. The only thing that kept me from being mediocre in my races was my commitment to repeating the training formula.

We tend to get lazy. We think we don't have to work so hard once we've attained a certain level. We think that once we know how to do something, we will be able to do it forever without practice. But that's not how it works. Life is a process. Show me a great pianist, a great ballerina, or a great artist. Every day of their life they're committed to improving their art. If that commitment continues they can maintain high standards and perhaps reach even higher ones.

The average person doesn't want to strive for anything. Most people don't expect to see mastery, and so they stop when they have the most modest success. But by doing that, they're actually stopping their whole life process from going forward.

Everyone can progress toward his or her higher self. In that way, a person learns that no one is gifted. We're all given gifts that must be honored to be realized. Everybody can do something special if they simply work on mastery.

Do artificial boundaries keep you from growing?

People would like to grow and usually start out with the best of intentions. They say, "Today is the day. I'm tired of my life being this way and it's going to change." Then, they hit a wall and look around to find boundaries everywhere. They start to think, I can't get through this, and find justifications for why they can't. They rationalize, I don't have the resources, the knowledge, the money, the support. But these are all excuses.

Why do we establish artificial boundaries that prevent us from being who we want to be? Part of the reason we do this is because we have learned to do it. We have taken lessons from other people earlier in life. We watched them set, manicure, and defend their boundaries and thought that this was the way we were supposed to live.

Another way we put up boundaries is by failing to realize that life can be different. We lack the awareness of having choices. That lack of consciousness is in itself a boundary since we cannot enjoy that which we cannot imagine. We're not going to find that which we are not looking for.

We also set up barricades to our growth by making too many choices simultaneously. In life, we need to focus on something like an automatic camera does, one image at a time. When taking pictures, if we try to focus on three images at the same time and they are several feet apart, we can't do it. The same is true of trying to focus on multiple possibilities for our life all at once. We get a blurred image, which makes us afraid to engage any one of them. This is what happens to the person who starts a lot of projects but finishes none of them, who goes to all kinds of workshops and lectures, has all kinds of relationships, and finds no real ultimate fulfillment.

We need to have a single focus and then master the art of taking one step at a time. That gets us outside of the boundary.

DO YOU ACTUALIZE YOUR INTENTIONS?

Most people don't even think in terms of intentions. No great intentions are in front of them. Instead, they just meander through a day, figuring that today will be just like the day before. In effect they're saying, "I'll put the day on repeat. I've done it so many times; I know what I'm going to do, what I'm going to eat, what I'm going to wear, how I'm going to put on my makeup, how long I'm going to be in the shower."

Intent allows you to make each day significant. Whatever you choose to put into it is what you will get out of it. But intent must be followed with action so that what you envision you can make manifest.

Fear can block the ability to manifest. You start to hear statements in your head like "I would like to do that but I'm afraid it won't work." "I can't succeed." "I don't know how to do that." "I don't have the skills." "I don't have a support system." "I can't afford the changes." Such thoughts stop us from creating the kind of life we want for ourselves. Physically, they drain us of energy and they can even eventually foster disease.

One of the ways we create health is to recognize and honor our intent. Create an intention and then prepare yourself for tangible results.

DO YOU USE EXCUSES TO AVOID CHANGE?

Commonly, we make excuses that prevent us from taking actions that move our lives forward. One excuse we often make is, "I don't have the time." What we are really saying is that we are making nonessentials a routine part of our lives. Once we stop doing unnecessary things, we have time to do what is truly important.

We often make excuses not to do things because we fear failure. We are afraid of not living up to other people's expectations of us. Essentially, we're saying, "I would try but I'm afraid that if I failed you would think less of me." Instead we need to accept failure as a natural part of growth. It gives us the opportunity to learn. We ought to follow the example of the many small business entrepreneurs who each year fail or come close to failure, learn from their mistakes, change some aspects of the way they were doing business, and ultimately emerge with viable, growing enterprises.

When we accept ourselves we don't see failure as a reason to lose self-esteem. We look at it as a beginning step toward growth. Growth takes effort, and every effort makes us stronger. We realize that our goals are not insurmountable once we acknowledge that failure is a necessary part of the process.

DO YOU PROCLAIM THAT YOU WANT A AND THEN SPEND ALL YOUR TIME PURSUING B?

Have you ever noticed that some people say they want something but then do nothing to make it happen? Some even sabotage themselves, such as the person who says he wants to make more friends and then declines invitations to social events. There are several reasons for this, including fear of failure, fear of the unknown, fear of change, discomfort, a lack of time, and scattered thinking.

Be honest about what you proclaim. If there is something you want, then focus on accomplishing it. That means that you should not do anything that works against your progress toward the goal. If you want to be healthy, you cannot eat junk food. When you think about eating something you know you shouldn't have, tell yourself, "Hold on. How can I be healthy and eat junk? I can't. So I'm not going to engage in something that's going to sabotage my efforts. That's my choice. I have free will and I will exercise my free will."

IF SOMEONE HADN'T SEEN YOU IN FIVE YEARS, WOULD THEY BE SURPRISED?

If they wouldn't be surprised, then you're doing something wrong. You should be able to surprise someone every year, whether he or she likes it or not. Don't be afraid to excel—it does not equate with being compulsive or needing to win. It means simply that you're bringing yourself up to your highest ideal and maintaining it daily. You will become energized by this and you will be able to feel and see new things. You will be able to breathe in new energy and accept people as you never did before.

BEFORE YOU MAKE A DECISION, HERE ARE FIVE STEPS YOU MIGHT WANT TO TAKE.

These steps can keep you out of trouble, and help you make some positive changes.

(1) Withdraw to a nonjudgmental space.

Did it ever occur to you that you don't have to become connected to everything that you are participating in? Simply take a moment before acting on something. Remove yourself from what you are judging. Try to remain neutral. That way, you won't be reacting from the ego.

Say you own a business. One day, a group unionizes it. They want workers to start off with $40 an hour and compensation packages. They are going to put you out of business. Your first reaction is "I hate unions," and their reaction is "We hate rich guys who own their own businesses." Both are wrong. You aren't rich and they aren't greedy. The union people might speak differently if you had a chance to explain that you're willing to pay fair wages, but wages based upon the necessity of making a profit and keeping the business going.

How many businesses have closed in America because unions have refused to pull back? They stay out on strike until they all lose their jobs and the business closes. Now the price goes up and the business is going to hire nonunion people. All of this is unnecessary if both sides can learn to work on a cooperative basis. The shops that do cooperate have succeeded and have created some security and respect. It has to work both ways. There has to be a point where both people have some form of common adaptation, not dominance. Withdrawing to a nonjudgmental space can facilitate that.

(2) Don't react to anger with anger. Instead, react creatively.

People expect you to meet anger with anger, but you don't have to fulfill their expectations. You, not they, are in charge of your reactions, and if you react creatively you can steer through a situation.

For instance, if someone writes me a critical letter, I do not immediately respond by writing another angry letter. I take a step back and become uninvolved. I ask myself, what does this really say? Then I open a dialog. I call the person and tell them that I got their letter. Then I thank them for writing me and say, "I'd like to know what it is that you want to share with me that could help me better understand why you wrote this. And maybe you could explain something other than what's within the letter." That catches them off guard because they're expecting me to say, "You're wrong, I'm right. I've got this. You don't have that. I don't do that." I don't try to make the other person wrong. One of the best ways in the world to resolve a problem is to ask the person who helped create the problem to be a part of the solution for you. See if that doesn't work.

Think of a time you reacted to someone who upset you. That person knew what to say to get you to react. What would happen if you didn't react? What if you didn't give the word power? The word doesn't have any strength. It has no reality unless you make it real. You've got to give it life, and the choice to do so or not is yours. Don't let words hurt you.

(3) Allow time for reflection.

You often have time to make a decision. Why not use it? Think your situation through. How are you affected? What changes might you need to make, both short- and long-term? Write all this down, and write down your options, plus the pros and cons of each. Then wait and reconsider these the next day.

(4) Ask for others' input.

While you're taking time to make your decision, talk to others. How do they view the events that are affecting you? If you talk to several people, you may receive several conflicting pieces of advice, but of course you're under no obligation to follow any of them.

The value of getting others' input is frequently that they can open up perspectives and possibilities that you didn't even know existed. For example, you're wondering whether to buy a house in town A or town B. You talk to friends and acquaintances, some of whom extol town A's virtues, and some, B's. But then a friend tells you about town C, which you didn't even know had the things you were looking for in a place to live. And someone else suggests not buying a house at all, but renting, so that you can remain relatively mobile. You hadn't thought of these last two possibilities at all. Suddenly your choice of options is widened.

(5) Before being critical, place yourself in the other's life.

Ask yourself, "How would I feel if I were in the other person's shoes? How would I be inclined to act?"

Recently, I saw a doctor denigrating a patient. I walked up to this doctor and asked to see him for a moment. We went into a room. I asked him if he was aware of what he had done. And I reminded him that a sick person comes to him because he or she is suffering and in pain. The doctor is supposed to nurture the emotions as well as the body. Patients see him as an authority figure, and he used his power to make someone feel bad. This is something the patient does not need to feel on top of his disease. Before you lash out at someone, I reminded him, ask yourself, what would it be like to be at the other end of that abuse? How would it feel? If it doesn't feel good, don't share it.

The doctor realized his error and apologized to his patient. Then he went over to the other people nearby and told them that what he had done was wrong. At least he had the decency to realize his mistake and correct it. Many people wouldn't, but he is the better person for it, and he'll probably be more empathetic in the future.

DO YOU EXPERIMENT WITH LIFE?

When we experiment, it's often with drugs or sex; witness the 1960s and 1970s. But these can be destructive ways to experiment. There are many other ways to experiment that are not only non-destructive but healing as well. We could experiment by reading a book a week. Or we could walk into a bookstore to purchase magazines we have never read before. What if we began to experiment by changing our hair? If it's short we could let it grow long, and if it's long we could cut it. If we're used to subdued colors, we could wear brighter clothes. Or the reverse.

We can also break some rules and do things that are not socially acceptable. For example, when was the last time you saw an adult skip down the street? The only thing that used to be socially acceptable for adults was walking down the street, with running permitted only to catch a train or bus. Now, it's okay to run or jog for health. But skipping by adults is still not acceptable in public places. Why not? It's fun, aerobic, and not harmful to anyone. Contrast this with public smoking, which for years was socially acceptable. Smoking might have been fun, but it was anti-aerobic and harmful, both to the smoker and to those nearby. So here's a thought: Maybe skipping in public will be the next frontier, especially for those who have had to give up smoking and need something to do. All we need is for somebody to start experimenting and breaking the rules.

Remember, if you always live by the rules, then you become part of the social contract. Yet there's no reason you have to, in effect, sign this contract. As long as what you're doing is legal and moral, why not experiment?

DO RELATIONSHIPS HAVE TO BE PERMANENT?

We like to hold on to people. We gain a lot by saying that we have had a long relationship, judging relationships by the length of time we spend with someone, rather than by the quality of the time that we spent when we were with them. I feel, though, that if there is a time when it is naturally necessary to separate, you should simply part with peace and allow yourself to go on with your life.

In my book *Who Are You, Really?*, I discussed characteristics of the different life energies and how they tend to relate to others. Adaptive supportives, a particularly stable group, tend to have relationships that last longer than those of other groups. These are not always quality relationships, however. Then there are other life energies, such as dynamic assertives, dynamic aggressives, adaptive aggressives, and creative assertives, who tend to have people as points in their life to enjoy. I don't consider this less lasting way of relating to be inferior. Unless someone is at your level, sharing the same energy at the same time, there may well be a time when one of you grows away from the other. This doesn't make anyone bad. It doesn't make one person right and one wrong. It means you are no longer compatible.

Let it go, if this is the case. Look at your relationship as an experience of the moment, without expectations for the future. You're living now. You're respecting, honoring, sharing the best you can now. Sometimes, we want to hold on to a moment and repeat it ad nauseam. When something happens and the person cannot repeat what we had shared in that magic moment, we get angry with the person. We question the person, we question ourselves, and we ask, "What's wrong with me?" Then all of our time is spent challenging the relationship and what went wrong instead of enjoying the relationship. There's no time to enjoy the other person anymore because we're so caught up in the past.

Remember, nothing is ever the same again. No two moments are ever lived the same way. No kiss is ever the same. It's different. That doesn't mean it's worse. It's just different. Why do we have to stay in the circle of the known? "Well, I know how you smelled, and looked, and responded, and now it's not the same. I want you back the way you were." And you start thinking, "Maybe I should go back." But of course you can't.

Don't look at relationships as permanent. For that matter, don't look at your job or your home as permanent. Look at everything for what it means to you at this time. And enjoy it. Engage it. It is rare to meet a person who can enjoy the moment for what it is. People spend so much time in anticipation, and then in jealousy and envy.

CAN YOU POSSESS PEOPLE?

I can't possess another human being. I have no right to. I only have the right to direct my own life, not anyone else's. If someone wants to share a moment in time with me, that's what they've got to share. Sometimes you'll share longer than a moment and you'll continue to evolve together. Sometimes you can share years together, possibly even a lifetime. But it's because you are growing together.

You can stay together if only one is growing, but then you don't find joy in what you're sharing. You are sharing insecurity. You're afraid to be alone. I have a buddy who's terrified of growing old alone. Does he honor his relationship? No way. Does he love the person he's with? Not at all. She fills certain sexual and emotional needs. He simply needs her. So he holds on.

You can't hold on, really. I think of life as a series of passages. For instance, you have a passage with your children. It comes and goes. When they grow up they're still your children, but the passage is gone. You can't relive it. If you've put too much energy into getting ahead and gaining possessions, your passage with your children will have gone right by you. Then if you say, "I'd better get back there and do something," it will be too late. You can never undo something once it's done. You can only do something new.

Think about what would change in your life if you looked at everything and everyone as a passage, not a possession.

WHAT YOU THINK, YOU CREATE.

Thoughts have power. You believe someone gives you a headache, for instance, and then you get one. The truth is that you—not the other person—give yourself the headache. Something I've always found is that if you think small, you get small results. For example, driving up Route 17 from Harriman, New York, toward the Catskills, you see a cluster of suburban homes all stacked together. Two miles away is beautiful countryside. Every time I pass this area I ask myself, "Why would anyone want to live around all those people, with no privacy? Why wouldn't they want to live two miles away?" They think small. They think in terms of cloistered, protected, walled communities, and that's the reality they create.

It you think big, everything in life becomes big. If you think beautiful, you see beauty where otherwise you wouldn't. I choose to believe that all people have beauty in them. I choose to acknowledge that everyone has a warm heart. That doesn't mean that they act beautifully or that they exhibit warmth. But at least I know it's there. If I try, and if I touch something in them that resonates, maybe they will open themselves up and allow that to come out.

I also believe in thinking happy. When I get into a cab, I look up front for the driver's name and then address him by his first name. It adds a personal touch and it brings a smile to his face. When I go into a restaurant I give a bigger tip than what is expected, not to impress anyone but to let the employees know that I consider their service special. I simply extend that connection.

Think excitement! I do. I believe life should be exciting all the time. There's no rule that says it can't be, so I get excited by everything. Most people are afraid of excitement because they don't know how much freedom they have to express themselves. So they restrain themselves. They become passive spectators.

What if you get actively excited when you feel good about what you are doing and you express yourself with happiness? You are sending out a powerful healing energy, and you will attract people.

WILL YOU FIND *IT* WHEN YOU ARRIVE AT YOUR GOAL?

I know people whose goal is to work twenty years, get a pension, and get out. What are they going to get out of? Life? Is the pension a substitute for life? Is a pension a reward for a life misspent? I can't imagine that kind of mindset.

Why not reevaluate your goals and ask, what is the heart of what I want? Is it amorphous? Is it real? Look at your goal. What makes it important? Why are you working at something? Or are you merely working *for* something? Know what it is that you want. If you're working only for a distant goal, there's a danger. Processes, not goals, make a difference. It's what you experience and learn along the way that's important. Otherwise you reach your goal and your life becomes vacuous.

IS TOO MUCH OF YOUR ENERGY INVESTED IN THE FUTURE?

Frequently people put so much energy into the future, and what it might mean for them if things change, that their happiness and fulfillment depend upon what happens out there two months, two years, or five years down the road. I know people who spend nine years in a doctoral program, completely shutting themselves off from the rest of the world. Well, life can't be repeated. You can't live those nine years over again. Unless the extremely cut-off scholarly lifestyle is in itself rewarding—which for a few people I concede it might be—I don't think it's worth it.

Don't postpone your life. Don't sacrifice yourself to the gods of status or to someone else's concept of the path you should take. So you don't get a Ph.D. So you don't buy a million dollar house or work behind an office door with a title on it. Realize that you have enough to enjoy, to accept, to do, to utilize, simply because you are living and it is now—it is this morning, or this afternoon, or this night—and you are here.

What can you do to be in this moment? Just stop everything and say, "What if I started to look at the actual energy that exists right now, instead of at what could be? What do I have right at this moment that can make my life work?" Put some energy into your life right now. Each evening, take an inventory of what you have learned and how you have gained from it. The next day that comes, you will be wiser, smarter, and better able to enjoy life.

Mistake Number Three:
Planning for the Future

1. Right now—do you have a half hour? Go to the most beautiful place you know of within ten minutes of where you are. It could be a park, a corner of your backyard, a spot near a window, or a seat on the couch next to your cat. Spend ten minutes there, relaxing. Return.

   Your reactions? _____

_____

_____

2. Start reading the book you've been saving for a rainy day today.

3. Watch the movie you've been saving for a rainy day tonight.

4. On the next rainy day, walk; don't stay in. (Dress for the weather.) The idea is to see how you can enjoy the moments that make up your life in new ways.

5. We always want to look our best on our birthday. Today or tomorrow, wear what you were planning to wear on your next birthday. Also, eat what you were going to eat (you can omit your name and the candles from the cake!), and see, or at least talk to, the special people you would see or talk to on your birthday. You can enjoy it all again on your real birthday because happiness, like work, will expand to fill the time you give it.

Avoiding Risk

AVOIDING RISK ISN'T necessarily a mistake. It would be fool-hardy to go mountain climbing if you're totally out of shape, surfing if you can't swim. But there are other kinds of risks that are good to take because chances are great that they will enhance your life. Some examples might be, accepting a job offer that doesn't pay well but is in a field that you love, touring Europe alone if you have no travel partner, enrolling in a course in computers even (or especially) if you have no clue as to where the "on" button is.

We've got to remember that, unless we spend life sealed in a room, everything we do is going to have at least a small amount of risk attached to it. Every opportunity comes with a set of unknowns, which you can interpret as risk. It's been my observation that most people don't take advantage of their opportunities. They look at an opportunity and see only the risk, rather than the up side of what life is offering. "No thank you," they say, because they want to play life as safe as possible.

Again, I don't mean that everybody should strap on a parachute and jump out of a plane. But what percentage of people, especially members of the baby boom generation, do you see taking risks such as the ones I've just mentioned? Or, here are some more: leaving a high-status job because it was too high-stress; saying no to social obligations that didn't feel right or weren't mutually fulfilling; changing one's diet completely in order to maximize health; setting a rigorous exercise goal and then actually sticking to the plan, rain or shine; cutting off a negative relationship (when it's possible to do so), rather than just complaining about it for years; deciding a distant place would be a better living environment, and then picking up stakes and moving there. Most of these risks involve breaking away from the mold of what's expected or comfortable, and most people don't want to do that.

I know some individuals who have done these things, and you may know some too, but they're the exceptions rather than the rule. Most people prefer a lifetime of what they see as security— coupled with a low level of satisfaction—to a life of opportunities seized, joys experienced, and yes, risks taken. Such a journey through life can be bumpy. But the "secure" life has its own bumps too, because you can't control every circumstance. So why not increase the risk factor in your life just a little and really try to optimize your time on the planet?

Baby boomers seem particularly risk-averse to me. Maybe this can be explained when you remember that risk often involves breaking away from the safety of the expected or comfortable, and that safety, comfort, and doing the expected were all prized values of the era that molded the boomers. This generation's parents valued safety and comfort, and you can't blame them. The nation had recently been through one of the most traumatic periods in its history—World War II—and had triumphed, but at great cost. What's more, just before the war, baby boomers' parents had lived through another scary time, the Depression, which had left psychic scars on many of them. Emerging from these two difficult periods, young parents set out to make their children's world a better, happier, safer place than their own world had been. They were determined that their children would not have to deal with the perils they had.

Think about where a lot of baby boomers lived growing up— the suburbs. The new "instant" suburbs that sprang up after World War II provided a lot that was good for the children who grew up in them: nice new houses, fresh air, and safe places to play. On the down side, though, these safe havens may have been a little too safe. People in them tended to be from one economic stratum, so that children growing up in the suburbs were not usually exposed to a mix of economic classes. Or races—blacks were excluded. Adding to the sense of the residents' sameness was the way these communities were built. For affordability's sake, the new developments were created the cheapest way possible—by putting up similarly constructed dwellings on clear-cut lots. This meant that people's houses were just about identical. It also meant that everyone could see what their neighbors were doing—not just in their yards but in their houses too, because picture windows were coming into vogue at this time. So it was hard to be different without the Joneses noticing!

They'd certainly notice if your parents weren't fitting into the prescribed mold. The paradigm we had for the family in the 1950s and most of the 1960s was an unambiguous one: All fathers should work full-time. All mothers should stay home full-time. Fathers were responsible for making money, fixing things around the house, and yard work. Mothers were responsible for housework, for the children, and for interacting with the school when necessary. A friend who grew up during the 1950s recounts, only half jokingly, how it felt when her parents deviated from this norm: "I was in the third grade and my father came into school in the middle of the morning to drop off something I needed. I was embarrassed; having a father show up in school seemed like something only a foreigner would do. And this was in New York City, where there *were* a lot of foreigners, and people whose mothers worked, and other un-American phenomena. Imagine if this had happened in the suburbs; it would have been totally mortifying!"

With strict unwritten rules about how people should live their lives, the 1950s and early 1960s were not a time that encouraged risk taking. The idea was to live within acceptable guidelines and concomitantly get rewarded with all the good stuff that modern suburban life had to offer. You could call this a Faustian bargain, but it seemed fair at the time.

After all, modern suburban life did have a lot to offer: pretty streets, green grass, and homes chock full of the latest in wonderful appliances and other fun things, ranging from washing machines and TV's to cake mixes and TV dinners. It was the golden age of ever-improving "labor-saving" devices and the beginning of feverish domestic consumerism as we know it. People talked about "cocooning" in the 1990s, that is, using one's house as a comforting and entertaining refuge from the world. But it was in the 1950s that the ideal of the suburban home as a safe and fun-providing cocoon was really glorified. That safe haven was so important that it required a full-time manager, Mother, who was always supposed to be there, a welcoming, comforting presence. Father went away each day to work, but there was even a safe feeling about that too, because you knew that he'd have his job until he retired, and that the salary the company paid him was taking care of the family, enabling them to enjoy life in their domestic safety zone for years and years.

I'm not saying that this was the life actually lived by most people in America, but this was definitely the ideal. People who are today middle-aged lived with it growing up, and however sophisticated we are now, what was imprinted on our brains in childhood does have an effect. All of which is why taking risks may not be a baby boomer's strong point.

WHERE WE ARE NOW

During the past half century the roles men and women assume have become much more fluid, so that now, for instance, fathers are no longer unusual sights in schools, and some are even their children's main caregivers. Conversely, the fact that mothers may work full-time is accepted, and in fact this often seems expected. It's as if the pendulum has swung in the opposite direction in the expectations department, so that now many stay-at-home moms feel a stigma attached to their *not* being in the paid work force.

Nevertheless, things have improved overall in that there are more options open today to both men and women, in terms of flexible work schedules, telecommuting, and the sharing of parental responsibilities. The latest news in 2001 is that fathers are indeed spending more time caring for their children and doing housework than was the case a few decades ago. Also, recent reports note a trend among both men and women in high-powered jobs who are leaving their prestigious positions in order to spend more time with their families. Some reporters, implying that there are other reasons behind these people's quitting, have been skeptical. I'm not (for once). I believe these people, and I salute them for deciding what's important to them and then going out and pursuing it, at a cost. This is exactly the kind of risk-taking I am talking about.

Taking risks is not easy. For those who suspect they could improve their lives by living a little more "dangerously," exploring the following ideas and questions related to risk-taking, and to associated issues, may be helpful. Again, my answers aren't necessarily the right ones for you. I offer them in the hope that they'll be helpful as a catalyst as you start your own exploration.

FIRST, WHAT *IS* RISK ANYWAY?

The dictionary defines risk as exposure to the chance of injury or loss. That sounds bad, and like a sensible person should want to avoid risk altogether. However, there are three things you should keep in mind. One, the chance of injury or loss may be a very slight one. For instance, when you take a plane flight, there is a risk that you'll be involved in a crash, but the probability is minute. Two, the injury or loss itself may be a slight one. Example: If you give up smoking, drinking, and junk food, there's a real risk that some of your party-animal friends may feel threatened and stop talking to you. But if that happens they weren't true friends to begin with, so it's no great loss. Three, as we've mentioned before, just about every activity beyond breathing carries some risk. (And even that you have to worry about, given the quality of the air!)

Taking on new risks is often both terrifying and exhilarating, like your first roller coaster ride. I went on America's largest roller coaster. It was ten stories high, which is four times as high as the Cyclone in Coney Island. It was so high and steep that we sometimes couldn't see the track in front of us. I thought the track was gone at one point. When we started our downward plummet I screamed at the top of my lungs. I was scared to death. But when it was over I wanted to do it all over again!

Of course doing it over is never the same because you know something that you didn't know before—what the experience is like. I find it exciting *not* to know what's going to happen. That's why I try to change everything in my life every three years. I want to recreate my life by doing and seeing different things. I don't want my life to become predictable and my attitude to become complacent. I want more than just comfort and security; I want to see different sunsets and feel different ambiance. I know this will bring my mind and body up to their highest capacity, and I like the idea of being able to survive in any environment, with all senses present and all my energies balanced.

HOW CAN WE GROW?

We can grow only when we transcend our pain and fear. Unfortunately, society is not going to help us do this, because society wants us to maintain the status quo (i.e., to *not* grow). Thus, we'll work at the same job for forty years, live in the same neighborhood our entire lives, or maintain abusive relationships. It's easier for society that way.

It's not easier for us, though, because we limit our existence. Consider the average person's state of chronic ill health. Most people could be healthy and functional for decades longer than they are. But most are afraid to challenge the dictates of the established medical system even though they rarely, if ever, get better. Society has conditioned people to adhere to traditional standards, even at the cost of their well-being. So people in this country accept, for instance, that it's normal to get next to no exercise during the course of daily life. They accept that the way to eat is to ingest highly processed and sweetened foods. Then they accept that it's normal to suffer from heart disease and other serious illnesses in middle age. Further, they accept that it's appropriate to treat these illnesses using potentially toxic drugs rather than through lifestyle change. Only those few people who are willing to transcend the fear of breaking out of the American mold and do things differently are going to enjoy optimal health.

FROM WHAT DO WE HIDE?

We hide from the truth. It makes us uncomfortable because it shows us what we're doing that's dishonest. If we know the truth but deny it, then we are denying the responsibility to be who we are and to honor the true self.

If we don't confront fear, it will always be present. Only when we confront something can we change. I can't imagine going to a nine-to-five job that I didn't like; I can't imagine being with someone whom I didn't love. It would be abhorrent to me to spend time doing anything that wasn't meaningful. This moment and this day will never happen again. So why not treasure this day? What I want to do now has nothing to do with what I've done. This is the concept of recreating yourself. If we don't try to create an image to please others, then we can create a life based on what we really want to do.

At what point do we say, "I don't need excuses to keep from having a life"? It requires a commitment to oneself and not giving power to the false images of others who are trying to control our life.

DO WE GROW THROUGH
ACTIVE OR PASSIVE FOCUS?

I believe we grow through active focus. Otherwise nothing happens. How many times in life do you focus on something but not act on it? You have what you want in your sight, but do nothing about it. You don't take steps to make it happen. You are passive.

Society, and not just the individual, benefits through active focus. If no one is willing to go out and protest a war, that gives government the message that no one is against the war. When a few people protest, a few more join in, and before long many people are united. Now legislators respond and political changes occur. This is all as a result of people who are actively focused.

ARE CHOICES OR CIRCUMSTANCES
MORE IMPORTANT?

Never allow circumstances to become more significant than the choices that you make. People sometimes do this when they don't want to risk committing themselves to a choice. For example:

Charlie: Do you want to catch a movie tomorrow?

Gary: I'm not sure. Let me call you back later.

Charlie: Well, okay.

This is an example of bad communication. I was afraid to risk making a choice and, as a consequence, I've given Charlie two messages. I've said it might be okay, but I've also said that I might have something better to do. In effect, I've told Charlie that he's not important to me.

Now Charlie feels a little uneasy. But *he* has a choice. Charlie can confront me and say, "Gary, yes or no? Either yes you want to go with me, or no you don't. Which is it? You've got two choices; 'maybe' isn't a choice." By speaking these words, Charlie is asking me to be straight to the point in my communication. He wants me to put choice before circumstance, and he's right.

WHEN FACED WITH A CHOICE, ARE YOU ALWAYS AFRAID TO CHOOSE THE SEEMINGLY MORE DARING ONE?

If so, it may help if you can creatively balance the positive and negative aspects of each. Here's a case in point.

Several years ago I was in upstate New York looking at two pieces of property. I was planning to build a holistic center where people could go to learn crafts, to detox, to meditate, and to be close to nature. I was looking for a place that was within easy traveling distance to New York City but that was in a secluded, inspiring setting. It wasn't easy to find everything I needed.

One of the properties I was looking at was a beautiful, remote sixty acres, but nothing was on it. The other property also had spectacular views. In addition, it had a pond, a barn, and a 200-year-old house. The difference was that the price of the second place was two and a half times higher than that of the first.

I was with a friend who said that of course I should get the land that was less expensive. At first, that seemed the natural choice. But I did this. I said, "Let's look at the pluses and minuses of each one." We started adding them up. In the more expensive property, we had a giant barn that could be turned into a craft center. The cost of that would be approximately $10,000 for insulation and repairs. Also, the more expensive place was located in a community that lacked a health food store. We could create that. In the giant barn, we could press apple cider. We could make everything from wheat-free pasta to sprouts, tempeh, and tofu. The other place did not have a single structure. We'd be looking at nine months to a year and probably $800,000 to build it up.

This process allowed us to see that the more expensive land was better in the long run. It would allow us to function and to start paying off some of our debts right away. After adding everything up, my friend saw my point. What initially looked like a problem became a logical decision.

Follow this process whenever you have a decision to make. Use it in your work, in personal relationships, and in all other areas of life. Add up the pluses and minuses in everything. And in your personal-decision balance sheet, don't forget the intangibles, such as the emotional value of having an adventure, or your need for novelty, or the way a particular place makes you feel. Then, make your choice, realizing that no option is going to be perfect.

ARE YOU A PERFECTIONIST?

Have you ever been around a perfectionist? No matter what they're doing, they're going to find something wrong. It's very annoying that they can never accept anything for what it is.

"Yes, I'll participate in this," the perfectionist says, "but it has to meet certain standards, and those standards are extremely rigid, and I don't know anyone or anything that can meet my standards in any area." They make everybody feel uncomfortable by picking everything apart.

They make themselves uncomfortable too, trying to live up to impossible standards. Every project they're involved in has to go off without a hitch, or it's a disaster. Every experience they have has to meet all their expectations, or it's an unhappy one. And of course everything they own has to be "the best." If it doesn't bear the top-status label, if it hasn't received glowing reviews in *Consumer Reports*, it's not worth having.

Alas, all of the requirements of the perfectionist don't make for a very joyous or spontaneous life. Perfectionists won't risk a new experience until it's passed their personal standards test.

Part of being free to be in the moment is allowing things to be what they are. You don't have to make them over into anything else. You simply accept them. If I go to a restaurant and I don't have the service I want, I accept that, in that moment, that's what the situation is. Maybe it will change, maybe I can encourage it to, but I'm not going to get angry about it. And if you cooked me dinner and I'm eating a meal that you put all your effort into, I'm not going to be nitpicky about it. I'm not going to say, "I don't eat this with that. It's miscombining."

I go to friends' houses who serve me meat and whatever they've got. They're not chefs. Most of them never listen to me on the radio, never read my books. And I never talk about health with them. That's not what we share. So I'll take the meat on my plate and cut it up into little pieces. Then I'll take the white bread and mush it in there. I might find some peas I can eat. I might find some potato. And by the time I'm finished with the meal and talking and enjoying their company, it's too good. I can't eat any more. I'll say something like, "Why don't you put it in a bag? I'll take it home and eat it tomorrow." I don't want to make them feel bad. I want them to feel good.

What I'm getting at is that, to me, the joy is in being with the person, not in what they give me. They're sharing love and respect. How in the world could I be critical of someone sharing love and respect? I want to let them know that the most important thing is the energy that they've shared. It's not about the food on their table. I will never make an issue of that, because I never want people who are trying to be kind to me to feel that I don't respect what they've done.

Adapting to your environment is part of the art of survival. It's my belief that if we were to put more attention into how we can adapt to our surroundings we'd be a lot less stressed, a lot healthier, and a lot happier.

WHAT MESSAGE DO YOU SEND TO OTHERS WHEN YOU BEGIN TO TAKE RISKS?

You are letting them know that you are not under their control. You are your own person. That makes some people feel uncomfortable. You've broken out of their painstakingly maintained little boundaries, and they can't deal with it.

I've seen so many examples of this with people who have taken the risk of changing their diet radically as part of a program to improve health. Often, the people close to them can't deal with the change because they perceive it as a threat to their own ways of eating, cooking, and entertaining, and also to their own sense of fatalism about how healthy and energetic a person can expect to be. So instead of saying, "Fine, I wish you luck in your health program, and even though I'm not going to change my own eating habits, I respect what you're doing," these family members and "friends" will go out of their way to sabotage the person's diet, predict its failure, or disparage the person as a "health nut."

With friends like that, as the saying goes, who needs enemies? Actually, for people who really understand the value of risking new challenges, none of the disparagement matters. They know that while taking risks may mean displeasing others, you also become a more healthy, energetic, and exciting person, and happier with who you are.

YOU SEE THAT SOME AREA OF YOUR LIFE IS NOT WORKING AND YOU WANT TO MAKE A CHANGE FOR THE BETTER. WHEN DO YOU WANT THIS TO HAPPEN?

Most people are only going to change something when they have the confidence that what they are changing to is going to be better than what they are changing from. So they postpone their plans for change. However, if you need certainty before making change, then the change is never going to happen because the results of real change can never be certain. Real change requires you to embrace the unknown. Once you realize this, there is no clock that ever has to be stopped before you can start changing. You can immediately start to change because you are not waiting for certainty.

When you are insecure about change you don't truly let go of the old ways. You place so much of the old self into the new self that your new situation is not going to be any different. You go from one bad relationship to another, from one job you didn't like to another, similar job you don't like, from one unsatisfactory location to another place just like it.

Try making a change where you have no knowledge of the outcome. That is how you will make your greatest breakthroughs. When you don't know what the outcome will be but are willing to try something new, you start to come up with answers for yourself.

COMMITMENT TO CHANGE IS GOOD. BUT CAN YOU APPRECIATE WHAT *IS*—RIGHT NOW?

Focusing on change should not be an obsession. I may have a desire to change, and focus on getting there, but it does not pre-occupy my thoughts. Getting to where I am going is a process, and every step of that process is essential and vital.

How would your life be different if you lived every moment as if it were your last? Would you live it with more respect, attention, focus, acceptance? Would you honor that time? You bet you would.

Normally, we are so preoccupied about getting someplace else that we forget about where we are right now. Learn to appreciate the moment.

HOW DO YOU FEEL ABOUT SAMENESS?

I think sameness is overrated. People expect others to act the same way day after day, but if they do, how can anyone grow? People expect vacation spots to provide the same delight year after year, but it never works out that way, does it? Places just naturally change, vacationers grow up, and then there's the boredom factor too.

I believe in preempting boredom and complacency. In my restaurant, for instance, I like to challenge myself by changing recipes frequently. I'm always offering new entrees, desserts, salads, and soups, because sameness is not something I particularly value. I have certain core offerings, but outside of those, I love to experiment with new dishes. Yes, it's a risk for a restaurateur to vary the menu selections. People may not like the new dishes, and you may lose some business. Then again, other diners may be attracted to the new tastes, and even to the idea that they get to "audition" the unknown.

Shouldn't we be auditioning the unknown every day of our lives, in all kinds of ways?

WHEN YOU COME UPON A FEAR OR UNCERTAINTY, WHAT DO YOU SAY?
(A) I DON'T WANT TO KNOW;
(B) I DON'T KNOW; OR
(C) I COULDN'T KNOW.

If you say "I don't want to know," you are really saying, "If I know, I will have to do something about it; if I don't, then I won't have to do anything." If you say, "I don't know" when you are at a point of uncertainty or fear, you are saying that you are not afraid to find out. You are at least willing to find out, to learn, to do something about it. This attitude, at least, shows an openness.

And lastly, there's "I couldn't know." That's the victim. Often, when people say, "I couldn't have known," they could have. They chose not to know. To know would have meant that they should have been responsible. They chose, instead, not to take the effort to do what had to be done. An example is the laid-off worker who chose not to see the handwriting on the wall and prepare himself for the eventuality of a pink slip. Another example would be the person who eats junk food for years and leads a couch potato existence, and then acts surprised when he or she has a heart attack. I'm not saying that it's always possible to foresee crises, but that it often is, and that people become victims who don't have to be.

HAVE YOU CONSIDERED THE RISK OF *NOT* TRYING SOMETHING NEW?

All new ventures have some risk attached to them. But so does *not* venturing forth into a new endeavor, when you consider the possibility of later regrets as a risk.

No one goes down every single road that presents itself; that's impossible. So we all have had opportunities that we failed to take advantage of. We think back on the experience and wonder,

"What if?" How do you deal with missed opportunities? Do you get depressed thinking about what you might have done? That doesn't accomplish anything. Or does the experience of having missed out on what you could have had give you the courage to take advantage of future opportunities? That's a more constructive approach.

WHAT HAPPENS WHEN YOU ARE VERY SECURE? WHEN YOU ARE INSECURE?

What goes on in your mind when you feel most secure? You follow your own dictates. You relax. You stop thinking a lot. You're yourself. What happens when you are insecure? You try to escape who you are. You become nervous.

We wear a certain image and project an identity of who we want people to think we are. That stems from our insecurity. People then won't know who we really are. If they did, maybe they wouldn't accept us. Maybe they would. Maybe they'd like us better. But when we're most secure is when we're honoring the real self. We're relaxed, we're at peace.

My suggestion is, why don't we take that energy with us every single day? We should surround ourselves with friends who support us when we are in the workplace and at home. This may mean letting go of friends we currently have, or changing the way we dress or where we live. The idea is to have others around us who support our inner sense of peace and security.

If all you do is go through the motions of life, you will never feel secure about who you really are. There will be an underlying agitation. And there are millions of agitated baby boomers out there, from what I've seen. They've gone as far as they could go with their education and their careers. Still, they don't feel they have enough. They think, if only I had more work, more money, more acknowledgment, more success, more things, I would feel better. There's something inside that is insecure. They change everything out there to feel better inside. Unless they finally come to terms with the fact that the outer changes don't change anything basic, they will continue to feel this insecurity.

The insecure self is the one that makes the bad decisions. When you make a decision that's crucial about your life, your relationships, or anything else, from the insecure mind, it will always fail you. You should make important decisions only from a secure mind. That's the mind that allows you to take the risks and the chances, to be flexible and dynamic.

ARE YOU AFRAID TO RISK BEING ALONE?

Everybody talks about "the relationship." Am I wrong? How often do you talk about a relationship?

You can spend your whole life calculating where you're going to find the ideal relationship, especially if you're a woman. Women spend incredible amounts of time trying to figure out where they're going to find the right relationship. And then, if they have the right relationship, the question becomes, how do we know it's *really* the right relationship?

You must be healthy and whole as an autonomous single before you can be happy in a relationship. If you find someone along the way who can support you in a positive way, do so. But most of the relationships in America are codependent, fearful, and insecure. Most of what couples do is hold on to each other as if the other person is a life vest and they're in turbulent water. That's not healthy. Jealousy and envy breed in that environment because the whole reason you're in the relationship is insecurity. Where are you going to grow from there? If one person starts to grow, it makes the other person insecure.

It's better to be single, healthy, happy, and whole and then choose to share in a way that does not adulterate the rest of your life. Then you're choosing to share your strengths. That's not how it usually works in our society, though. We only nurture the relationship. We do not nurture the autonomous self.

WHY VALUE INDEPENDENCE?

Choices change when you say, "The control is with me." It takes an exceptional person to assume that they don't need anybody in their life in order to feel good about who they are. With this type of person, whoever is in their life is there unconditionally.

The whole idea of permanence in a relationship—"till death do us part"—is a societal thing. People need that because they're terrified of the idea that you can be autonomous.

Women, at least in some circles, are still encouraged to get married pretty quickly and have children. What if you could have had the choice not to get married, but rather to see the world, and experience more people? You would be a different person.

In our society, we're scared of the autonomous person. What does it mean to be that independent? It means that that is when you can begin to feel real love. It means you're going to be warmer and more honest in what you share because it comes from the heart, with no hidden agenda, no false motivation.

DO YOU DARE TO THINK IN TERMS OF ULTIMATES?

What could you do, be, or change, in an ultimate way? Have you ever thought about becoming the ultimate vegetarian, the ultimate athlete, the ultimate artist, the ultimate scholar, the ultimate humanist, or the ultimate traveler? Have you ever thought about being the ultimate at anything?

The desire to be the ultimate at something begins with your

imagination. Then, you need the desire and the conviction to try. Desire and passion fuel motivation. They keep you focused on believing that you can. See your ideal perception. It helps not to watch television, listen to the radio, or read the newspapers. Engage in the scholarship of life, not its distractions.

DO YOU EVER FAIL OR LOSE?

We never fail or lose at anything. The language we use must express that. When you accept terms such as failure or loser, you become those. You begin to associate with what you've lost. If you lose love you feel unlovable. If you lose a job, you lose self-esteem. You ask yourself, "If I was really any good, why would they fire me?"

What if you changed the question you asked? What if, every time something didn't work out, you were to say, "How can I use this loss and learn from it?" In that way, you could become stronger.

Think of the losses you've experienced and grown from. Think of all the job losses, the deaths of loved ones, the health problems, the financial losses, the relationship crises. You've made it through all of those. That counts for something. As a result, you are more confident and better able to deal with life.

Did you ever realize that people who succeed in life have had far more failures than most people? The difference is, they haven't given up. They've kept going. They've used their so-called failures as building blocks for the next step along the way.

Mistake Number Four:
Avoiding Risk

1. Write down what would constitute one step beyond your comfort zone in the following areas:

Your favorite sport_____

Meeting new people_____

Going to new places_____

Your career_____

Choose an area and take that step.

2. Consider the following:

What was the biggest risk you took in the past year?_____

_____

In your life?_____

_____

Are you glad you took these?_____

3. What small risk can you take tomorrow that may be worth taking? Examples: striking up a conversation with someone at your workplace whom you don't know but have been wanting to meet, eating alone at a new restaurant, playing tennis if you're not good at it.

Write it down._____

_____

Do it. What were the results? _____

_____

4. Are you currently involved in a conflict with someone? If so, take the initiative in resolving it peacefully.

5. Plan your next vacation in a place totally new to you.

Believing Our Culture Is the Best

THE GOOD NEWS about mistake number five is that we're making it less and less.

Let's look back at the 1950s and early 1960s. Then, the United States was the best country in the world—period. That's what people said, without any qualification. That's certainly what baby boomer children were taught in school. Today, you can make fun of multiculturalism and political correctness, but it's still a good thing that we're questioning that old idea of "the American way—all best, all the time." Generally, we have become more interested in learning from other cultures.

The baby boomer generation helped get this process going with the counterculturalism and activism of the late 1960s. Anther factor is the foreign travel that many people of this generation have undertaken. Not every American who's gone abroad has stayed in four-star hotels and eaten in foreign McDonalds's. Some have actually immersed themselves in the lifestyles of the different cultures they've visited, and some have even learned from them. For instance, many Americans have gotten to know something about France and Italy. They've seen how people in these countries shop for food, prepare meals, and dine. In America, shelf-life, convenience, and speed are the ruling virtues in the food world, but in Europe, finding quality fresh foods, preparing them well, and eating in a leisurely, social atmosphere are more important. Americans who have experienced this first-hand have come back home and tried to change their shopping and eating habits. We've seen such changes as the increasing popularity of farmers' markets and organic food co-ops, and of "the Mediterranean diet" as a healthful alternative to the American meat-and-potatoes dinner plate.

Child-rearing practices are another area in which Americans have adopted what would have been considered, several decades ago, foreign ways. In the 1950s, anyone carrying a baby around strapped to their chest or back would have been looked upon as a nut—that was what women in Africa did! Precisely. Mothers in Africa have always known that keeping an infant strapped close to your body, so that the child can feel your skin and move with you as you work, keeps that infant happy, and Americans, to their credit, have caught on. They've also caught on to breastfeeding and natural childbirth, which in the 1950s were the kinds of things that only so-called primitive people did. Or look at the "family bed" concept, where everyone—parents, babies, and young children—sleep together, as they do in many Native American and other cultures. This is not what we've traditionally been told is right in this country, but there are some American psychologists today propounding the concept, and some American families practicing it.

WHERE WE ARE NOW

I'm not saying that most people are sleeping in the family bed. Most people aren't even trying the Mediterranean diet, despite the fact that it could save their lives. Many may not even know what it is. So there's still a lot of horizon-broadening to do.

(In case you're haven't heard, Mediterranean cultures such as Italy, Greece, and Crete have some of the healthiest and longest-lived people in the world, and one of the reasons is their diet. The characteristic Mediterranean diet features fish in abundance; organic, cold-pressed natural oils, such as olive, almond, and flaxseed oil; olives; avocados; purslane and other herbs; grain-based foods, including lots of homemade pastas; low-alcohol, natural red wines; fresh fruits and vegetables; and nuts, berries, and seeds. The people in these countries are not generally vegetarians—they do eat meat occasionally—but their cuisine is delicious, and most Americans would be doing themselves a big favor if they tried it.)

It's important to understand that the issue of horizon-broadening goes beyond interest in other cultures. Here's what it's about at a deeper level: If a person's not willing to look at his or her cultural assumptions, he's not going to be willing to look at any of his assumptions about life. He's just going to plod through his days unquestioningly, following down the same narrow path that he's been following for years and that others have followed before him, stuck in the same old ruts that are getting deeper and deeper all the time. Were I to suggest getting off this path, and getting on a wider, fresher, more scenic one, he's going to give me reasons why making a change is not practical. When I counter those excuses, he'll say, "No, it's more complicated than that. You don't understand."

But I do understand. The problem is a closed mind.

Let me give you an example of what it is to have a closed mind. I take my shoes off when I come into my apartment, and I expect everyone else who enters to do the same. There's a sign near the door politely requesting that people remove their shoes, and I do this because there is no way I want the filth that's in our city streets tracked into my house. Think about what's out there—every excretion from the dog, cat, and bird body—not to mention some from humans—plus soot and auto emissions. (By the way, in the suburbs you may think the situation's better, but it's worse when you consider all the herbicides used on the lawns.) So why anyone would accept all this toxic, dirty stuff being spread across their floors when it doesn't have to be is beyond me. And in households where there's a baby crawling around, it's unconscionable.

Anyway, most people who enter my apartment comply with my request. But a few let me know they don't like it. They seem to find this shoe removal business un-American, maybe because, in the movies, John Wayne usually got to keep his boots on. For whatever reason, they just can't get their minds around the concept.

"Oh come on, Gary," they say when they see my sign, "what are you, Japanese?"

"You bet I am. . . ," I say, ". . . when it comes to keeping dirt out of my home. And everyone else should be too."

Then I say to them, "Did you every try to wear your shoes into a Japanese person's home? They're appalled! They try to hide how upset they really are, but they're appalled. And rightly so, because . . . ," and then I launch into a description of all the filth that's on our streets, something like I've done here, but in around ten times more disgusting detail. For instance, I describe all the germs for all the awful diseases that could be in someone's spit that you might step in on the street. I really go into the total picture.

Believe it or not, some people are not swayed. They nod, "Yes, but . . . ," and then they switch the subject to fashion, explaining that when a person goes to a lot of trouble to put together a look, their shoes are often an important accessory, and they don't want to spoil the look by removing them.

"I understand," I say, "but now try to look at this from a different perspective. When you put together a fashion statement, sometimes your overcoat is an important part of it. Still, when you enter my house, you're going to take off your overcoat. If you didn't, it would be like saying my house wasn't adequately heated, or like saying you didn't want to be here and you wanted to get out as quickly as possible. It would be insulting to me. Likewise, not taking off your shoes is insulting. It's saying you don't care about my health. So just think about a shoe as something like an overcoat. You come in, you take it off. It's only a small change in mindset."

Still, there are some people who can't make that small mental change. They can't expand their outlook. They can't learn. This is a shame because, with the world as your classroom, you can learn so much.

You can go to Spain and see how they don't have to say "Let's do lunch" there, because they "do lunch" every day with their families, enjoying a relaxed main meal for at least an hour. It keeps family ties strong, and is better for the digestion than our custom of eating our largest meal in the evening.

You can go to South Africa and see how the Bushwomen of the Kalahari nurture their infants, carrying them close to their bodies all the time and breastfeeding them for several years. These children do not have problems with insecurity.

You can go to Hungary and observe how young people there are guided by their elders through the difficult passages from childhood to adolescence to adulthood. Guidance there is not just something you get from an office in school.

You can talk to Native Americans about what the concept of nature means to them. It's a sacred part of everyday life. It's not merely a frill to be enjoyed on weekends, or a force to be controlled, owned, erased, or put on exhibit.

I could go on, touching down in dozens of cultures, but it all boils down to this: If you're open to the world, the world will open up a wealth of useful knowledge and perspectives to you. This is true on every level of experience.

Let's use this idea of openness as our jumping-off point in self-exploration.

CAN YOU ACCEPT NEW EXPERIENCES AND PEOPLE WITHOUT PREJUDGING THEM?

When you think of going someplace, your mind paints a picture. If I say to you, "Let's take a trip to London," you might see Big Ben, the Tower of London, and the little inns. If I suggested a trip to Haiti, your image would be altogether different. You might see poverty and crime.

London and Haiti are both beautiful places. They both have good and bad inhabitants. You could have a good or bad time in either place. But the image you create leads to a prejudgment that will cause you to accept or reject the possibility of a good or a bad time.

It's the same with people; you should never prejudge them. Unfortunately, many of us just can't resist generalizing about groups. For instance, say the word "teenager" and many people will conjure up a vision of a threatening, lazy, disrespectful individual whose hair is dyed green and whose skin is pierced in ten weird places. The reality, though, is that a lot of teenagers are the most polite, hard-working, socially adjusted individuals you'd ever want to meet. Yes, there are those with green hair and pierced body parts, and here's the interesting thing—a lot of *them* are polite, hard-working, and socially adjusted too! You don't have to be dressed in preppy clothes to be an honor student, just like you don't have to be between the ages of twenty-five and sixty-five to be a model citizen.

A friend of mine has an interesting story about how prejudging doesn't work. "Up until my late thirties," she says, "I'd just sort of assumed that you were friends with people in your own age group—maybe give or take ten years—people going through roughly the same stage of life you were. So moms with young children were friends with moms with young children. That was my stage of life, and those were the people I was seeking out.

"There was a woman in my neighborhood whom I only began talking to because we'd both gotten involved in a local political struggle, to save trees in an area park. It seems silly now, but I found her a little scary at first because she was in her seventies, her skin was all wrinkly, and her eyes were slightly crossed. When I saw her, my first reaction was 'strange.' She'd never had kids, and was not the type to pretend interest in other people's.

"Here's what I found out: I had more in common with this woman than with a lot of fellow moms my age. Like me, she truly cared about the local park and its trees because, like me, she liked to walk on a trail there. She had the kind of spirit, energy, and interest in the world that some people call youthful, but that are really ageless. When I talked with her it was like being back in the exciting world of a college campus, where exchanging real ideas was an important part of conversing. . . .

"I later met this woman's husband. He was even more off-putting in appearance, in that he had Parkinson's disease and he shook a lot. But he had a really innovative mind; he was an inventor, and was particularly interested in extended-time photography. You could talk to these people for hours. To tell the truth, getting together with them was a whole lot more stimulating than talking with other mothers about the cutoff date for kindergarten. But I never would've suspected this at first glance."

What if you were to simply refrain from prejudging everything you think about? You wouldn't reject all the places you hear negative things about. You wouldn't dismiss people until you got the chance to know them. Think of how much more of the world you'd be open to experiencing.

WHAT'S INVOLVED IN ACCEPTANCE?

To me, the ideal of acceptance connotes openness. I chose to accept everyone early on. Because of that I now accept different belief systems. I can sit and talk with a communist, a capitalist, or a socialist without feeling angry, without trying to "correct" or change them, and without trying to make them see my reality.

You never change anyone in life, not that you have the right to. If you think you're smart enough to change someone, think again. We live in a world of multiple realities. There is a place for all of them. If you don't accept other people's realities, they may close off a side of themselves. All you are doing then is accepting someone who has changed superficially to be accepted. As a result, you never expand your outlook on life, and you pay a price for that.

If you can accept a person who is completely different from

you, and honor those differences, you will have the opportunity to build a rich relationship. The differences can enhance you as much as what you have in common.

WHAT HAPPENS WHEN YOU ARE HONEST?

When you are honest, you are in harmony with your true being. Being honest is easy, because you do not have to pretend to be something you are not. Conversely, being deceptive takes time and attention. You always have to remember what you said and did so others won't figure out the lies. The lies lock a door to your soul, which is your true self.

In actuality, you can never really lie to yourself. When you suppress feelings, desires, and thoughts, you create guilt at the subconscious level. People who uphold vows of celibacy, for example, consciously believe in the rightness of what they are doing. The politic part of their being believes it. But their body doesn't, and their physiological sensations tell them so. To assuage their guilt, they often become more radical in their beliefs. They begin an emotional flagellation of self. They say, "I'm not worthy because I don't have the strength to keep from sexual arousal." In reality, though, it is all biological.

Ultimately, your truths must coincide with universal ones. For example, a person is conditioned not to trust someone because of his nationality. On the surface, the person believes this to be true, but his inner consciousness knows it to be a lie. It is not a universal honesty. You have to match your individual beliefs to universal truths. To do this, you frequently must take a big step outside of your belief system.

How do we know what is universally true? That which honors life is true. No one has the right to take another life, for instance. And no one has the right to dishonor anyone. If I am growing food organically, I am not adulterating the soil, water, air, or human body. I am following a universal truth. If I am not an organic farmer, I may be growing food with pesticides, and I may be growing only one crop at a time. I believe that this is the way I must farm to prevent insects from eating my crops. My individual truth, then, is that I can't grow anything but corn or wheat, and that I have to use pesticides. That's my truth, and it's correct as far as I know. But it's not a universal truth. To understand what is universal, we have to look at the consequences of our beliefs. How will what you believe manifest? How will it affect other people? Once you think of the consequences of your beliefs, you will see whether or not they uphold universal truths.

Being honest is the first step toward genuine communication. How in the world are we going to communicate meaningfully if we're always communicating with partial deception? Of course being honest means that we will not always be accepted. People can say to me, "Gary, I appreciate your being honest, but I don't like what you're saying and I can't accept it." That happens all the time, and it's okay. Others have a right to reject what I say. At least people know where I stand, and I know where they do.

Being honest makes some people uncomfortable, but I can't help that. If I were to stop and think before I ever said anything, and edit what I said based on expectations of acceptance or rejection, no one would come to my lectures because I would be saying nothing new and vital. I know my questions make some people uncomfortable, but I also realize that I do not create that feeling. Something within the person triggers a reaction. You can see it in people's bodies; they start to recoil, to become physically defensive. Of course my intention in being honest is not to hurt anyone, but rather to communicate the truth.

What's nice about committing yourself to honesty is that you can never go back to deception. It's like being in a straitjacket and getting out. You'd never want to be restricted and limited again.

When I go to sleep at night, my head hits the pillow, and I'm asleep. I have no unresolved worries on my mind. Truth assuages everything.

WHAT MAKES SOMETHING RIGHT OR WRONG?

Being right takes more than your perception of being right. As we've just discussed, your truth must be right according to universal principle.

Some people see what's right for them personally, and then they stop their thinking right there. I interviewed people who worked in a company that made pesticides that were banned in the United States, but sold legally overseas. I checked and found out that hundreds of thousands of pesticide poisonings, and tens of thousands of deaths from those poisons, had occurred in China and other countries. I asked these people, "Is it right for you to be working in a company that makes a product that hurts people in another country?" Their answer, almost uniformly, was, "I'm not doing anything wrong. I'm just making a living." They were making a living by taking other lives, but that didn't seem to matter.

People do not feel connected to their extended reality. That's why a bomb maker doesn't think about where the bomb is going to be used. Imagine working in a factory that makes land mines. Every day, children throughout the world are getting their limbs blown off because someone went in and planted a mine, but no one ever cleared it. There are millions of these planted mines. No one knows where they are, and no one is taking the responsibility to clear them.

I couldn't work in a factory where I knew that something was being made that could destroy someone. I have to live by universal truths, and my reality honors all people. Don't forget that everything you do extends to others. See the larger reality that affects us all.

DO YOU JUDGE PEOPLE?
OR DO YOU SIMPLY TRY TO COMMUNICATE?

We are always measuring people. We ask ourselves, are we equal? Are we more? Are we less? Within two minutes of meeting someone, we've already made innumerable judgments about them. What we have usually not done is think about how we can communicate with the person despite our differences.

You see this in the way people socialize. If you dress up like a bag lady and then go to an upper-middle-class party, you are sure to be ignored or asked to leave. But if people are led to believe that you are famous European nobility, they will treat you differently. You'll receive enormous respect, and everyone will vie for your attention.

People just don't get that others who seem different from them are still people. They try to compensate for the differences by ignoring or being disrespectful of those they think are their inferiors, and by fearing and playing up to the ones they believe are beyond them.

We respond more to image than to substance, when in reality we are all just people. If you deal with famous people, you will soon come to realize that they are just people. You will begin to look for your commonalities and associate along those lines. Then you recognize one another's humanity. It's the only way to communicate.

This is not to say we can't appreciate other people's differences. We have to, because all of us are different, and in fact one of our goals should be to learn about and become more sensitive to how these differences are expressed. Our culture favors people who respond in certain ways and discriminates against those who act differently. Consider, for instance, that Cherokee Indians are brought up never to answer questions that would in any way denigrate others who can't answer. But in the average American classroom, when one person doesn't respond to a question, another is immediately called on, to the first person's humiliation. If you were a teacher, you could be in a situation where understanding this cultural difference might be vital.

Have you looked into history on your own?

History is constantly being perverted to serve the interests of those who are writing and interpreting it. As a result, most people where I grew up believed that blacks were stupid. If they weren't stupid, then why weren't they successful and rich? I had to argue constantly with so-called educated people that it wasn't the blacks who were at fault.

I wrote a book called *Black Geniuses* that showed the creative insights and unique contributions of over 2000 African Americans who helped civilization advance, although they themselves had no financial means whatsoever. Their contributions include the fire extinguisher, the safety traffic line, open-heart surgery, blood plasma, the couplings and overhead lines on trains, and the first incandescent light (which was not created by Edison, but by Lewis Latimer). George Washington Carver alone created hundreds of innovations; his output was never surpassed by any other inventor in history. Admired by Henry Ford, who wanted this prolific inventor to come work for him, Carver developed a wide variety of useful byproducts of sweet potatoes, soybeans, and peanuts. This was important for the south's agriculture, which had become too dependent on cotton. When that crop was threatened by the boll weevil, finding uses for other crops was an invaluable contribution, but one we don't learn that much about in mainstream education.

I recommend reading one book per month about a group other than your own. Find out about a different perspective on history. Read about other races, cultures, and religions. You'll find strengths and weaknesses in all. Once you understand the strengths and weaknesses of each, you can put it all in a proper historical perspective. That way you'll be less prone to be manipulated and lied to.

DO YOU THINK BEFORE YOU ACT?

Correct choices are conscious choices. But these rarely occur. More often than not, choices are based on reactions to emotions felt in the moment. You're in a traffic jam, for example. Traffic is stuck, and you're frustrated because it's hot outside, and you have to be someplace. You're afraid that you're going to be late and judged irresponsible for being late. Automatically, you grab the wheel hard, and you bang on the horn, even though it's not going to mean anything. No one's going anywhere, because everyone's stuck in traffic. Now your adrenaline's pumping. In the course of a few seconds, you have created a cascade of stress hormones that could lead to premature aging and illness. The body can't differentiate the stress that arises out of an emergency fight-or-flight response from the stress of just having a bad day. It can't say, "This isn't serious, so I'm not going to put adrenaline out right now."

Every time you have a negative thought you create stress. Every wrong thought creates the wrong emotion. Then you have the wrong reaction. That's a problem in our society. That's why we're forever saying we're sorry. We're sorry because we don't think before we act.

CAN YOU ACHIEVE EVERYTHING FROM A STATE OF CALM?

Yes, you can. We're used to thinking that we have to be on an emotional roller coaster because we're a society that's addicted to the adrenaline high. Normal nuances of everyday living, subtle expressions, gentle teachings, no longer catch our attention. We're at a loss when we're confronted by something that's subtle. That's why we read and watch the news. Did you ever watch what's on the news? Murders, rapes, burnings, disasters—the news media supply us with what they feel we need.

But we don't need that. Stop reading newspapers. Stop watching television. Stop the negative input, and regain a sense of calm. Only the quiet mind can heal, but we're a society whose mind is constantly chattering. So we need to slow it down. When you slow down the mind and you quiet it, then you can hear your inner voice. Otherwise, you're always looking here, there, and everywhere, and listening to external clatter. And you can't feel the subtleties.

Healing energies are subtle, and are a contrast to everything out there, which causes excessive stimulation. Movies, such as *Armageddon*, now have to cost $200 million in order to get our attention. They have to spend $100 million on promotion. That's ridiculous, especially when you consider that all they're about is violence and destruction. Once again, they think, let's take Americans up to the top of the roller coaster and put them on a fast trajectory down. That's the only way we're going to get their attention. And it's true. The masses don't want to see subtle, poetic, gentle movies. If it doesn't have the violence, sex, or high drama we've come to expect, we don't want to see it. We don't want to see movies where there's a happy beginning, middle, and end.

Women's movies are designed to show the victimization of a woman, a broken heart, unrequited love. In the end she dies, and then everyone's happy. Audiences walk out happy, visualizing themselves as the heroine. It's crazy, when you think about it—we can't be happy with happiness! We don't get off on it. It doesn't ring a bell. Good news doesn't sell. Good news is bad business. Bad news is good business. Something is wrong with that.

We can change everything by realizing that we can answer questions from a state of calm. The more calm you are, the more options you have in the selections that you are willing to make. When you are creating from a state of anxiety, you limit your options. Fear restricts them. Anger, fear, and loathing all limit what you're willing to do when making a decision, and these negative emotions will almost always result in the wrong choice. When you're calm and relaxed and feeling at peace with yourself, you're honoring who you really are. That's when you should make your choices.

Never make choices from anger, depression, anxiety, fear, uncertainty, or pain. If you do, they will probably not be the right choices. They may be convenient, but they won't be right. Wait until you have clarity. Then look at your options and make a choice.

CAN YOU CONTINUALLY CHALLENGE YOURSELF BY THINKING WITH A NEW MIND?

That's the ideal, I believe, because with that new mind come new ideas and a broader perspective. Broadening perspective, not knowledge, is key.

We've come to accept knowledge as growth. I would challenge that. We've been led to believe that all we need is new information and new facts. If we have enough facts and equations, then somehow we can figure things out. But if that were truly the case, why do we have so many problems in society? And why do so few people have a life that works? They certainly haven't been deficient in information. What they've been deficient in, rather, is new perspectives, new ways of framing problems that leave the old biases, prejudices, and bigotry behind.

DO YOU BLOCK OUT WHAT YOU FEAR OR DON'T UNDERSTAND?

When you are in denial, you deny everything. The person who says he doesn't like Jews, or blacks, or Catholics, or WASPs is substituting hatred and racism for a fear of the unknown. When people feel good about themselves and are in a natural rhythm of living, they can appreciate everything for what it is. They can appreciate people for who they are, not judge them by color. There are both good and bad people of all races and religions. When you are in harmony with life, you can see that. But if you are insecure about yourself, and if you lack inner love and peace, you're going to allow artificial boundaries to exist. Then you'll overreact and overjudge and do everything you possibly can to justify yourself.

DO YOU TRY TO CHANGE THE PROBLEM OR YOUR PERSPECTIVE ON THE PROBLEM?

Most problems start with an inappropriate perspective. When you are able to change your perspective, you can change the problem.

Here's an example: One day, I was walking down my street. A man from the sanitation department was writing me a ticket because my garbage bags were open. This was not my fault. I had closed the garbage, and tied it up. He didn't want to hear anything from me, though, and proceeded to write me a ticket.

That night, I was by my window. Sure enough, at about 11:00, a man came along with a big shopping bag and a big, black garbage bag. He opened up the garbage, took out cans, wrapped the bag back up, and moved on.

A little later, another man came by and punched holes in the garbage. He threw everything out. I went outside the next day to talk to them. I asked the first man, "What is it that you are doing?" He said, "I'm trying to make a living. I don't want to be in a shelter. I don't accept money from people. I want to take care of myself." This unfortunate man had enough self-esteem that he wanted to do something constructive, so he was recycling cans, trying to make enough to get himself a little room in a hotel. He was hoping to get beyond all this soon.

The other guy was just looking for something that he could sell on the street. He didn't care. I said to him, "We have a situation here. If you continue to leave the bags this way, I will continue to get tickets. I don't deserve that. I'm willing to help you by asking people in the building to save anything of value for you by putting it downstairs outside of bags. Would you work with me on this?" He agreed to do it, and he did. People in the building began to put out old phonograph records and other things he could take.

By changing my perception—not looking at this person as bad, but with the perspective that this man was without a home, poor, probably uneducated, probably without a support system, and probably without self-love, I was able to understand his actions. Without self-love, he could easily feel indifference toward others. When a person has no love or respect for himself, then he is less likely to extend these feelings to other people. My perception was, deal with the person on his level of need.

It was this perspective that allowed the problem to be changed.

IS YOUR REALITY CREATED BY WHAT YOU BELIEVE OR WHAT ACTUALLY IS?

Is a reality something that is, or do you create what it is? It is what it is, but we often end up creating something else. We misinterpret reality all the time. For example, I once had a guest at my ranch.

The person said, "My purse is missing. Someone here stole it."

I said, "You're jumping to conclusions. I don't think anyone stole your purse."

"Someone had to. It's not here. My door was unlocked. Someone stole it."

I pulled back and this person whined and moaned the whole day. She was very upset and didn't attend any workshops.

It turned out that she had put the purse in another room when she had gone to visit someone.

That night, the person who found it said, "By the way, you left your purse on the bed when you were here."

"Oh," she responded.

I said, "'Oh' isn't good enough at this point. You should go to every person here and apologize to them for assuming they were thieves."

"Why?"

"Because that's what you were thinking. You blamed the others. You were wrong."

Jumping to conclusions is always wrong. You create something other than what is, and you don't see things for what they really are.

DO YOU PLAY THE BLAME GAME?

We're constantly blaming. Only, I don't think we've noticed that this approach doesn't work, on a personal level or on a societal one. Look at our legislation, for example. Right now we want to build more prisons and give longer prison terms because we have more drug addicts. But increasing jail-time is merely one possible reaction to the circumstance that we've got people selling drugs on our streets. The truth is that if you put every drug dealer in jail there would still be someone else managing to sell some drug.

We can never build enough prisons for all the people willing to commit crimes. So why not look at the reasons they commit the crimes, sell the drugs, take the crack—and then try to get at the causes. If we did that we'd have to become more egalitarian, more humane, more understanding, more ethical, more spiritual. We'd have to be concerned about people's essential needs that we're not willing to meet.

It's a "me" society—I got mine; you get yours. You can't get yours—too bad. I like yours; I'm going to take yours and put it with mine. Now we've got super-rich people who have got theirs and everybody else's.

Take away everything people have and they're going to be depressed. That's going to lead a lot of them into some very aberrant behavior, especially when they feel that no one cares. If you care about someone, you nourish that caring, and you watch how that person starts to look for reasons to be healthier and happier. As a schoolteacher, if you find the child that the parent has not paid attention to and you give him some real one-on-one time and energy, you start to see the attitude of the child change. And if you make that child feel that he's smart and good and creative, and make him an important part of your class, he's going to be less likely to want to go out and do drugs. The drugs were merely a replacement for the unconditional support and love that he should have been getting from family or from the system around the family.

Unfortunately, the support and love that children need are often lacking. Instead we just say we'll have a 10:00 curfew. We'll confiscate arms. We'll put more officers on the street. We'll legislate longer prison terms. None of that is going to change the underlying cause of the problems.

DO YOU LOOK AT THE LARGE ISSUES?

People ask me how I come up with the ideas for the talks that I give and the books that I write. They come when I am completely relaxed, and not thinking about any specific issue. I go out on my Versaclimber and I start doing a long workout. During this hour and a half, thoughts come into my mind. In sorting through them, I always start with the larger issue. When you start with a big issue and you work back, you suddenly see where you are, and where you've been in your previous mindset. Hence, you see how prejudiced, or biased, or limited your thinking was. Our society has an interest in keeping us really specific in our thinking, thinking the so-called right thoughts, for which we are graded in school, acknowledged by our parents, rewarded at work, and honored by society. Everyone has a notion of what's right. Hence, everyone has a stake in our sense of reality.

Rarely does a person get a chance to take a big step out of all that and take a look at what really is. That's why you'll hear me ask questions such as, how does medicine continue to arbitrarily, seemingly, and capriciously, sacrifice tens of thousands, if not hundreds of thousands, of lives, when the protocols are clearly flawed? Look at chemotherapy, anti-inflammatory steroids, Prozac, and electroconvulsive therapy. This is not to suggest that some people do not benefit from those modalities. But as a whole, none of them are healing. At best, they stop some of the symptoms. Our society doesn't want any bad feelings, physically or emotionally. So it does everything it can to provide people with things that will take them away. As a result, we're in a lot of denial. And when you are in denial, you never see what you are a part of. You see only the problem right in front of you. But you're not aware of what the problem is attached to.

That's why I look at governments and ask, in whose interests are they run? Who benefits from the policies that are made? Is the whole process of selecting people to make decisions for us truly democratic? Are the people chosen really objective? I don't believe so. Our so-called representatives don't care about our interests. If they did, they wouldn't be enacting laws that are self-serving and selective. No one in office is saying, "You're from Mexico, you're from Israel, you're from Jordan, and you're from Northern Ireland. We'd better make sure that all of you are respected for your backgrounds, your perceptions, and your realities. We can form a coalition that allows for everyone's interests to be acknowledged." At least that way you could start the process of bringing people together. But our society separates people with a passion. And we don't always acknowledge it.

We're too busy looking at the little conflicts and problems to step back and view the whole picture.

DO YOU NEED CONFLICT? IF SO, WHY?

We pride ourselves on our conflicts. We prided ourselves on the Cold War while it was going on, and we still seem to delight in the differences between Democrats and Republicans, the North and South, labor and management, blacks and whites, Christians and Jews. We maintain conflict instead of asking ourselves what would happen if the conflict were resolved. When you remove the ego's need to be part of the conflict, you will find all kinds of options for its resolution. Most people in our society, though, don't seem to be interested in this.

I was invited to be a guest on a TV program to debate a doctor who didn't believe in vitamins. Since I advocate such supplements, the producers were hoping to start a fight. They know that ratings rise when there is a conflict. The problem is, I would have had to yell and scream to make my point heard, since the other guest provokes such scenarios. We wouldn't have been able to debate the issue in an intelligent way, and the audience wouldn't have gotten to make choices based on sound reason. I declined to appear on that particular show, because the conflict format doesn't make sense to me.

DO YOU FEEL THE VALUE IN ALL THINGS AND IN ALL PEOPLE?

If you are like most people, the answer is no. Don't feel guilty about things; do things. I believe anything constructive you can do you should do. And if you can't, just honor the fact that you can't. It's better to be honest than to say it doesn't matter. This affects your inner voice, which can never be lied to. Every human being has an inner voice. We're born with it. That is our spirit. When the spirit is allowed access to our conscious states, thoughts, and actions, we will never live in disharmony with other people, nor seek conflict, because we will find that all things have value.

How can any culture feel good about itself if no one values them? Wars are created when people are given no power and are acknowledged no value. As a result, they're the ones who starve, who are made homeless, who are made victims. They're the ones who end up in the ghettos with no future. And after a period of time, someone comes along—generally a dynamic energy—and says, "Hold on. This is not right. Let's overthrow this." And the rebel movements start throughout South America, Africa, and elsewhere. Now you have conflict.

We ought to look at conditions in developing countries and see how they got this way, how they are being maintained, and what we can do to change them. In this way, we value these people and their children. Do you think that the mother of a Bolivian child is so unaware of the importance of her and her child's life that she doesn't care if her child dies? Of course that person knows the value of life, just as we do. The difference is that she has had all power taken away from her.

Spend time, as I do, with poor people, and see where they get their strength, purpose, and meaning. They'll show you that without anything that we think is essential for life, they have everything that's truly essential. Most people in this country—living with conditions that anybody else in the world would grab in a second—whine and complain, "Woe is me." I have no pity or sympathy for people who have so much and appreciate so little. I can take you to places where the population has nothing, materially, that we have, and yet they are still able to have meaning, purpose, and spirituality in their lives, and live at a higher level. This is because they still have a sense of values.

When I look at life, I start by saying that all life has value. You are what you manifest, not what you think, not what you'd like, not what you're guilty about, but what you are—that is your value. Are you a caring person? I've never met a truly caring, giving, and nice person who couldn't be nice, giving, and caring to everybody, not just to those in his/her own group. It's easy to be caring to those in your own circle. But what about all those who are out of the group, those who may seem different, or whom you may even fear?

What if you had no boundaries? What if you accepted everybody as being equal? Then you wouldn't have an allegiance to anyone. Therefore, no one could manipulate you by using the concept of group loyalty. You would be a more powerful individual because you would be beholden to no special interest beyond that of your own personal integrity.

ARE YOU POSSESSED BY POSSESSIONS?

We're a thing culture. Our minds are possessed by what we possess, and we're so used to this state of affairs that we don't even notice that our daily lives are largely devoted to the acquisition and maintenance of things. We think it's normal to be deluged with advertising from morning to night, and to wear brand names on our clothes. Even our relationships are pervaded by materialism.

It's unfortunate that people don't understand that there's a purpose to a relationship that goes beyond just shared possessions. Many couples start off a relationship with a sense of wonderment, excitement, exploration, and enjoyment from being with someone. A year or so later, they're working on careers as a way of getting things, without enjoying each other. The wonderment, the joy, the love, the affection, are all gone. Now they're working on a condo or a house or something else. The relationship becomes a convenient way of working together to possess things. That's not a real relationship anymore. That's using each other. Unfortunately, this describes a lot of relationships in our society.

DOES THE "I'LL SHOW THEM" ATTITUDE MOTIVATE WHAT YOU DO?

Never do anything just to show what you can do. The moment you have that attitude, you are in trouble. The Chinese have a saying: "Those who seek vengeance must dig two graves." Having to show people only proves that you're not confident about who you are. Do something for you, not for them.

Do something because it's a natural part of your nature. If it's something good and other people benefit from it, fine. But don't do something negative just to get even, or something good just to get attention or acknowledgment or to hear someone tell you that you are really good at something.

WHAT IS MISSING WHEN NO AMOUNT OF SELF-IMPROVEMENT IS ENOUGH?

There are people who always seem to need something more. They put their lives on hold until they get it. It could be an achievement or a thing. "I've got to lose twenty pounds," people will say. "Once I lose twenty pounds, I'll be more attractive, and then I can go out to parties and be happy." Or they'll think, "Once I get this car, I'll have a whole new image and feel really good about myself." Here's a big one: "I've got to get this degree. If I get this degree I'll be able to get the job I want, and then I'll have time for our friendship. But for the next two years, I've got to get my master's degree. Oh yes, and then for three years after that I have to get my doctorate. I'm not going to have time for anything except that because I've got to get these in order to get this, that, and the other."

Think of all the times you thought, "I would be happy if only I had x." But it never works out. Once we get x, we quickly go back to feeling lonely, empty, and disillusioned. We start looking again, refocusing our energies on *y* or *z*, or something else that will be the ticket to contentment.

I live on the upper west side of Manhattan in an apartment that overlooks the whole city. At night, I go out on my balcony and climb my Versaclimber. It's a nice way to relax my mind and enjoy the city, because it's quiet up there, and I get to see all the lights left on in the mid-Manhattan buildings where people are still working. I see people coming home 11:00 at night with their briefcases. They're carrying take-out Chinese food and looking tired. In the morning, as I'm coming back from my 6:30 run, I see them going to work again. I ask myself, "What is missing in their lives that they're willing to sacrifice everything for this?" They're willing to work that hard and be that committed to prove their value, because proving one's worth is what it all boils down to.

Do you know what's going to happen when you die? All the things that you still need to get done will still be needing to get done. You'll never have enough time in your life to do all the things you feel you need to do. So why work so hard to get them all done now? You're not going to get a merit badge. What you're more likely to get is a heart attack or a stroke.

Slow it down. Stop trying to prove your life through your work; it's the wrong vehicle. You shouldn't have to prove yourself in this way. These provings are artificial ego acknowledgements. Start to live a balanced life, one in which the simple things you liked or wanted to do as a child you still have time to do.

You can't have it both ways. You can't spend all your time and energy working for the happiness that you're sure is going to come your way with the money you're going to make while, in the meantime, all those books, newspapers, and magazines that you haven't yet read are still there. You're going to get to them, you say. And there are the hobbies you're going to get to and the places you're going to travel to. It never happens. Start cutting out the extra stuff today, and get back to a simpler, uncluttered life.

Consider that time is all you really own. You don't own your home. Don't pay the taxes and watch who owns it. You only have a lease on it, basically. You can exchange it or sell it, but you don't really own it, the way you do your time. Making the choice to do something positive with your time is crucial.

DO YOU SURRENDER TO YOUR IMPERFECTIONS OR EXHAUST YOURSELF BY TRYING TO ACHIEVE PERFECTION?

Neither way is ideal. A lot of people surrender to their imperfections, saying, "I'm never going to be perfect, so why even try?" Other people say, "I'm going to achieve perfection, and I will accept nothing less." Both approaches are wrong. We should never be defeatist. On the other hand, we shouldn't be trying to achieve perfection, because it can't be achieved. And the effort to do so will limit our capacity to enjoy life.

What we have to do is take both of those extremes and realize that they are extremes. Both are negative; neither is going to give us positive results. We should choose instead to raise the standards of our expectations just a little higher than where they are right now. We must stretch intellectually, physically, and spiritually. But we must not stretch so high that we miss the mark entirely, imbalance our life, and cause others to feel uncomfortable with the efforts we're making. We should stretch just enough so that we can say, "I did it. And that feels good." And then we should do it enough times so that we have a new level of comfort and ease in the new standard.

Many people in my health support groups have done this with their diets. At first, they thought it was impossible to give up something that had been a staple of their diet, such as meat, milk, caffeine, or sugar. But now that they have done it for a while, it's easy. Their diet is effortless, and they feel good. Now that it's effortless, they need to raise the bar again to a new, reasonable, nonexcessive level of expectation.

There is an expectation that I think is reasonable for everyone, and it's this: As many of your choices as possible should be conscious ones. If you strive toward this, at the end of two or three years you're going to be a much healthier, happier person. You'll be honoring who you are with the choices you make. You may have taken a lot out of your life. You may have downsized your life. You may have become a minimalist. But you'll be happy with what you've done, because every day you'll be with who you really are. And you'll truly love that person.

WHAT IS TRUE SELF-LOVE?

True self-love involves a sense of completeness. You don't need anything more. You don't need more money; you don't need another car; you don't need another stock; you don't need more vacations; you don't need a more beautiful partner. You feel complete just waking up each day. You're happy just to be alive. You smile at the adventure of having a new day to recreate your life. That's healthy. That's the right choice. That's when you know that you're going to do something positive for yourself. And that's when you're able to relate in a positive way to others.

WHY NOT WORK WITH OTHERS, COMBINING ENERGIES TO CREATE SYNERGY?

Let's say a friend and I work side by side on two separate, independent projects. Assuming we're both competent, the result will be two well-done, but small-scale projects. But if we combine energies on one project, the result will probably be bigger and bolder and more impressive than the sum of our two separate efforts. That's the amazing force of synergy, or combined energies, and that's why working with others is often a good thing. Of course you have to put aside your ego if a partnership or a committee situation is going to work. Otherwise you'll get bogged down in conflict, and produce nothing.

Get your ego out of the picture. Look for ways to work with others. I hardly ever work on important projects alone. I could organize retreats or run a restaurant, for instance, on my own, but I generally want other people to engage their energy along with mine. I look for people with a similar excitement, passion, and even impatience about getting the project done, but with their own unique outlook on how to do it.

DO YOUR ATTITUDES PROTECT YOU?

Protective attitudes generally are those that exclude other beliefs and realities. Living with protective attitudes is like living in an exclusive, security-patrolled neighborhood. Anyone who innocently walks by gets arrested and is quickly shown out.

Many of us carry around biases involving culture, religion, race, and gender. These attitudes are usually based on outdated or downright incorrect messages we received growing up, yet they color our expectations of people, our relationships with them, and our very picture of reality.

WHAT'S ATTITUDE GOT TO DO WITH IT? EVERYTHING!

Your reality is shaped by your attitude—that is, by the thoughts and feelings on your mind each moment. The thoughts and feelings you have in the present are related to the ways you have been conditioned to think and feel in the past.

There is no such thing as a fixed reality because there is no such thing as a fixed thought. Every moment of the day, thoughts flit in and out of your mind. You immediately react to the thoughts coming in.

If you have been properly conditioned, your reaction to your thoughts and feelings will not cause you turbulence. You will not feel bad, become depressed, and react negatively or irresponsibly. If you were improperly conditioned, you will have negative reactions.

Most of what happens in the world is unalterable, but your reactions to those events are not. You can't change whether it's hot or cold out, but you can change your response to the weather. You can't change the fact that diverse groups of people visit Central Park, but you can change your attitude toward different types of people. You can embrace their differences instead of fearing them. Once you alter your perception of what is happening out there, you change something you perceived as negative into something positive.

It makes all the difference in the world if you are walking around in a negative frame of mind, or a positive one. If, for instance, someone tries to bring you down, they can't do it unless you already have negative emotions. If you're feeling truly good about yourself, then you will remain positive.

Always make your most important decisions in a positive frame of mind, especially decisions about separations, hiring and firing, and leaving something or someplace. If you act out of anger or negativity, you are more likely to do something stupid. Then it's done and nothing you do can change what you're already done. Apologies won't undo the impression people have formed about you. That's why there's that old advice about counting to ten before saying something out of anger.

Your thoughts and feelings constantly change. Two or three positive thoughts will be followed by a negative one. You'll have two thoughts that build confidence and then one that creates doubt in yourself. You shift moment to moment throughout the day.

You may think you're smart enough to control all of your thought processes. But by trying to control them all, you limit yourself. Only when you allow every thought—both positive and negative—to enter your mind, can you sift through them and decide which ones to focus on and which to ignore.

ARE YOU WILLING TO CHALLENGE WHAT DOESN'T MAKE SENSE?

If you get into that habit, you won't have what doesn't make sense cluttering up your days, and your mind. Soon, you're going to be able to wake up and say, "This is a great life!" You're going to be able to smile.

Mistake Number Five:
Believing Our Culture is the Best

1. If foreign travel is an option for you: Visit another country but do not stay in the capital. Stay, rather, in a small city, a town, or a village.

2. Take a free mini-course in another culture by using the books and videos in your library. Be sure to learn some of the language as part of this.

3. If you are a city or suburban person, arrange to spend a few days on a farm. Conversely, if you have never done so, live for several days in a city.

4. Use a cookbook featuring the cuisine of other countries, particularly Mediterranean cultures—Italy, Greece, Morocco, etc.—and Asian countries. Vary not just one dinner, but several days' worth of meals, including breakfasts.

    How did this experience affect you, physically and otherwise?

_____

_____

_____

_____

5. Read a contemporary foreign novel (in translation) from a country you know little about.

Looking for "Magic Bullets" to Solve Problems

"What supplement can I take for more energy?"

"Can you recommend a doctor who'll cure my arthritis?"

"I've been using an herbal remedy for depression, but I'm still depressed. I must be taking the wrong dosage; how much do I need?"

"Which exercise machine will get me fit?"

"I need inner peace. Should I move to New Mexico?"

Working in the field of health and nutrition, I'm asked dozens of questions on a typical day. I like to help people by sharing information, but sadly, most of the questions I get are like the ones above; they're based on the assumption that there's a "magic bullet" that's going to wipe out the problem. Which is why, often, my answers to questions are not ones that the askers expect. In their minds, people are ready to hear quick answers like, "See Dr. X; he'll fix you up," or "Take three a day," or "Yes, move to Taos, or better yet, Santa Fe." Instead, I have to sit them down and explain that there's more to combating arthritis or stress or whatever their condition is than taking just one step. You have to change your lifestyle—your diet, exercise habits, even your way of thinking—to really make a dent in most conditions. Even moving across the country is not going to help you if that's all you're doing that's different.

In short, I often find myself telling people that, to solve their problems, they're going to have to do some hard work. This does not usually go over well. I get the glazed-over look, the denial that the problem is as broad in scope as I'm making it out to be.

"Yes, I know about all that lifestyle stuff," people say, trying to lead me back to their agenda, "but for now, just tell me the correct dosage. Should I take two a day? Or three? Should I take them with meals? Or before?" People want to shoot their magic bullets off at just the right times, in just the right way. That's all they want to do.

Sometimes I give up and just provide the short, easy answers. But what I really want to do is yell, "Wake up! You're living in storybook land! You're waiting for some fairy god-doctor, or some magic beans, to transform your life. But look, even Jack in the beanstalk tale had to so some work before the magic beans transformed his life. He had to climb the stalk a couple of times, confront the giant and his wife, steal the golden-egg-laying hen and the magic harp, and chop down the stalk with the giant in pursuit—all before *his* life changed for the better. And you're expecting to do even less than a fairy-tale character in order to reap the benefit of your magic beans? I don't think so."

How did we get so ready to accept the premise of the magical, easy fix? For members of the baby boom generation, it wasn't hard. We grew up with television, a seemingly magical medium in itself, telling us that advertised products were the marvelous keys to health and happiness. Commercials were heavily into fantasy when we were growing up. There was bread that was soft as a cloud but was supposed to wondrously build strong bodies. There was toothpaste said to have an invisible shield that would guard against cavities. There were cigarettes that, with one puff, would change the season to springtime, and hair dressing that, with one little dab, would make you a magnet for the opposite sex. If you're of a certain age, the jingles and slogans are probably etched in your mind. Most probably you absorbed, on some level, the idea behind it all—that you could do anything you wanted just by buying the right package, tube, or box, or by using the right technology.

After World War II, the world of science and technology seemed to offer some veritable miracles. Nuclear power was the biggest. It would remake the world. In the mid-1950s, the Disney-produced movie and book called *Our Friend the Atom* likened nuclear energy to a genie that could give the world power, food, health, and peace, if we dealt with him wisely. "The magic power of atomic energy will soon begin to work for mankind throughout the world," said the book, with an optimism that was characteristic of the period. Other developments that seemed to hold vast, magical promise were antibiotics and vaccines. With the burgeoning of our medical arsenal, we really seemed on our way to wiping out disease.

WHERE WE ARE NOW

Disease is still around. Yes, antibiotics have accomplished wonderful, life-saving things, but as everyone knows who's read a newspaper lately, germs have mutated to resist them, and there are now some bacterial agents that are beyond the reach of just about all the antibiotics available. Likewise, today we have to acknowledge the problems with vaccines, and the accidents that have occurred at nuclear plants, health and environmental disasters that have irreparably tarnished the promise of nuclear power. So the world, as it enters the twenty-first century, is no longer naive. We've seen how magic bullets sometimes miss their targets. We've seen them hit the wrong targets, as with chemotherapy drugs and anti-HIV "cocktails" that have devastating side effects. We understand that the answer that seems too good to be true often is.

On a personal level, though, many people are still caught up in the magic-bullet mentality. As I've mentioned, I meet them every day—the people who are still counting on the promise of the miracle pill, or the exercise machine of the moment, or the self-improvement guru. Are you one of them? It's an issue worth exploring.

INSTEAD OF THINKING ABOUT THE LONG-TERM PICTURE, DO YOU CHOOSE TEMPORARY SOLUTIONS?

Has this ever happened to you? You're on an airplane, and you're landing in forty-five minutes. You eat the airplane food instead of waiting for a better option upon landing. That's reliance on a temporary solution. What if you were to take a different approach? You could say, "I'll eat something good when I get there."

There are many times I've walked out of restaurants after viewing the kitchen hygiene. I won't eat anything that's bad. Yet people go into a restaurant and intentionally try not to know what's in the kitchen. They don't want to know about the lack of hygiene or sanitation. And even when they do, they are frequently blasé about it.

Someone in my audience said he recently noticed that the commissary next to his workplace was run by a person with dirty hands. The person was chopping heads of lettuce and tomatoes, not washing anything. He was working on a dirty board and mixing the salad with dirty hands. Bacteria and parasites had to be all over his hands. Someone's going to eat that and later end up sick. The average person's system is not going to be able to withstand that assault. He went back and he told his co-workers about how unsanitary this place was. They didn't care.

Here's another example. I was driving down the Mexican Riviera with friends. They were hungry, so they stopped at a stand selling mystery meat on skewers. I said, "While we're here, why don't you just jump off the cliff? That way you won't be able to feel the diarrhea and maybe dysentery tomorrow."

"Oh, Gary, lighten up," they said. "It's not that bad."

The next day I heard, "Gary, what have you got to help us? What will work?"

The idea is, let's remember that we have to look at the long-term picture, and not always go for immediate gratification. And when faced with a problem, let's start looking beyond the temporary fix and ask ourselves, what is fundamentally wrong? What is the nature of the problem? Unless we deal with the nature of the problem, all the temporary solutions in the world are not going to make a difference.

HOW MANY EMOTIONS, ATTITUDES, AND RESOURCES DO YOU USE WHEN CONFRONTING MAJOR PROBLEMS?

Say you've got a problem. What do you generally do? First you are going to feel something. You feel something because you think something. Thinking creates a feeling, but do thinking and feeling change the problem?

The only thing that resolves a problem is action that is more creative than the problem. You have to proceed with creativity, uniqueness, ingenuity. You need to use a multitude of different emotions and approaches.

Most people are limited in their emotional spectrum. They've been taught to limit their emotional range. This is why some outbursts are disproportionate to what they should be. In our society, we're very concerned about behavior that's not controlled. Of course when you have a society that is chronically repressive in its zeal to control, then you end up with people going out and shooting each other. You also get a lot of people who vent and sublimate through unhealthy outlets, such as gambling, drinking, drugs, and pornography.

With so many people participating in so many things that are bad for them, we've got to ask, "What do they need to do that for? What are they not doing with their life that is causing that behavior?" The answer is, they are living within a narrow emotional range. They're not engaging in free-form expression; they're tight, not loose. They're not using a multiplicity of emotions and thoughts to deal with problems.

Remember, the more flexible you are, the more resources you can use in problem solving, and the more likely the problem will be solved. The total self has everything it needs to resolve any problem because it is enormously flexible. It can stretch in every direction.

HOW DO YOU CONTINUE TO CREATE YOUR CONFLICTS?

We continue to create our conflicts by continuing the same patterns. Every time we eat ice cream or pizza because we're anxious or lonely we continue to support the belief that food equals comfort. Once we break the patterns, we end the conflicts.

We need to change our behaviors; then changes in belief will follow. If we feel uncomfortable we can call someone close to us and talk to that person about it. We can join a support group to help us break our physical addictions. Then we can break our emotional ones.

WHAT DO YOU HAVE TO DO TO GET SOMETHING?

If you're a marathon runner, or if you've completed a detox program, you've disciplined yourself to go through a certain process. Average people, however, are not committed to taking the steps they need to take to make change happen. Yet they still want the results. What do they have to do to get there?

You need to identify the problem and focus on what needs to change. Getting a direction is key. You see something you want. Now make it a priority.

Before you do that, however, make absolutely sure that what you want is a priority. Ask yourself, "How important is this to me? Is what I get worth what I will have to go through to get it?" Ask yourself, "Is this going to give me something more in the way of awareness, spirituality, insight, creativity, fulfillment?"

These are basic questions we often do not bother to ask ourselves. We just get excited by something and say, "This is what I want." Then we go after it. But unless we are sure that what we want is worth the effort, we most likely will not put all the effort necessary into getting it.

Where do you focus?

Do you focus on what you can or cannot achieve? Generally, we focus on what we can't do. We put up barriers to keep us from doing things differently. We are afraid of the unknown because there is a lack of predictability there. We can't control how we are going to react or feel.

When we look just at the problem, we begin to take all of our messages from the same repeating negative cycle. "Can't," "Won't," "Would, if," "If . . . then." These are ways we rationalize staying the same. If you want to continue to repeat patterns, you will continue to have the same mindset and the same results.

Look at the things you *can* do, and you will get a totally different perspective. When you focus on what you *can* achieve, then you can do anything.

Do you focus on a few or on many choices?

Most people focus on a lot of things. That's perfectly okay if you have the kind of mind that can achieve that many things. But most people don't work that way. If you really want to get something done, focus on a few things, and then prioritize them.

Don't forget to include hobbies—pleasurable, creative things you can do in your leisure time. Otherwise, when you are not working, you won't play. You will, instead, use your time in non-constructive ways. You'll just sit and veg in front of the television, for example, or waste time gossiping on the phone.

At the beginning of the week, make a list of what you want to spend time doing when you aren't working. Your list can include simple things, like going for a walk. It can also include important life-changing activities. When you write these things down, you get the focus to act on them.

LET'S TALK ABOUT LEARNING.

When I first came to New York City, I met a red belt master in the martial arts. I was running in the park one morning while he was out doing his exercises. He had heard from some of his friends that I had a background in nutrition, and he wanted some advice from me. He offered to teach me martial arts. In turn, I could teach him and one of his friends about nutrition. I agreed, as I wanted to learn.

I learned, first, that there were multiple lessons to be learned. This was one of them. He asked me to give a dog a bath. The first time I did, I got bitten twice.

He said, "That's a very good lesson."

I asked, "For me or the dog?"

He said, "Could you have done it so you didn't get bitten?"

I thought for a moment and said, "I don't know."

He said, "Let's try again."

I said, "He's going to bite me again."

He said, "Not if you learn to pay attention to the lesson."

He was good enough to show me what I had not paid attention to. And he was absolutely right. There are certain ways that dogs will allow you to handle them. When I was patient and did what honored the dog, I was not only not bitten, but while I was shampooing the dog, he licked me on the side of the face. What a difference from just an hour earlier, when the dog was snapping at me!

The difference came about from focusing on the problem and concentrating on what I was doing. I discovered that giving the dog a little piece of cheese as I began washing him really changed his mood for the better. I now saw that if I massaged the dog—particularly his neck and ears—as I worked with the shampoo, and if I was very gentle in the way I rinsed him off, he seemed to enjoy the process. Drying him off, I discovered that the dog liked being cradled in the whole towel rather than being worked on piecemeal. Concentration and focus helped me discover these things.

I see the importance of concentration all the time. In Central Park, when we're trying to teach people how to run, we tell them to be sure to keep their legs straight and in a certain position when they plant the foot. They'll learn, and two minutes later they'll forget. The mind loses its power of concentration. It's no longer focusing. When the mind is not focused on what it's supposed to do, that's when accidents occur. Then we blame the accident on something else, rather than on our lack of focus, our not paying attention to what should have been done.

This is why we have to learn things in stages. We need patience. Otherwise, we will continue to repeat the same error over and over again, and wonder why we're victimizing ourselves.

CAN YOU MAKE ONLY POSITIVE CHOICES?

Yes, you can. You can even perceive so-called negative experience as positive. Sometimes, through accidents, pain, discomforts, and crises created by wrong choices, we become much stronger and learn to make right choices. Think of the people who are not dressed properly for the marathon who get hypothermia. Think of the people who go too fast. They made choices. They could have gone faster or slower, they could have dressed better or not. In reflecting on the experience, they are probably saying, "Let me learn something from this experience so that I can make better choices next time." That's how we grow. That's how we make better choices, not by beating up on ourselves, not by feeling bad about what we've done.

I had detached retina surgery. Someone got his elbow in my eye during a race. During the surgery, which lasted two-and-a-half hours, I simply focused on what I was learning from the experience. By doing that, I was able to keep my pulse at fifty-two beats per minute throughout the entire two-and-a-half hours, without an anesthetic. I was able to deal with the pain, and didn't even spend the night in the hospital. I got up after the surgery, and went back home. I didn't look at the experience as being painful. I prepared my mind by saying, "I'm going to learn something. This is going to be a new experience."

Think for a moment about what it's like to accept that an experience isn't going to be bad, but instructional. By using your mind in a dynamic way, you can change a negative experience into a positive one.

DO YOU OVERLY GLAMORIZE SOMEONE OR SOMETHING THAT CANNOT LIVE UP TO YOUR FANTASIES?

We like to take certain people and say, that person's the ideal. Then we bestow upon that person certain virtues that they have not really demonstrated or do not represent in their honest, natural life. We set them up for a fall. We are good at doing this kind of moralizing. We establish a standard that no one can meet. And when people don't meet our standards, we tear them to pieces.

Who in the world would ever want to be in the public eye if what we are going to be doing is making them into someone that they can never be? All they can do in return is lie. They know they're a fraud, according to the high standards the public has set. The best they can do is to try to prevent us from knowing.

IS THERE SUCH A THING AS TRYING TOO HARD?

You may have heard me say on the radio that the sickest people I've ever met are in the health movement. It's true. And why? They're trying too hard to prove that what they're doing is right.

When you have to prove that what you're doing is right, then you don't truly believe in it. I never think about health. I never think about being good or kind. I never think about exercising, or praying, or any of that. It never comes across my mind. I simply do it. I do it as a natural, integral part of my life. And it's not done with pressure. I never feel pressure. If I did it would be self-imposed, and that doesn't make sense.

I can go without eating unless I can eat something good. But I don't get angry about a lack of good food. If I can't eat, I enjoy the benefits of a fast. Most people, however, are overly concerned about their intake.

"How many calories did you eat today?"

"Did you get two scoops of this and one of that?"

"Did you take your 800 units of E?"

"Oh my God," some people say, "I didn't! Father forgive me, for I forgot my E."

When you try too hard to be healthy, you're automatically sick.

Almost everyone I meet in the health field is sick, even though they're taking all these vitamins, because they're not healing on the essential level. They're thinking all they have to do is fill the body up with all that it needs. The body needs, first and foremost, a positive attitude—a healthy disposition—and that doesn't come from a supplement.

WHAT HAPPENS WHEN YOU SURVIVE A CRISIS?

Once you've survived a crisis, you become a survivor, in the admirable sense of the word. We admire people who have been down and are able to get themselves up again without whining, moaning, and complaining. They pick themselves up and go forward. It's important to keep this in mind because there are times when we are down on our luck. That stops us for a while. But it needn't stop us forever.

As long as we have the courage to go on, there will always be people to help us with whatever it is we need to get on with our lives. We should never believe that just being down makes us a failure. It's only when you give up that you fail.

WHAT DOES THE CONCEPT OF STRENGTH MEAN TO YOU?

The image of strength is one we want to be associated with. Usually, when we think of strength, we don't see ourselves. Instead, we see some hero out there.

Strength is often thought of in physical terms, but what about equally important receptive qualities? If a person is known for being strong, we don't usually ask ourselves if that person is smart, sensitive, kind, humanitarian, or giving. These associations don't usually come to mind. We think of a six-foot-six, 325-pound football player, a monster in motion, when we think of strength.

Often we think other people are stronger than we are, especially when they are part of an organization or movement. Movements project an image of being protectors and problem solvers. That image increases our own feeling of weakness and makes us feel the need to belong to some group.

In reality, groups are made of individuals like ourselves. They have flaws just as we do. Often, seeing this is disheartening and we feel let down. The truth is, they've never betrayed us. They were just being themselves. We feel let down because our image of who they are has changed. We believed that they could be stronger than us.

Often we feel that we first need to change our circumstances before we can honor a new reality. That's unrealistic, though, because no circumstance will ever change that completely. A right setting will never manifest that will allow us to feel comfortable enough to take off our masks and be completely vulnerable and flexible.

I'm suggesting, instead, that in one second we can give ourselves a positive association to go along with a word—such as strength—and follow through with the emotions that allow us to honor that word's suggestion. Keep your words positive irrespective of what is occurring around you. Reality is always a state of mind. It's just that we think of the world outside ourselves as greater than our inner being, when it's not.

The more positive thoughts you honor, the more adept you will become at following through with constructive action. You will be better at discriminating between the positive and negative thoughts and choosing to act on the positive ones. At some point you will even feel comfortable redefining who you are by engaging in those things you want to do but somewhere along the line "learned" that you couldn't. By doing something completely out of character, you will gain the confidence to do something else unexpected. Before long you will no longer feel it is out of character to act this way. You will realize that you are in fact honoring your character by allowing yourself to do something different and live in the moment. You will realize that you don't need to have things out there change in order to change within. Your thoughts alone are all that need to be altered. The belief that you can do will gear your emotions toward positive change.

HAVE YOU TRIED TOO HARD TO FIND
THAT MAGICAL MENTAL FIX?

I've heard it said, about the generation that came of age in the 1960s, that this was a generation that looked within and didn't find anything. They had mantras, out-of-body experiences, and meditation. But all these experiences meant nothing because it was all just a creation of their minds that had nothing to do with the real world. I wouldn't make such a cynical generalization, but this does describe some people, or perhaps some facet of many of us.

A friend of mine meditates an hour each morning. Despite this, he frequently gets into raging arguments. How can someone practice meditation for thirty years and still not get it right? We all have these contradictions. We think we just have to find that special moment to find ourselves, to rebalance, and then we can come back and tolerate more stress, craziness, and contradictions.

But we need more than that special moment. We need to learn to *live* in the moment. Every day we are different. Every cell in our body changes. Our perceptions, then, should also be changing.

If we have fixed beliefs we are afraid to make changes. We then must guard an ever-narrowing spectrum of life. We see everything as passing us by. We wish for the "good old days" because we glamorize them. For instance, people look nostalgically at a bucolic scene of cowboys sitting around a campfire, without thinking about the fact that such a scene would not, in reality, be comfortable. There would be red ants, scorpions, and rattlesnakes, and it would be cold. There are many factors that we don't take into consideration when we project idealism onto reality. Once we change places and we're in that environment, it's not what we thought it would be. That disappoints us.

We escape the moment in many clever ways. We watch television and films and engage in superficial relationships with our families, friends, and even ourselves. These fantasies never require us to commit ourselves and simply be in the moment, accepting what is, not making judgments, and learning from the experience.

The resourceful mind stays protected and safe so that it can maintain its fantasies and illusions. Most people reside with the illusions of life and not with the reality. That's why they generally don't change until they're in crisis. They give up smoking, for example, after they're diagnosed with cancer. That's the kind of reality evasion we need to get beyond.

WHOM CAN WE RELY UPON TO SUPPORT OUR CHANGES?

Many of us start to make changes. Then we start thinking about our limitations, which stops us from going further. We use the word "but" a lot, saying "but I will be criticized," "but I don't have enough financial resources," or "but I don't have the time." Why not look at what we do have that allows us to make changes, and then stay with those changes?

Supportive people can encourage us greatly and act as role models. If we want to run a marathon, we can associate with people who will aid and encourage us. There is no shortage of people who have made fundamental changes in their lives and who enjoy sharing what they've learned. These people can support us. There are also support groups across the country for every kind of activity or undertaking. They can help keep us on track as we take the slow, steady, uphill journey that is true change.

Mistake Number Six:
Looking for "Magic Bullets" to Solve Problems

1. What about yourself would you like to change? Don't do a thing about it for two weeks. During this time, write a detailed year-long plan for change—dividing the time into months, and preferably weeks. Then start to implement the plan.

2. Is your house cluttered? Clear one surface, such as a table, or one shelf. Then stop. Tomorrow, if you're motivated, you can clear another one.

3. Is your house dirty? Clean one object—e.g., a sink, a countertop, a windowsill. Then do nothing. Tomorrow, if you're motivated, you can clean two objects, and the next day, three. Work up to five.

4. Are you overweight? Make your next meal a healthful, well-planned, low-fat meal. Then don't think about your weight until tomorrow.

5. Think about the best time in your life, up until now. Write a few words describing what it was. _____

_____

The idea is not to make any plans to recapture it, which is probably impossible. The idea is simply to appreciate it.

Trying To Do Too Much

Here's a 1990s quiz. Bill and Jim are having a conversation.

Bill: Hey, why don't we get together for lunch?

Jim: That's a great idea. When?

Bill: Let's see . . . next Monday and Tuesday are out . . . how about next Wednesday?

Jim: Okay.

Bill: Oh, no, wait a minute; I've got something then. Next Thursday?

Jim: Sure, no problem.

Bill: Oh, hold on a sec; I may have a commitment next Thursday. That Friday's booked too. How about the following week? I think I can clear a day then. Is anything good for you the week after next?

Jim: Yes, any day. In fact, I can make it any day *this* week. . . .

Here's the question: Which person is there something wrong with? And your answer is Jim—isn't it?—because Jim isn't busy enough. To be a normal 21st century person you have to be busy all the time. The first thing out of your mouth when someone asks you how you are has to be, "Busy!" Your appointment book has to be bursting at the seams, and if someone wants to get together with you, it can't be too easy. You always have to be doing a lot, and you always have to be trying to do more. In fact, if everything you're trying to do each day can reasonably be expected to fit into twenty-four hours, you're one step away from being a lounge lizard.

The busywork standard is particularly high for women, who are expected to be totally frazzled all the time. There was this "juggler" ideal put forth in the media several years ago; the concept was that the modern woman should juggle the responsibilities of career, husband, and family all at once, and enjoy it. Surprisingly, this idea is still around; society hasn't seemed to notice yet what the act of juggling actually entails. Think about it. If you're juggling, at any given time most of the things you're working with are going to be up in the air, so you've got to be pretty tense as you try to prevent them all from crashing to the ground. This is okay for a five-minute performance, but a life of perpetual juggling would be torturous. That's what we expect, though. Then we wonder why we have millions of women suffering from anxiety and depression. They're trying to live up to an ideal that's too much to ask of a human being.

Nevertheless, women's magazines try to "help" women live up to this ideal. A staple of these magazines is the how-to article on ways to save time, which generally involve doing two things at once, like folding laundry while watching TV, or having a heart-to-heart talk with your child while driving on the interstate. The problem is, how are you going to live in the present and enjoy the moment when your attention, every moment, is divided between competing activities? If you try to focus on too many things, you can't focus on any of them very well, and nothing provides real fulfillment. That's a situation with which too many women, and men, of the baby boomer generation are familiar.

How did we get to this point? Maybe it has something to do with the fact that this generation has been particularly materially blessed. Starting from when baby boomers were children, they were told by advertisers and society that, with a little effort, they could acquire an almost unlimited amount of things. And—guess what?—that actually turned out to be true, so that today we have a middle-aged generation that has accumulated more stuff than any previous generation in history. That's why many thirty- to fifty-somethings have bought ridiculously large houses; it's not because they've had gigantic families, but because they need a place to stow all their stuff. Anyway, maybe these people have felt that since it's possible to *have* an almost unlimited amount of things, it's also possible to *do* an almost unlimited amount of things. Of course this doesn't follow; you can't buy a calendar with more months or a clock with more hours the way you can a house with more rooms. But sometimes we don't reason things out; we just unthinkingly assume them.

So we follow along and live like everyone else is living, even though it doesn't make sense. Many of the activities people try to cram into their schedules aren't things they really want to do, but things they feel that people around them expect them to do, like belonging to the right groups, or signing up tiny little kids for organized sports teams, or going to trendy health clubs, or shopping at upscale malls for yet more stuff. An interesting exercise is to look at your day planner and see how much of what's on it you really want to do, and how much of what you've planned for your kids they really want to do. Then see how many of those activities you can get rid of. An even more interesting exercise is to look at your day planner and see how many of the activities in it didn't even exist a few decades ago. That might give you a new perspective on paring down your schedule.

WHERE WE ARE NOW

We're in a ridiculous situation, when you think about it. Today we have more labor-saving devices than ever before, and they work better than ever, and yet we have less time. We have a wide variety of convenience foods—not that I'd recommend most of them, but people do use them—and yet we have less time. We have instant entertainment with our VCR's. We have libraries at our fingertips with home computers. We have instant communication with all parts of the globe. We even have a longer average lifespan than we used to, and still, we have less time. What are we doing wrong?

We're simply trying to do too much. The world today is offering a vast array of opportunities, and we, like gluttons in a supermarket, are trying to grab them all. Think about being a glutton for a minute. You can't be a glutton and really enjoy your food. For one thing, you're cramming food into your mouth too fast to really savor it. Second, whatever you're eating, you're always thinking about the next thing you're going to eat. Third, you're destroying your health. It's exactly the same when you try to cram too many activities into your life: You're not really savoring them; you're always planning for the next thing; and if the frenetic pace gets too stressful, you're endangering your health.

If you're someone who generally tries to do too much, the following section can help. In it, we'll be looking at issues related to how people spend their time.

DO YOU SPEND YOUR TIME IN A QUALITY WAY?

Most of us do not. The average American wastes six hours a day in front of the television, another two on the phone, and frequently another two in a shopping mall. That's ten hours a day wasted.

I don't believe in wasting time. As a result, I both work and socialize, create and play, all within a day. I never just sit in front of the television and watch unless there is something I am specifically watching. Watching whatever happens to be on TV is like eating whatever happens to be in front of you, or talking to whomever you happen to pass on the street. Why would I want to do any of these things?

Also, I don't turn on talk radio, because I find most of it vacuous. What am I going to learn? About prejudice and anger?

Every day I spend some quality time with my little dog. I don't care what's going on in the world; it's her and my time to bond. By the way, I did the same with my daughter when she was growing up. Nothing in the world came first. It really makes a difference when you don't allow anything to distract you from what you are sharing. So in my house, if the phone rang, no one answered it, unless it was time to answer the phone. I would have certain times that I answered the phone, and people would know to call at those times. What if there is an emergency? some people would ask. So what? If someone dies, they are probably going to remain dead for some time, so there's no pressing need for me to find out about it immediately. I never understood that whole urgency thing.

Another kind of quality time is complete, uninterrupted relaxation. This is especially important if you're by nature a hard-driving person who does actually enjoy having tightly scheduled, activity-packed days. You have to be capable of interspersing those with periods of total rest.

If I want to just relax and do nothing, I go away to the islands. When I went to Jamaica with some friends, the first thing I did was find a hammock and gently sway in the breeze for about nine hours. I was totally at peace and rejuvenated enough to enjoy the rest of the night.

HOW MANY DAYS DO YOU LIVE WHEN EVERYTHING IN THAT DAY, TIMEWISE, IS UNDER YOUR CONTROL?

It's a scary question. The answer may well be none.

Every day you wake up and put your time and energy into something. Is what you do irrelevant to your real goals? Is what you do more important than doing something for yourself? You can't put your energy everywhere. If where you put your energy isn't essential for you, then shouldn't you be putting it someplace else? You may be falling into the same patterns day after day for reasons of insecurity and the belief in the wrong choices.

Alternatively, your time is under your control if what you do during a day is honoring your own priorities, and not anyone else's.

DESCRIBE THE ROUTINE OF YOUR DAY. DOES IT CHANGE?

When our routine changes, we're being flexible. When it doesn't, we're being predictable. If we tend to have nonchanging routines we are more likely to make a lot of excuses. We'll think, "I have no time. There's too much in my life already." Instead, try saying, "I'm willing to make room for some change in my life. Outside of my Monday-to-Friday nine-to-five commitment, I've got lots of extra time."

Make a list of the things you do that take your time. Consider everything. Here's a partial list to get you started: work, sleep, friends, TV, eating, shopping, nurturing, self-grooming, walking, meaningless business, gardening, movies, crafts and hobbies, travel, reading, telephones, addictions, daydreaming, planning for the future, workshops.

Look at your list and note how you can make adjustments that will let you do what you want to do. What is helpful and what should you eliminate from your routine so that you'll have time to do the things that will make your life more meaningful? What do you need to change even if you can't do it immediately? Let's discuss these different areas of life.

Work

Ask yourself if you love what you're doing. If you are like most people, you probably don't. Your work is boring and meaningless.

It leaves you with a paycheck at the end of the week, but you don't feel rewarded by the work itself. In fact, your Monday-through-Friday life could be something like a reverse prison cell, where each evening you go out and enjoy the freedom, but each morning you return to the cell. The question then becomes, "Why not break free completely?"

If you ask this question, the one that follows is, "What can I do about changing jobs?" At this point, you may hear lots of doubts surfacing, such as, "I need the money," "I don't have the skills to change," "There's no time to look for a new job," or "I can't risk losing my job and not finding another." All of these excuses are limiting if you accept them as legitimate.

Get past the excuses and ask yourself the following question: "If I could do anything, what would it be?" Brainstorm and let the ideas surface to your consciousness. Think of things you love to do. Perhaps you'd enjoy being a landscaper because you love flowers and trees. Why not do it? You may think there are too many people in that business already. So what? There are many people in all kinds of businesses. Still, there are always new businesses that succeed when someone is committed to making them work.

Let's say you're worried about not having the necessary money or skills. You can deal with that by committing yourself to a two-year period of change. During that time you can re-educate yourself, gather the resources you need, and network. You can use those two years to do what you need to do to make the transition.

Be persistent. Many television producers were once $150-a-week assistant bookers. They were the people who booked guests, and nobody paid attention to them. But they saw that the hotshots at the top are always moving. When they leave, there's no one to fill the void. That's when the people who know all the guests move in. Suddenly, opportunity for advancement is available.

Being innovative and not stopping at rejections also helps you to reach your goals. When PBS wouldn't show my AIDS documentary, I got the names, addresses, and phone numbers of 800 cable stations. I sent them explanatory letters along with the tapes. Ultimately, 150 of them played the documentary several times. It is important to keep your mind flexible, creative, and open. There is more than one solution to a problem.

Sleep

Sleeping too much usually stems from a toxic system. As you detoxify your body you release poisons and, consequently, need less sleep. Working with thousands of people in health support groups, I've found that the average American—pre-detoxification—does need, as common wisdom has it, eight hours of sleep. But that's because the average American is not healthy. Once people detoxify, sleep requirements lessen.

We should note that when people are just starting the detox process, they go through a kind of withdrawal. Giving up such substances as caffeine, sugar, meat, and dairy products can, during the first one or two weeks, cause some unwanted effects, such as a need for *more* sleep—perhaps eight to twelve hours a night, or erratic sleep—with cycles of two hours of sleep followed by wakefulness. However, taking the right supplements, particularly melatonin, can minimize this. Soon, the unwanted side effects are gone, people are feeling vital and energized, and the overwhelming majority need only about six hours of sleep a night.

Friends

Take an inventory of the people in your life. Stop relating to those who are not really friends. They may be good people, but people you no longer have much in common with. Let those relationships go.

Now you have more time, both for other pursuits and for your truly meaningful friendships. Some of these can last a lifetime; some may be excitingly new. Never take friendship for granted. Consider what you need in a friend and what you are willing to offer in terms of time and emotion.

Television

The average person can easily reduce the amount of television he or she watches, freeing up several hours a day.

Eating

Most of us think we enjoy eating, but we could be enjoying it more. We could start by thinking in terms of dining, not eating. We could then enjoy the experience more by preparing better quality food, by seeking out interesting and exciting restaurants and markets, and by trying new foods. As we dine we need to be conscious of the experience, rather than just gulping food down in haste as we read or watch TV. This is one activity that we might want to spend more time on, rather than less.

Shopping

Try shopping one day twice a year. Think of all the time and money you'll save. That's what I do. I shop the last day of February, when all the winter clothes are about to be taken out of inventory and stored. Then I can get a 75–80 percent discount. Since I like certain designer clothing, economizing that much is a considerable savings. In September I buy my summer clothes. I travel around the world, so sometimes I'm heading into summer when it's New York's winter anyway.

If you're like most people you wait until Christmas to go shopping for that holiday. What a nightmare! You're fighting with everyone else to get something that's overpriced. With a little bit of planning, you can avoid that trap, and then sit back and relax while others are fighting traffic and long lines.

Get out of the mindset of having to shop all through the year. Make a list of what you need, and shop at set times to free up your days for other important activities.

Nurturing

When you consider the pace most of us live with daily, as well as the excessive amount of responsibility we take on and the to-do lists that just keep getting longer and longer, you can see that at the end of the day, most people's essential needs are not being met. Where is the chance to have a relaxed conversation with the people that matter to us? When do we get the time to sit on a swing and think? Or to listen to music? These days we're listening to music while we're cooking, or talking on the telephone, or helping the kids with their homework—or all three. It's as if we're the signal-master in Grand Central Station and all the trains and passengers want our attention simultaneously.

Derail those trains if you have to! Allow yourself time to nurture and be nurtured every day. It's important for your emotional health, as well as for the emotional health of those who are close to you. When I raised my daughter, I spent every day nurturing her. I would give her a thousand hugs, a thousand kisses, and a thousand "I love you's." That way she knew she was loved and that she would never be abandoned.

Also, as you consider those in your life whom you want to nurture and be nurtured by, don't forget animals. Animals have enormous patience. And they're nonjudgmental; they'll come to us, wag their tails, jump up on us, and give us their love without caring how old we are, what we look like, or whether we have bad skin or bad breath or not much money in the bank. When you bond with your pet, that is a bond for life, and you're not ever going to have to worry about being betrayed or lied to. In my view, everyone should have an animal.

Self-Grooming

Grooming is very important. It's a statement about how you feel about yourself and the world. It creates an image. If you want to present a counterculture image, that's okay. If you want pink hair and polka-dot eyelashes, that's still okay. But spend time on how you look, because it's a statement about how you feel about yourself.

Many people in our society have become lazy. They don't groom themselves, or they groom themselves in a lackluster way, without thought. They don't experiment with a look. They don't try something new. Guys with short hair don't let their hair grow long. Guys without moustaches don't try growing one. Guys who wear white don't ever wear black. People are afraid of how they'll feel about themselves and about how other people will perceive them.

Help groom someone else. In the animal kingdom you will witness this. It's a kind of bonding. And it's important. Grooming is a simple thing that we have gotten away from.

Walking

Walking every day is healthful, but, beyond that, it helps you to appreciate your environment. Every day of the week, I walk someplace in New York that I haven't been to before. The other day I discovered a building on 69th Street with Gothic architecture. It was a club. This made me wonder about the kind of club it was. I thought, "Who owns this whole half a block of prime New York real estate?" There are always interesting new sites you can discover if you take the time to walk, no matter where you live.

Meaningless Business

Get rid of the meaningless business in your life. For example, is it really worth your time and effort to cut out coupons from the paper, or mail in rebate forms? And you're not actually obligated to read your junk mail. Other time-wasting activities that people perform unquestioningly are towel-drying dishes, when they could air-dry in a rack; separating laundry by color (you don't usually have to once the items are no longer new); and, as we've mentioned, excessive shopping.

The shopping thing can get silly; it can become like a second job for some people, especially around the holidays. When it's

Christmas, don't ask people, except for young children, what they'd like as gifts. People do this, and then they have to spend days slavishly hunting around for the exact items requested. The holidays are supposed to be about the joy of giving, not the job of completing others' shopping lists.

Also, stop taking on other people's responsibilities unless it's really necessary. Parents, especially mothers, sometimes continue to do things for their children long after the children are old enough to do these tasks themselves.

If you're habitually short of time, ask yourself whether you spend your energy on essentials. Simply go through a day and make a list of what you do. Where do you spend your energy? How many of the things on the list are really essential to your life? You may find that you have spent a whole lot of time and energy on nonessentials. You may then want to live the next day totally differently.

Gardening

You don't need an acre; you can start a garden on a rooftop, a windowsill, or a countertop. You can grow sprouts in your kitchen, or start a community garden in an empty lot. Gardening is nurturing and healing. Each day there is something new to see and some manageable task to perform.

Movies

Movies help us learn about our lives. I like to see films because they frequently reflect the excesses or deficits of society. They can help us to release our feelings; we can safely cry during romance films or let go of inner rage by watching violent films. So movies are vehicles for helping people to express themselves. More important, we can learn from them by paying attention to what they are expressing, to who is expressing what. We can see what issues they raise, such as those of gender, power, and race, and see how they reflect our own experience.

Crafts and Hobbies

If you are over forty, you probably remember a time when people actually engaged in crafts and hobbies. Today few people do. Their free time is taken up watching television or playing computer games. Crafts and hobbies are wonderful, though, for engaging the mind. The more difficult they are, the more exciting.

I frequently run down Riverside Drive in the morning. I pass a man who makes sculptures from large pieces of wood. He works on this every day. It's a hobby. One day I talked to him and discovered that he used to do the same thing in Jamaica. This is what he loves to do, so he does it here.

A hobby can take up a lot of time, but if you have a passion for what you're doing it's time well spent, and you hardly notice its passage.

Travel

I travel the world over. Before I traveled to lecture, I traveled to learn. Perhaps you think you don't have the time or money to travel. These shouldn't be excuses, though, because there are ways to travel that don't cost a lot, and there are places to go that are nearby. If you live in New York you can go to Amish country in a couple of hours and be in a completely different world. Once there, you can learn about these people's austere and principled way of life. You can find out such things as why traditional Amish jackets fasten with hooks and eyes rather than buttons (the Amish are pacifists, and jackets with buttons look too militaristic), and why their curtains are pulled to the side (the Amish usually eschew electricity, so they need to maximize natural light). You'll be fascinated, and you'll have expanded your world.

You can save money by traveling as part of an exchange program, by working in another country, or by driving someone else's car to a specific destination for free. There are always ways to travel if you take a creative approach.

Reading

Reading helps you to travel in your mind. It also helps you to understand your own nature. Nonfiction can expand your knowledge. Try reading at least one book a month.

Telephones

Telephones are one of the biggest time wasters around. Do you know people who feel that just by virtue of their having dialed your number and your having picked up, they're entitled to an unlimited amount of your time? That's pretty presumptuous when you think about it, but a lot of overly polite folks let others get away with this. They let their callers talk for half an hour, even though, after a few minutes, a phone call is usually just the same things said over and over in slightly different ways. A couple of such extended phone calls can really wreck your schedule.

Try limiting yourself to four minutes a call; you will significantly free up your day.

Addictions

I don't believe in the traditional 12-step-program view of addiction. I don't believe that addictions are genetic problems, or that they're necessarily life-long problems that you have to label yourself with, as in, "I am so-and-so and I'm an alcoholic." They're simply a matter of people making wrong decisions.

Why does this happen? People make wrong decisions when their essential needs are not being met. Often, they do not even recognize what their essential needs are. Maybe no one's ever asked them, "What do you really want?" and it never occurred to them to ask themselves. Maybe they've simply been honoring everyone else's vision of how they should spend their days, and they have no real sense of who they are. After many years of this a person can get pretty frustrated—and never really understand why.

I don't believe we have stupid people making stupid choices when it comes to addictions. Rather, we have smart people who make choices that they're fully aware are foolish. But these are *their* choices. Whether it's out of frustration, anxiety, or anger, they want to get to a place with the addictive substance that allows them to alter how they feel in the moment. What they must sacrifice to do so—their health, respectability, family trust—becomes secondary to gaining a sense of euphoria, or at least a dulling of their pain. And they're never going to break completely free of their bad-choice-making until they address what's missing in their lives.

Addictive behaviors can range from the illegal—using heroin—to the socially acceptable—drinking coffee, overeating, gossiping. Notice your addictions and how they're affecting your life—in every area, from health and fitness to the amount of time they take up. Work on breaking bad habits and replacing them with healthier ones. But most important, see what essential needs are not being met in your life, and how you might meet them.

By the way, we've just discussed telephones as time wasters, and in extreme cases, talking on the phone can be an addiction that eats up all a person's spare energy and motivation. Talking can become a substitute for doing. If you're addicted to the telephone, my advice would be, "Just hang up!"

Daydreaming, and Planning for the Future

After a certain point, the more you daydream, the less you live. Excessive daydreaming tells you that you don't, as they say, have a life.

Planning for the future in a realistic way is a better activity than daydreaming. Still, you don't want to spend too much time thinking about the future and not enough time living in the present. I know people who, five years into their civil service work, start talking endlessly about the pensions they will be receiving twenty years down the road.

To live fully, we need to spend more time focusing on what's important to us now. Planning for the future should be only one of our activities among many, and should not take all of our energy.

Workshops

Workshops help us to grow and see life in new ways. They help us to keep on track, enable us to meet people interested in the same things we are, and give our lives an added dimension.

DO YOU THINK CAREFULLY BEFORE YOU COMMIT YOURSELF TO ANYTHING?

How many times in life do you wake up and feel overwhelmed by all the priorities you have? You've got too many competing priorities and you're afraid to give any of them up. Who is going to think what of you when you give up one of your priorities that affects them? Now shame, guilt, and fear are dictating your priorities. You're walking around with an enormous number of obligations, thinking, "If I could only get rid of them, I'd have a chance to do what I really want to do." But every time you go to get rid of a priority, someone comes around and reminds you, "Hold on a second—you're successful. We like you. We honor you because of that priority you're committed to." And you think, "Gee whiz, how am I ever going to change my commitments?"

Think of what you commit yourself to. Think of who you commit yourself to. Then think, if you had to do it all over again, to make different choices, would you choose the same priorities and the same commitments?

We are known by our word and we want to honor our commitments. So then others bring in words that they know are going to keep us locked in. "Well, you've got to honor your word. You've given us a commitment. Now honor it." Now we have to. But what if it's the wrong commitment to the wrong people for the wrong thing? Therefore, take a good look at the values of the people that are around you. If these people gossip, are petty and miserable, reconsider your association.

In order to get along, most of us lower our standards. We bring ourselves down to where others are so we can belong, because we're told that we're nobody unless we belong to somebody. We belong to guilds and clubs, societies and fraternities, Republican and Democratic parties. If we don't belong to somebody or something, we're considered an outsider. We're nobody, we're a loner. So, we make belonging important. Maybe it is, at times. But it's not as important as being who we really are and spending our time in the most meaningful way we can.

List the commitments that are no longer in your best interest to honor.

Listing the commitments you have that are no longer in your best interest to honor can be painful, but it is the only way to face what you need to let go of in order to make room for new activities that help you to create a new reality. Remember, don't bother trying to convince everybody that what you're doing is right. Some people are not going to understand what you need to do, and will try to persuade you to hold on to what you no longer deem useful. Their perceptions are different from yours. Only your own perceptions should mold your reality.

How much time do you need for yourself?

Late at night, it is very important for me to be alone. I spend that time looking out the skylight and visualizing. Through visualization, I get new ideas that challenge my present values and beliefs. I love new ideas. Every night, before I go to sleep, I have to have at least five. That is how I begin new articles, books, and lectures. Every lecture I do is completely different from the others I have done before, and late-night visualization is a large part of how I do it.

One time, I was in a relationship with a woman who tried to change my style. This is the dialog we had:

"It's late."

"It's late for you, but it's not late for me."

"Well, I can't sleep."

"You mean you can't sleep unless I'm beside you."

"That's right. You're being selfish."

"I don't think so. I am in my creative time. It's time I need for me. I don't want anyone in this time, except me. This is not a shared experience. There are times to share experiences and times to do things exclusively on your own. If you can't draw the boundaries, and have people in your life that respect those boundaries, then you don't have a healthy relationship. Do you understand that?"

"Yes."

"Then please do not use any words that try to make me feel guilty about making time for myself."

That person couldn't really understand. She got very angry at me for taking personal time. That ended the relationship.

Typically, when you tell someone that all your time in a relationship isn't going to be spent together, they don't like it. They don't like the idea that there is anything that they are excluded from, because society's belief system says that two people in a relationship should always spend time together. In effect, you are supposed to become the other person in your relationship. People transgress boundaries and try to make you feel guilty. That is very unhealthy.

What is healthy is being honest about how much time you need for yourself. When you actually write down why you need the time and list the things that you are going to do with the time, you can start to rebalance yourself. You cannot rebalance yourself if all your time is out there and not in here. So, write down how much time alone you need, and why. I know people who need a lot of time, and some who need little. Neither style is "right," but the key is to take an honest survey of who you are and what you need in order to function.

IS YOUR EMPTINESS DUE TO A SENSE OF MEANINGLESSNESS?

Many people fill their lives with busywork, trivial responsibilities, and the acquisition of things. The moment they have a respite, they feel restless and find something else to do. That prevents overwhelming feelings of melancholy from arising.

Instead of covering up your feelings, explore them. Then you can transform your life so that trivialities don't take up all of your time. Start by asking yourself, what is the meaning of my life? Write it down. Identify it. If feelings of loneliness surface, write down your thoughts and their implications.

Until you put real meaning back into your life—one that is equal to your capacity to live—you will have no life; you'll just be busy and have things. Define for yourself what the meaning should be. Identifying your real needs will help you to stop hiding behind masks and busywork, and to become liberated.

ARE YOU TOO MOODY?

Moodiness is not conducive to self-actualizing. Here's a scenario.

"Why don't we go out? Let's start a culture week. Every week, every Wednesday, let's set it in our schedule that we're going to do something culturally. One week we'll go to a play; another week we'll go to an opera; then we'll go to a concert."

"I don't know. It's such a hassle. We'll have to get the tickets. The bad weather. You know."

"I don't know. Do you want to do it or don't you?"

"Yeah, I want to do it. I'm just kind of moody."

"For as long as I've known you, you've been moody. Can you do something other than have a bad mood? Talk to me as if you're not in one of your moods."

"Alright, but it's hard. Every day I have to put the same expression on. Everybody in the office expects me to be moody. 'There's Helen. She's moody.'"

Do you know people who are always moody? What would happen if everybody in the office started acting like them one day? Ask them. Say, "I'll bet you've got another mood in you you're not sharing. Give me a different mood. I want to see it. I know you can do it."

Moodiness is a way that we limit our lives.

WHAT HAPPENS WHEN YOU PAY ATTENTION?

When you dress up, get your hair just right, and put on make-up, you are hoping that other people will notice you. These are times you really feel good about yourself; you've paid attention to yourself and now you want other people to pay attention too. When you don't feel good about the way you look, you don't want others to notice you.

When you pay attention to your life, it becomes better organized. You create systems and know where things are placed. Organization allows your life to flow better. When you make a list of things you are supposed to do, those things get done. If you don't have a list, you are less likely to get important things done because they won't be in your mind.

I believe in having a life that's organized. An organized life is a life under your control. When you want to do something, you have the tools there to do it with.

I have two friends. One is very organized and the other lives a life of total disarray. When I visit one friend, and go into his garage, everything he might need is in place. The other friend doesn't have any sense of organization. As a result, he never gets anything done.

One day I said to him, "Have you ever thought about all the things in your life that you constantly complain about that you are the direct cause of? Your life doesn't have the organization it needs. There are no systems." He said that he never thought of himself as organized because as a child he never was. Someone else always got things for him and picked up after him. He grew into an adult who was always making excuses for himself, blaming the past for who he is today, which of course is an unproductive approach.

The productive approach is change. If you're like my disorganized friend, you can change if you pay attention to your needs and start creating systems that allow you to be organized. Organization is everything. There are many opportunities you can take advantage of if you are organized and ready to go. When you're not organized, there are very few things you are going to do right.

DO YOU HONOR THE RESPECT YOU HAVE BEEN SHOWN?

If you are shown respect for something you have done, do you then honor the fact that you are held in esteem? It is very important that you do. If someone says, "I respect what you've done," they are acknowledging you. Look at that. Examine it. Think about what you can do to maintain that person's respect. It feels good to have other people admire you.

When you start something and you see that it's working out well, maintain your standards. Your standards will be maintained if your systems are maintained. Having organizational systems, as we've just discussed, allows things to happen.

Before going to bed at night, I lay out what I'm going to wear the next day. I also make a list of the meals I want to eat the next day. The next morning, when I finish my run, I can go into the health food store and know what to buy for dinner that night. I save money because I only buy food that I use. My meals are more creative because I think them out. I have a sense of purpose and balance in my daily schedule because I've taken fifteen or twenty minutes to think it out the night before. Simple systems make your life far more efficient.

HOW DO YOU PLAN A DAY?

In addition to laying out my next day's clothes at night and outlining my meals, I often like to take fifteen minutes at night to write down all the things I want to do in the next twenty-four hours. If I want to go to a museum, I write that down. If I want to run in the park, meet with a friend, work on an article, go to a movie, or read a book, I put that on paper too.

When I wake up the next morning, my ideas are fresh and I have the mindset to accomplish what I set out to do. If someone calls and wants to chat on the phone, I won't get distracted. I have plans to go to the museum and intend to carry them out, not forego them for a phone conversation. I get a lot done that way and I enjoy my life so much more because I give myself time to do my planned activities.

Without a plan, you are more likely to spend your time watching television, listening to the radio, and talking on the phone. This is time that could be better spent doing other things.

WHAT IS SOMETHING?

Is something *(a)* what we see; *(b)* what we expect; *(c)* what we think; or *(d)* what it is? Which is correct?

Only *(d)*. Something is what it is. When you understand something for what it is, and make your decision based on that, you can withdraw your support from it or you can give your support to it. Be very clear. Look at something for what it is, and don't try to make it into something else.

For a long time, I was never invited to lecture before any health group in America. Here I was, one of the most prominent health authorities in the country, and I was not invited to National Nutritional Food Association meetings, health food conventions, or any similar gathering. The reason? The organizers knew I refused to play along with the politics and two-facedness of these groups.

You see, at a very young age I'd had a best seller in the health and nutrition field, and suddenly I was up there with the top names in the health world. It was an exciting situation to find myself in. But then I went to a major conference, and was quite disillusioned to find that some of those top people were not practicing what they were preaching. There they were at the health conference, smoking and drinking, eating garbage for dinner, and seemingly without any holistic notions of living, on either a physical or a spiritual level. Not only was their dinner menu toxic, but their talk was; they were gossiping like gossip was going out of style.

I was totally depressed to see this world for what it really was, and I actually said so then and there. I said something like, "If I have to be a hypocrite like you people, I don't want to be a part of the organized health movement. I'll just go out and talk directly to the average American."

Hence my subsequent lack of invitations from the organized health and nutrition community. Not that I'm complaining: the time I saved not participating in their affairs I put to better use elsewhere.

WE ALL MEET EXCEPTIONAL PEOPLE.
ARE YOU OPEN TO THE EXPERIENCE?

Some people leave us feeling wonderful. They touch our souls so profoundly that it opens us up to who we really are and how we really want to spend our time and direct our thoughts. They are so enlightened themselves, with such unconditional love and giving, that when we are in their presence, we feel the deeper sense of our own presence. We have no denial, no blocks, just inner peace and harmony.

Then they're gone. The key is to honor them when you have that moment, and to realize how important they are to what you've become.

I remember once sitting across from a great artist, Paul Swan. He was about eighty-five. I knew I wouldn't be sitting across from him for too many days. I was a young kid in New York City. Here was this great thinker, artist, painter, sculptor, mime. He did it all. He was the ultimate Renaissance man. He was in the Van Dyke Studios painting on a rainy night. It was about midnight. I was watching this old man. I froze that in my mind and said, "I have been gifted to have a moment in time with one of the greatest creative energies in history." I never forgot that moment because I honored it. When I felt it, I recognized it. It's always been with me. That's what we should take with us—the passages in life that are important.

When I was going from West Virginia to New York, I remember it being hot and stuffy. They didn't have air conditioning on the buses, and it was a seventeen-hour ride. I remember a woman sitting so peacefully and calmly that outside of Pittsburgh I asked her, "Aren't you uncomfortable?"

She said, "No, I'm just thinking nice thoughts."

I thought, "I'm thinking about how uncomfortable I am. And this guy is smoking a smelly little cigar behind me. I want to punch him out."

And here was this woman. She taught me something. Again, it touched me. It was a passage that I went through and yet kept. It strengthened me.

Mistake Number Seven:
Trying To Do Too Much

1. Drop shopping: *(a)* Shop for clothes twice a year, for one day each time. Do whatever you must to arrange this. *(b)* Shop for greeting cards once a year; this is easy if you use blank note cards from UNICEF or a museum. *(c)* If you buy gifts, shop for them once a year from whatever one or two book or gift stores fit your style. Consider never shopping for wrapping paper at all. Also, consider using catalogs for most of these purchases.

2. Clear your schedule for a weekend. Plan nothing new. Then, during those two days, do activities as your mood, energy level, and the weather dictate.

What did you do?_____
_____
_____

How did you feel about it? _____
_____

Will you be doing things differently next weekend? _____
_____

3. Learn to cut meandering phone callers short by practicing the following phrases: "This is not a good time for me." "Unfortunately, I've got to go." "Can I call you back tomorrow?"

4. The next time you're having a conversation with a child, other family member, or friend, pay full attention and don't do anything else. (I don't generally advocate the common advice of trying to do two things at once; many times you'll be shortchanging yourself or someone else. Instead, drop one of the activities. Or drop them both.)

5. Do you really need to belong to all those organizations? Chances are there's no one up in heaven with a clipboard checking off who belongs to what. Quit at least one organization that you belong to.

Neglecting the Power of Silence

RECENTLY A COMMUNICATIONS satellite malfunctioned, with the result that a lot of the nation's electronic paging devices did not work for a couple of days. This technological breakdown was serious enough that it was page-one news, but the interesting thing was, if you read beyond the headlines, that many pager owners weren't all that upset. They were, rather, relieved. With their beepers temporarily silenced, there was one less bit of noise they had to experience and respond to. Their world became a little quieter, a little calmer.

This led me to imagine a scenario. What if all our nonessential telecommunications could go on the fritz for awhile? Emergency services would still be in place, but for ordinary life, there would be no telephones, faxes, TV, radio, e-mail. The effect would be like that of the satellite breakdown ten times over. People's lives would be much quieter, and the subtle sounds of nature would come to the fore. People would be able to think more clearly. They'd have more time to look into the meaning of their lives, instead of just scrambling to keep up with the trappings. In short, they would discover the power of silence.

This kind of selective power outage probably won't happen. But on an individual level we can make it happen to some extent, simply by turning off the appropriate switches when we can. There's another simple step we can take—we can stop talking so much. Then we can sit back, or go for a walk in the open air, and revel in the quiet.

Members of the baby boom generation are sorely in need of silence, because many have been silence-deprived all their lives. This is the first television generation, and if you think TV is mainly about visual images, think again. Many people use it as a noise box, keeping it on all the time to fill the air with sound. Plus consider the quality of the sound that comes from TVs versus the sound that comes from the home entertainment modes used before TV was introduced: radios and record players. With radios and records, the sound is the whole point, so care has to go into the music and talk that comes out of them. With TV, though, the picture is ostensibly the main point, and sound is a sort of window dressing. So TV music and talk can be junkier than radio or record music and talk, because, since we're distracted by the visual element, we won't necessarily notice. Some people have spent their whole lives not noticing exactly what kind of noise they're bombarded with, day in and day out.

In addition to television, other elements have made the baby boomer generation's formative years noisier than their predecessors'. This generation was the first to grow up with telephones as a birthright, not an option. The number of automobiles in the United States boomed along with the number of babies in the 1950s and 1960s; and along with this came increased traffic, noise, and destruction of natural environments. Rock and roll came on the scene in the 1950s, and has been getting more amplified, and pervasive, ever since. Add up all these factors and you can see why silence is something that many of today's adults did not grow up with. Some don't even know what they're missing.

WHERE WE ARE NOW

The Monks of New Skete are a group of monks who make their living raising and training dogs, and writing books on the subject. They have a holistic approach to their animals, and one of the things they suggest is silent walks with your dog, as a way of training him and of forming a deeper bond with him. A friend of mine tried this approach recently, with interesting results.

Every day she'd been in the habit of taking her dog for a walk, and attempting to teach him how to "heel," "sit," and "stay," by authoritatively saying these commands, while putting pressure on his training collar and using hand gestures. He was a frisky, energetic dog, and sometimes he'd listen, and sometimes he wouldn't. Then one day she tried the silent walk approach.

"It worked at least as well as when I was constantly talking to him," she reported. "Everything he needed was already there, without the words." But the benefits went beyond the training aspect. The dog seemed more relaxed. There did seem to be a new kind of nonverbal communication happening between them. What's more, she herself felt more relaxed, and like she could spend some of the walking time thinking about things other than whether her pet was obeying. Now, she doesn't walk the dog silently all the time, but she does so periodically, and it continues to be a positive experience. She tries to incorporate quiet into other parts of her life as well.

Some people, like my friend with the dog, have learned to appreciate the power of silence. But many haven't, and with today's proliferation of instant communication devices, it can take a real effort to try. On the plus side in the area of new technology, one great development has been the personal headset radio. At least with these, people are less likely to inflict their own noisy entertainment choices on others.

Is your daily life too noisy? Could you benefit by building some tranquil time into it? Also, what are some of the issues you might be dealing with during periods of quiet introspection? These are the areas we'll be exploring in this chapter.

HAVE YOU TRIED QUIET?

A woman came down to my holistic ranch. She attended all the workshops, but she and a small group of people talked nonstop. There was no introspection. I kept telling them that their best time here would be spent in quiet, doing nothing except being with nature. No one listened. They were talking every time I turned around. The woman wasn't going to stay a second week until I sat her down and told her that she had learned nothing. Of course she disagreed. She thought she had learned a lot. I repeated that I thought she had not learned anything because the most important message is always the silent one. I asked her to spend a second week there in silence, and she did.

During the second week, I asked every guest to eat in silence. I used candlelight. I played soft music. There were flower arrangements. There was no conversation. For the first time, people knew what it was to eat properly—not just to eat vegetarian, organic, gourmet food, but to eat in an environment conducive to inner tranquility. Now they were aware of what they were eating. They lost weight. They felt energized. When I took them out and had them sit by a rock, listening to the wind, they were able to be in nature. Suddenly they could hear a symphony in the wind. And they could let every distracting thought out of their minds.

People would tell me, marveling, that they could hear a thousand different sounds in the wind. "I heard the top of the palm trees moving. And I heard the grass moving. I heard the animals in the background, and the birds." All the sounds had been there before. It's just that they tuned them out because they were focusing on their own chatter.

Most people are nervous. This is especially true of intellectuals. I think intellectuals are the most insecure people in the world. They're always trying to impress you, always talking and never listening. Or if they are listening, they're simultaneously planning to get you to shut up so that they can correct you.

Trying to get them to be silent is like putting them in handcuffs. They fight it.

When a person finally breaks through and places his or her energy in the moment, he is able to transcend the normal boundaries of visual perception, smell, and taste. The person becomes integrated. Suddenly he knows what it is to be a bird flying. Like a bird, which never contemplates its death while flying, the person doesn't think of himself as falling out of the sky.

But we fly with fear. Any time we function from fear, we automatically respond before we think, because fear causes a hasty response. It's preconditioning from our families and our background. We learn not to take chances. We learn that good girls don't do that. We automatically let these old messages affect our energy and our thinking. Then we wonder why we keep on having the same problems. Why don't things get better? They don't get better because new thoughts are not replacing the old ones. We're not allowing ourselves to become integrated. We need to change completely to see how we can integrate.

So, this woman simply experienced a new way of being in an environment. She had been there all week, heard all these sounds, and saw all these things, but she had never allowed herself a sense of focus. And that's the difference. What do we focus on? She focused on the integration of all things, herself included.

If you do that, you'll never go for a walk again in the same way. When I walk, I walk in silence. When I eat, I eat in silence. My friends will tell you that when they come over to my house for dinner, it's a relatively silent dinner. I want candlelight; I want soft music; I want to enjoy the occasion in a quiet and integrated way.

It's interesting how an experience changes completely when it is experienced with integrated thoughts. I could have you sit down for an hour and meditate. And you could wonder about whether your children are alright and where your husband is. If your mind is somewhere else, you are not integrated. On the other hand, you could be there in the moment. That's where healing occurs.

WHAT'S GOOD ABOUT BEING ALONE?

I find taking time to be alone a valuable experience. A time of quiet, during which I do not engage with people, is crucial. That is one of the reasons I do not, at this point in my life, choose to be in a relationship. When I am involved with someone, every moment that person is creating a chattering in my mind. Now I have that quality time to focus on me.

Most people never think about how good it is to have quality time to themselves. If you're in a relationship, you may have to ask the person you're with to allow you time alone. Such time is not a luxury. I've never seen anyone have a healthy, balanced life without it.

HOW DO WE BALANCE OURSELVES ON EACH LEVEL?

Physically, we must change our diet and detoxify. We must eat only healthy foods. If we're eating only because we're frustrated, or anxious, or not dealing with our problems, we need to recognize this and stop. As long as we take in only the best food, and only what our body requires, our body will detoxify and we'll be healthy. If we add exercise to the mix, within a year we'll see a body that we'll be happy with.

We often don't believe we can be both sexual and spiritual. We feel we must repress the body in order to enhance the spirit. But that's a limited perspective. We can have a healthy, sexual body and a dynamic and free mind and be spiritual also. The problem, as I see it, is that we feel we need interpreters between us and our higher being, that we aren't capable of making our own determinations of how our spiritual self can be manifested. But we don't need interpreters. As long as I love life and nature, and am a good-hearted person, then I am as spiritual as any other human being. It's that simple. Spirituality is the unconditional giving of the love we all possess. We were born perfect but we spend our lives denying it. The person who is spiritual accepts his or her perfection and then manifests it.

I don't believe that we have to suffer in order to grow. That is part of the dogma used in controlling people. If we control a person's sexuality and his or her mind, then we control that person. Very clever people throughout history have sought to control our natural impulses. If we believe or feel something that doesn't conform to the prevailing view, we are made to feel guilty or we are punished. If there is a long history of people being punished for following natural impulses and being spontaneous, then people won't, unless they are very courageous.

HAVE YOU EVER HAD A BLISSFUL EXPERIENCE THAT YOUR MIND COULDN'T FULLY COMPREHEND BUT YOUR BODY COULD EXPERIENCE?

Some of us are afraid of feeling anything unless we can analyze, control, and manipulate it. We are never free, though, until we disengage our minds. If we disengage the conscious mind, we allow the present to exist. A sense of overwhelming euphoria and bliss can occur only when the conscious mind is suspended. We try to do Spirituality 101 on the weekend and wonder why we don't get it. It's like my friend who meditates every morning and then goes into rages.

The only time we usually surrender to the moment is when we are one with nature, looking at a sunset or smelling fresh-cut grass. Then, we're not thinking of anything, just enjoying the moment. The things that give the most pleasure, innocently and honestly, are those we experienced as children. We don't often allow in that innocence when we are adults. We can't explore bliss if our mind is controlled. We have to get out of our mind to have the moment.

WHICH EMOTIONS HAVE
YOU LOST TOUCH WITH?

You need to identify the emotions you have lost touch with in order to get back in touch with them.

Many people can operate in only two emotional modes—rage and calm. These people are difficult to deal with. One minute everything is alright. The next moment they don't like something you say, and they blow up at you. When you deal with these people, you generally hold back your true feelings to avoid becoming the recipient of a hostile overreaction.

What precipitates rage? Most people who react this way do so because they feel that their power is being challenged. As soon as you say something, they contest whatever you say. They have a difficult time being quiet and listening because hearing what another person says honors the other person. Not listening is a defense mechanism.

People who react with rage need to realize that nothing constructive ever comes from their outbursts. The people they deal with only pull back or retaliate, and real issues get lost. Once this realization occurs, they can step back and try to hear what other people are saying. By listening to others, you're letting people know that they aren't going to be yelled at or rejected for sharing their feelings. That gives them a chance to express themselves in an honest way.

Re-analyze your communications on a day-to-day basis. Realize that you can express yourself without rage and still be firm. When you replace rage with determination this doesn't mean you're turning yourself into a passive person, but, rather, that you're becoming a more effective communicator.

On the other hand, if you tend to be too passive, you may feel better when you express yourself in a more determined way as well. Express yourself with passion. In our everyday world, we assume that it's best to appear passionless; everyone is supposed to maintain an emotional monotone. To compensate, we then look for people who exaggerate their emotions. We find these people in films, in athletics, in the press, and even in politics, and we use them as emotional surrogates. They express what we wish we could say, and feel what we wish we could feel. Isn't it better to get in touch with your own thoughts and feelings and express them yourself?

HOW IS ANGER POSITIVE?

Not long ago I produced a documentary on cancer, providing a forum for many people to speak. It was surprising how many patients were angry. Anger is a very positive emotion in that it is energy. But realize that there is a difference between anger and rage. Rage can hurt; anger can create change. In fact, I can't understand people who never feel angry. It seems to me that if you don't get angry at things, you have no passion for life. There are so many things we *should* be angry about, as the first step in constructive change: genocide, racism, injustice, and environmental abuses. I use my anger to create a constructive process. Anger at the complacent and ineffective conventional medical establishment has been an impetus for my documentaries on AIDS and cancer, for example.

Most people get so comfortable and secure in their predictable lives that there is no anger left to project as a positive emotion. Remember the anger of some of the baby boom generation as they protested the Vietnam war? What happened to that? We could use some of that anger today to improve our society. Anger can be very constructive—it depends on what you do with it.

WHAT DO YOU SAY OR DO THAT CREATES
A LACK OF TRUST, COMPASSION,
OR INTEREST IN OTHERS?

If you have been negative, uncaring, or insensitive to others, those people will not be there to support your ideas, dreams, and goals. They may appear to encourage you, but actually not care. You need to be aware of how you treat people. If you want other people to be interested in you, you've got to be interested in them. If you want people to care for you, you've got to care for them.

You've also got to undo what you've done in order to go forward. You can't just walk away from someone pretending that what you've done to them doesn't matter. Merely saying you're sorry isn't enough. It doesn't undo what you've done. You've got to recognize the negative qualities you've attributed to other people and take ownership of what you've done. In other words, you need to acknowledge to the other person that what you've said or done has come from you and has nothing to do with the other person. That realization will clear the air and restore sanity and caring into your communications.

What do we say or do that creates a lack of trust, compassion, or interest? Gossip is one good example. Why do we generally talk about people behind their backs? We're bored. We thrive on the negative energy that's created. We feel part of a group. We envy the people we're talking about and want to pull them down and make others think less of them to build ourselves up. But by putting someone else down we're showing that we don't feel very good about ourselves.

Do you trust people who gossip? You shouldn't, because they're going to do the same thing to you. It's better to tell someone who gossips that you don't want to hear it.

When you're talking about someone behind his back, you're dishonoring the person. It's always better to talk straight to someone. Tell him or her what you feel. Say what's bothering you. Be honest. Then you at least have a chance to resolve issues and clarify misunderstandings.

Gossip is not about the person being gossiped about. Gossip is about the people who create and perpetuate it. Be aware of your actions and stop gossip when you can, or at least show others by example when you don't participate in it. You can't make the world like you, but you certainly don't need to engage in any behavior that would debase you or anyone else.

A person of spiritual commitment doesn't engage in gossip, never casts aspersion on others. There's no purpose to this kind of talk, except a negative one. The rule is this: If you don't feel good being on the other end of what's being shared, don't share it. It's plain and simple—just say to someone, "Don't share this with me."

Another way we undermine people's trust is by breaking our word—lying or not following through. How many times do you give your word and then break it? That shows people that they can't trust your word. They may not tell you about it, but when you make a promise they'll know you are lying, and not honor you for it.

It's important to make people aware of their deceptions. Years ago my aunts and uncles used to get together for Sunday canasta games. On one occasion, when my cousin was there but had left the room, my uncle asked, "Doesn't he realize that he exaggerates everything and that we know it?" I said to my uncle, "Why don't you tell him? He's going to spend the rest of his life exaggerating, thinking that it's normal, unless we tell him what he's doing." I proceeded to tell my cousin about it. He hated me for it and never spoke to me again. But that's his right. At least he knows what I feel.

You also create a lack of trust if you have a lack of principles. Some people stand for nothing. They go with the popular trend. Whatever allows them to survive, they accept for the moment. Those people can never be real friends because they can turn at any time.

Giving only half-hearted help shows people that you aren't really interested in them. Let's say you're moving and a friend who offered to help helps only a little bit. You relied on that person and were disappointed. You won't want to have that person help you ever again.

We definitely won't trust people who are inconsiderate and unkind. These are the very first traits we notice about others. We like to think that we have the right to be unkind when we don't. Being that way immediately takes us to our lower self. It denies our higher virtues. If you can't be kind to someone, don't be around that person.

WHERE DOES INCONSIDERATE BEHAVIOR ORIGINATE?

It originates in our youth. As children, we are innocent and honest until we're conditioned to become what our parents or guardians expect of us. That's when we start changing. But this is not to say that we can lay the blame at others' feet. Yes, at one time we had to conform to others' expectations. We were vulnerable little people and it was a matter of survival. But now, as adults, we act that same way because we are stuck in a pattern that was formed in our youth. We're not even consciously aware of not being ourselves.

We can begin to break out of our unnatural behaviors by identifying what we do and how we feel that makes us uncomfortable. We need to notice when we act in these ways, and we need to ask ourselves how and why these behaviors served us in the past. One of the ways we can do this is by journal writing.

DO YOU THINK BEFORE YOU SPEAK?

Always think before you say something. See what the reaction to what you say could be. A credit card company owed me a lot of money. I had paid the bill, and my secretary then paid it again without knowing I had already done so. The company promised a refund would come, but it didn't. Three months passed.

I simply called and said, "I have a question for you. I'd like your help. Do you think you can help me?" The person said, "That's what I'm here for." I explained to the person that the company owed me a large amount of money, almost $23,000. And I explained that I have to pay interest every single day on anything that I owe, but that they had had my money for three months and had not paid me interest and had not paid me back my money. They had just kept promising it was coming. Then I simply asked the question, "How would you feel if this was you?"

They resolved the situation that day. What if I had called and said, "You jerks. . . . " etc., etc. I'd have been verbally assaulting someone on the other end who would have taken it personally and who would have then figured, "I'm not going to help this guy. The heck with him. He can wait forever to get his money back." In short, it pays to think, what is the feeling we want to create? What result do we want? If you want a result that is supportive, cooperative, and helpful, then that's the energy you have to share.

You see, we have choices. First, think, what result do you want? Your results are going to be directly based upon your choices. So think well before choosing because once you put an action into play you cannot control the reaction. That's crucial. You can only control your action. Anticipate what kind of reaction you're likely to get. In all probability you will get that. You can create a spiral of negativity. Or you can create a spiral of positiveness.

Do you usually communicate positive messages, or negative ones?

Most of the time, you probably let people know your problems. Instead of telling people about all the good things that have happened and how good you feel, you let them know what does not feel good, and what is not working.

What are they supposed to do with this negative information? Should they be sympathetic and agree with you? That won't change anything.

Watch how you communicate with people. If you catch yourself dumping a problem in someone else's ear, ask yourself, is there a purpose to this? Can this person do anything about it? Can she help me? Have we already discussed this problem time and time again, ad nauseam? If there is no real purpose to what you're doing, you may want to take the conversation in a more positive direction. Or simply terminate it.

IF YOU GAVE UP ALL DENIAL, WHAT WOULD CHANGE?

If you gave up all denial, you would create a new life, because you would allow yourself to be who you really are. Most people never wake up feeling truly themselves. They know their name, their job, what they do in life, their routines and responsibilities. But those don't necessarily fit the real self. There may always be an emptiness that can only be filled by getting other people around you. Look at the people who are afraid to be alone. These are the very people who should be alone, because they'll never help themselves by being with other people. They'll just use the other people. I see it every day.

Only by being alone can you have a silent mind that allows you to think about who you are, not who you were told you are. Then, the people in your life will be there unconditionally. No relationship will ever take precedence over self. We have the mistaken notion in our society that the high point of our adult life is a relationship. I find that for most energies that's very unhealthy. It's one thing to relate to people, to be with people, to share with people.

That's normal, that's human, that's important. But you should never *be* your relationship. Because what happens is that you cannot differentiate self from the relationship. You never have a sense of being a complete and whole person. You're always attached at the psyche to someone else. And then you get engaged in the conflicts. Then your mind must be coinciding with the other mind to create harmony before you can do something. Everything must be a mutual decision. There's never any space that's really your own.

Here's the question: How are you going to grow, how are you going to give yourself time, if everything you do is always explained to someone else, with the expectation of acknowledgment?

Most people do not communicate honestly about what really concerns them in relationships. They know that if they did so, that might jeopardize the relationship. So holding on to the relationship, which at least gives them companionship, becomes more essential than being honest about what really bothers them and how they want to grow.

The only person you should really be relating to is one who is growing, so that you can grow together. Unfortunately, relationships generally stay together longer when both people are stagnating. Both are insecure about stagnating alone; they'd rather stagnate with someone else. You'll know you're in the wrong relationship when most of what you hear are complaints. Trust me— that's the wrong relationship. It's people using each other.

Someone called me whom I haven't spoken to in a long time. The person has a health problem and said to me, "Gary, I want to see you. Remember, we go way back. I need to come over and see you."

I said, "No."

"No? Why not?"

"Because we have nothing to share. And if you want my help as a stranger, you've got to get in line behind all the terminally ill people that I do see. They come first. They're strangers too, but that's my priority. The fact that we spent time and intimacy together means nothing. It's what we are today. To call me after years of not speaking to me, because you have a problem, doesn't honor me. That just shows that in desperation you are looking for a person to help you."

And that's what we do in this society. We use people in ways that are convenient for us. It's not healthy.

I wouldn't allow a relationship where what a person did was whine, moan, and complain about a problem. If you've got a problem, fine. Resolve it. And how do you resolve it? First, change your perception. That changes the problem. If you are not willing to change your perception and live by a new perception, then you're not honoring yourself, which means that you cannot honor the relationship. It's just a dumping ground. How much negativity do you want dumped into your psyche before you say, "Enough!"?

I wouldn't treat anyone less well than I would treat a rose. What would you do for a rose each day? Give it sunlight, positive energy, and what it needs to grow. Why wouldn't you do the same thing for a human being? Give them love, unconditional acceptance, and a sense of caring. When you do that with people who are ascending and honoring their spiritual self, then you've got two spirits sharing a higher consciousness. That's a positive relationship. We see so few of these, we think we are not capable of them. But we could be.

WHAT POSITIVE AND NEGATIVE IMAGES DO YOU FOCUS ON?

You focus on the things that people say to you or about you. You also focus on the things you say about others. Once you say something, your energy goes out there and you're connected to it. Now you've aligned yourself either positively or negatively to something.

Power is not in the emotion. Emotions are overemphasized. Psychologists and other therapists focus upon the significance of emotions. They focus on whether we're emoting enough. It never occurs to them that some people do not overly emote because they don't need to. With all due respect to the feminist movement, I take exception when they state that men don't know how to express emotions. I know an awful lot of men who don't express emotions because they're happy campers. They express happy emotions and that's it.

When you fill your mind with a lot of self-doubt and negative thoughts and destructive images, the emotion is automatically going to be negative and destructive. Everyone knows when you're negative. When you feel good about yourself your actions show it. But in our society, people think you're not responding enough.

Fortunately, there are lots of people in this society who require very little for happiness. That gets other people bent out of shape. They'll question another's right to be happy because they're steeped in misery and all their thoughts are negative. They're always on the attack. They're always trying to disempower somebody else to empower themselves.

You come along without the need to disempower anybody. You just feel good because you have good thoughts. You're happy and so you make everybody sick.

WHY NOT CHANGE YOUR PERCEPTIONS ABOUT PROBLEMS?

Take your negative thoughts and reverse your perspective on what is happening. Ask yourself, how can I make this situation into a positive one? What good can come from this? Doing this will allow you to change negative patterns that bring you down. You may not change another person or the circumstances that are bothering you, but you will change your perception of what is happening.

I learned this lesson a long time ago. While driving my car in heavy traffic, I saw two men yelling at each other just because one had cut the other off. They got out and fought. I thought, how stupid; what's the purpose? Someone is going to end up with broken teeth for nothing. At that point, I decided that any time traffic was slow, I would use that time as an opportunity to think. Now, whenever I am in a traffic jam, I don't get upset. I'm glad to be where I'm at because I have a couple of extra minutes to think. I didn't change the circumstances, but I changed my reaction to them.

List your problems and ask yourself, how can I alter them? There are always options. You will only find these options, however, by facing your problems and looking for positive solutions. Then, suddenly, they are not such a big deal. If you ignore your problems, they will remain on your mind. They will rob you of clarity, balance, spontaneity, and relaxation.

Facing a problem is itself part of the solution. You can't always change the problem, but you can change how you feel about it.

YOU CAN HAVE HAPPY, POSITIVE FEELINGS ONLY IF YOU HAVE HAPPY, POSITIVE THOUGHTS.

What comes first—the thought or the emotion? The thought is always first. But thoughts can have delayed responses. Something that you've been thinking about can cause a reaction a week later. It will eventually appear because your thoughts are energy that you put into your being.

A thought is a word or a sentence or a whole paragraph that you've created. Consider how many times you've thought about something that you didn't do and should have done, or that you did and wished you hadn't. Or perhaps you should have done more or you should have said something and you didn't. How many times do you think about that? How many opportunities have you had and lost, and then relived a thousand times in your mind? Every time you relive a moment, you relive it by creating thoughts.

The thought, then, is not the reality. But how many times have you made thoughts reality? Most people assume their thoughts are reality. For instance, we're in a small southern town. There's an all-white audience. Suddenly, a black person comes in and sits down. How many people are going to think a negative, fearful, racist thought and make it seem as if it's real?

Thoughts are not real. They're merely images. Allow the image to come in and go out of the mind. Empower only that which you want to make real. A thought has no power until you let it have power. Therefore, I can allow every thought to come into me and then say, "That's a thought I want to act on, and that one I will give power to."

No one can have only positive thoughts. Even if you meditate, you're not going to have only positive thoughts. I've never met more unbalanced people than people who meditate. I have a friend who's a producer. He's a maniac. And yet he goes out every day to meditate. He'll eat vegetarian food. But he's a crazy person. He thinks that as long as he's meditating he's normal. But he hasn't dealt with his underlying fear, anxiety, and insecurities.

Imagine what would happen if you decided that it's not meditation, or yoga, or correct breathing that's going to make you lose your stress. It's not health food that's going to make you healthy; it's not vitamins or juices that are going to change your life. Rather, it's your attitude that is going to change your life. Your life's going to change because you're not being overly critical about anything you do wrong.

There's nothing more damaging than an overly critical mind. If you need to do everything right you will invariably fail because mistakes are inevitable. Then you're going to beat up on yourself. Say you eat only organic produce. Then, one day, you don't. You beat up on yourself as if now you've broken the perfection. Or think about the people who will eat only organic produce, but become so anxious about it that there's no flexibility left in their temperament. That kind of highly rigid mindset may appear normal, but it's not. It is not an integrated mind.

Stop blaming your feelings on circumstances. Otherwise every time you get abused, every time you get spoken to in a way you don't like, every time anything less than perfect happens, you're going to overreact. Allow yourself to be much more fluid, and much more flexible. Allow things to go through you. You cannot control your thoughts, so just let them be. You can control your reactions to circumstances, however. Remember, if someone says something critical to you, don't react. They're just words. They're just syllables, vowels, consonants. They have no meaning until you make them have meaning.

Only actualize what is constructive. Think in terms of watching your thoughts parade in front of you and going, "No . . . no . . . that one I like. That one supports my intentions. That's healthy. I'll take it in." Let go of all the rest. They mean nothing.

When you dwell on something, it creates your emotions. And when you dwell on something that's not positive, the negative emotion is going to come right behind it. Maybe you're wondering why your blood pressure is high, your cholesterol's high, and the stress hormone cortisol is being pumped into your system. These things are partly a result of your focusing upon negative issues. The negative emotion that automatically follows sets off a negative biochemical reaction. And if you're habitually negative, it will take a long-term physical toll; you may even be setting the stage, physiologically, for conditions as serious as stroke, heart attack, and cancer.

So get out of this destructive pattern, if you're in it. Switch from looking at problems to looking at solutions.

DO YOU FOCUS ON PROBLEMS OR IDEALS?

You can't focus on problems and ideals at the same time. The ideal is where the solutions lie. If you focus on problems, you look at the negative in everything. You make excuses that keep you from going forward by saying, "I would, but. . . ." You end up wasting a lot of time.

How do you keep from being tied up in the problem? How do you keep the problem from becoming more essential than you? Look at the ideal. Ideals always transcend problems.

WHAT ATTRACTS YOU TO THINGS?

What attracts you to jobs, people, activities, places? Why do you want to be in a place? Out of curiosity? Because you feel reverence for it? Because you want to be inspired by it? Because you want to connect to it? Because you feel you are connected to it? What attracts you to sex? Is it relief, loneliness, love, obligation, fun, exploration? What is it?

Keep a diary, or journal. When you start to identify in your diary what attracts you to things, you will start to see the real self. The real self will always attract you to something. Feel the real self. Feel its energy. There's an excitement that comes from an honest identification.

I have a friend who was a powerful attorney. Now, he's a game-keeper. He always loved animals and used to spend time in the Central Park zoo. He loved going there and looking at the animals. One day, he told me he felt successful, but not happy in his job. I asked him, "What would you do if you could do anything?" and he told me that he would love to be an animal keeper. I asked him why he didn't go for it, and he responded that he had too many obligations to consider. His family would never approve. I said to him, in essence, forget all that. If your family won't love you because you're changing your career, then go find another family. I know some people would berate me for that advice, and so be it. The man charted his own course. He followed his passion and is so much happier and healthier for it.

Too often we block our essential life energy. When we reconnect with it, we've practically catapulted ourselves into another dimension, a new universe of capability. That universe exists for each of us. If it didn't, we wouldn't have people able to do unique and strange things without ever having been taught. We have all had inspirational thoughts, times when we did not know how to figure something out, but an answer suddenly appeared. We weren't taught the answer. It was just there. In our most vulnerable moments, when we're truly ourselves, we can connect with that higher consciousness of life, or whatever we wish to call it. I'm suggesting we should make ourselves vulnerable and open to that all the time, and make our decisions connect with that. Then we have no down side to life.

WHERE DO YOU FIND MEANING?

No person can give me meaning if I don't have it for myself. People are forever seeking meaning through someone else who has meaning. Why do you think people join religious groups, become part of political campaigns, or follow those with dynamic personalities? It's because they seek meaning that is absent from their own lives. The healer must start by healing himself, and the warrior must start by ridding himself of fears.

I live my life in three-year increments so that my meaning and goals are for three years. Whether I'm dealing with environmental issues or health issues, I have that time to develop new attitudes, skills, and criteria. I can't keep using the old skills for every new task. We frequently do not want to learn new skills. We want to apply the old formulas to new challenges, but it does not work.

My attorney friend who became a gamekeeper was one of those who accepted the challenge of learning new skills. He had to learn a whole new profession, but he loves what he is doing—his life has new meaning. Perhaps he was a lawyer because his meaning came from his parents. But he discovered that getting your meaning from others isn't good enough.

If you're a middle-class person living in the city, chances are your meaning will be to maintain your security. You will not take chances. You will not exceed the boundaries—physically, mentally, or spiritually. You'll support a political system that will take care of you; freedom will not be important. You will live through other people's freedom by watching TV or reading magazines. You'll live a fantasy life but not be able to actualize it because security is so important.

The real you can't come out as long as you honor the old meaning. You can't have a new self and an old meaning. Your life is boring and predictable because there is nothing new. The problem is, every time you look for something new, you are besieged with fears and excuses. You must transcend the boundaries and fears and break off into whoever you are. You may not even recognize who you really are, but you must accept whoever you become.

Mistake Number Eight:
Neglecting the Power of Silence

1. Spend as many consecutive days as you can without watching TV, without listening to the radio or other electronic devices, and, if possible, without using a telephone.

How many "quiet days" did you spend?_____

How did the experience affect you? _____
_____

If you've turned everything back on, how do you feel?_____
_____
_____

2. Do you overeat? Silence can help you stop. For the next week, eat your meals without talk or noise (soft music is okay), and without reading. Focus on enjoying your meal.

Did you eat less than usual? _____
Also, did you eat more healthful foods than usual? _____

3. Observe animals whenever you can, for at least ten minutes at a time.

4. Go to the beach off-season. Bundle up, and actually sit on a blanket on the sand. Late afternoon or early morning are good times to do this.

5. Take a long walk or hike with a friend. Do not discuss your relationship. Do not discuss anyone's relationship—or anything. Speak as little as possible. Just hike.

Thinking We Have to
Age "On Schedule"

BELIEVING THAT IT'S necessary to age "on schedule" is one of the worst mistakes a person can make. You probably have a set of expectations in your head about how people are supposed to behave during each decade of life. If you let it, this set of expectations will become a template that molds your own behavior. The problem is, people's templates for aging are based on the way the world was when they were children, and today, our knowledge and our personal opportunities have expanded considerably. So those who are following the model they internalized years ago, in, say, in the 1950s or 1960s, are going to be shortchanging themselves throughout life. And they may actually be shortening their lives in the process.

If you're a member of the baby boom generation, think back to your early assumptions about how people were supposed to act and look during the various decades of life. They probably went something like this: The first two decades of life were when you were young. You went to school and had a few other responsibilities, but you also got to play a lot and have fun. By age twenty, though, you were a grownup, so fun ended. In your twenties, if you were a woman, you got married and had a few children. If you were a man you got a job; the marriage and children part of life could be pushed back a few years if you wanted, but not that many. In your twenties you could still look young.

People in their thirties, however, were not young anymore. (That idea stayed around till at least the late 1960s; remember the

"Don't trust anyone over thirty" mentality?) Women in their thirties who had worn their hair long now had it cut short; long styles were seen as too youthful. Most women had finished having babies by their early thirties. Men of this age were serious workers. Actually, all adults were serious. They were supposed to be like the parents on the TV show "Leave It To Beaver" or in the Dick and Jane readers—all-knowing authority figures who, although they could smile at times, basically meant business. Their posture was kind of stiff, and so was their attitude. By the way, remember the clothes that adults wore then? There was a sharp demarcation between adult and juvenile clothes that made grownups seem stiff, and behave that way too. It was hard to be really relaxed in a dress, girdle, stockings, and high heels.

People started to get old in their forties then. It's true that when John Kennedy ran for president he was called boyish in his early forties, but that was because he was being compared to past U.S. presidents, most of whom had been considerably older. (It was also, from some quarters, an effort to detract from his qualifications.) In general, men in their forties were supposed to wear suits a lot and look large and distinguished. Women could absolutely not have long hair, unless it was in a bun. Women in their forties were so far over the hill they had practically hit bottom on the other side, and they were not supposed to admit to their advanced age. Actually, admitting to one's age, beyond twenty-five, was never considered a smart thing for a woman to do.

The fifties were the beginning of "old." You were gray, you were a grandparent. You certainly weren't very active. If you were a man you could be distinguished. You could also be dead. If you were a woman you might not be that likely to be dead, but you couldn't be distinguished or attractive. You could be a nice lady in sensible black lace-up shoes offering tea and cookies to people.

In your sixties you could die without question; after all, you were truly old. You retired at sixty-five and it was all downhill after that; although in truth it had been all downhill for a long time before that as well. If you didn't die in your sixties you could sit in a rocking chair.

Expectations for your seventies were that you could sit in a rocking chair.

In your nineties and hundreds you could sit in a rocking chair.

That's the interesting thing: When this set of expectations was prevalent there *were* plenty of people living into their seventies, eighties, nineties, and even hundreds. But it was like all the decades starting at age sixty, or even fifty, were lumped together in the common imagination as "old." So a person could be old for fifty years. You could be old for half your life!

WHERE WE ARE NOW

We have different expectations now. Average life expectancy in America has increased almost a decade in the past half century (from sixty-eight in 1950 to seventy-seven in 1997), but beyond that, society now acknowledges that we don't have to act or look old at any particular time. It's up to us. So today we have many people working well past the traditional retirement age of sixty-five. We have people people in their eighties completing marathons, in their nineties lifting weights, people in their hundreds writing books, and they're not looked upon as oddities any more, but rather as the wave of the future.

We're really beginning to understand that youthfulness can be stretched well beyond the limits we used to place on it. What it takes is the will to make wise choices in the areas of diet and lifestyle, and to learn about the natural substances that can combat aging. Researchers have been discovering the benefits of so many of these—from the antioxidant vitamins and minerals, to the herb ginkgo biloba, to lesser known compounds such as acetyl-L-carnitine, coenzyme Q-10, DHEA, glutathione peroxidase, and phosphatidylserine—that there's a lot that's new out there to learn. But it's an exciting kind of learning because the knowledge can then be put to use in a personally rewarding way.

This is the positive side about where we are now vis-à-vis aging. The negative side is that all the knowledge in the world is not going to do you any good if you have a negative attitude about your life. If you feel like things haven't worked out in your life the way they should have, and like there's nothing to get up for in the morning, why would you want to start taking supplements, eating right, or exercising? You wouldn't, because nothing would be motivating you to do those things. Unfortunately, that's the situation for millions of middle-aged people today who, even if they aren't wearing "old-lady shoes" or rocking on porches, have, essentially, an "old" attitude. These people are functionally depressed—i.e., they're walking around and doing what they have to every day, but that's about it. There's no joy in their lives. It's as if the snap, crackle, and pop have gone out of their relationships and experiences, and all that's left of their lives is soggy and unappetizing.

In my work, I've talked to countless men and women who feel exactly this way. The situation is particularly hard for men. Women, at least, have been conditioned to be able to talk about their feelings, so that they can benefit from support groups or from candid talks with friends. In fact, that's a major aspect of women's socializing—getting together with friends for personal-problem-venting conversations. These conversations can be great stress-relievers for women, and to pejoratively call them "kaffeeklatsches" or "girl talk" or "gossip" misses the point. Mixed in with the gossip is an important exchange of ideas on personal issues.

By contrast, think about what men talk about when they get together—sports, TV shows, movies, computer games—anything but personal issues. Never feeling free to come out and discuss the really important things can age a person. It takes a toll on the spirit.

Think also about how we define success in our society. Women are allowed to feel good about raising a healthy family, or keeping a neat house, or being a nice person. But success for men is measured by work achievement; this is an old double standard that's still with us. Here's the problem: How many men have something substantial to show for their work after thirty or forty years? Yes, some can show a pile of books written, or money made, or a plaque with an impressive title on the door. But most can't. The reality is that the average job isn't particularly meaningful, lucrative, or prestigious. So unless a man has learned to disregard society's unrealistic image of success, he's got a morale problem when he hits middle age.

The average man dreads the next high school reunion; there'll be no big achievement to brag about and nothing new to show but his gray hair, or lack of it, and an extra roll of fat. The pizzazz went out of his marriage a long time ago. His kids don't seem to want to talk to him much. What's left in life consists of distraction and addictions—food, caffeine, cigarettes, alcohol, TV, spectator sports. The most active thing he does might be bowling. This is not a prescription for a long and vigorous life.

Women hitting middle age have their own set of problems. For instance, if they've made their main job in life raising children, once those children are grown they might feel useless. Also, our culture's standard of attractiveness is more forgiving of signs of aging in men than in women; witness Hollywood's pairing of fifty- and sixty-something leading men with actresses several decades their junior. So society's messages can be demoralizing for women too.

For both women and men of the baby boom generation the bottom line is this: If you're going to avoid the aging-on-schedule trap, you're going to have to—first and foremost—want to. You're going to have to feel good enough about yourself and your life to want to get out there and shine, for years to come. You're going to have to want to try new things and take on new tasks, develop new habits, and possibly make big changes. That's why the following section is intended to help you explore personal motivation issues, along with ideas about aging.

LET'S LOOK AT WHAT'S UNIQUE ABOUT THIS GENERATION.

This is the first generation that believes we can actually defy aging. The baby boomers have succeeded in many areas of life, where others have not. They're used to success, and so they expect it in this area as well.

Now, some of the popular trends in combating aging—e.g., the use of Viagra and conventional estrogen replacement therapy—I would not recommend because they are superficial approaches and because potentially serious side effects are ignored. I would advocate more natural approaches, encompassing diet, exercise, supplementation, and stress management. However, the point here is a positive one: This generation is doing something bold. Asserting that we can intercede in the aging process is something that no one in the past has ever done. People, myself included, make fun of baby boomers for being pleasure-seeking, self-absorbed, and vain. But there's an up side to all of that. This generation is now seeking to live long, pleasure-filled lives, and to look good doing it. We have to credit them for that.

When my father was forty, he looked eighty. All our parents, with few exceptions, looked much older than we do at our age. Part of this has to do with us knowing more; part of it has to do with our willingness to actualize what we know; and part of it is our willingness to challenge norms. If our parents smoked or drank, they were often not amenable to stopping. You could not talk them out if these habits, even if they were diseased as a result of them.

Our generation has woken up. We haven't woken up to everything, but when it comes to aging we certainly have. We are light-years ahead of our parents.

A LOT OF PEOPLE STILL GET OLD
BEFORE THEIR TIME. WHY?

The reason is that as most people age, they continue to live life as if yesterday was more exciting than today. They recollect things from the past. A person who has lived according to everyone else's notions, who never really honored his own life, but who lived just as a nice, obedient person who put in his forty years of civil service, has nothing to look forward to except death. So he'll try to recount those things that were meaningful. He'll go back even to high school where he still had a sense of wonderment, where there was still a chance to do something unique, where he still had the courage to challenge authority. Or he'll look back to college or to the few times earlier in a relationship where there was a sense of purpose. And that's what he'll talk about. He won't generally talk about anything newer than that unless it involves aches and pains or problems. Then he'll start to blame the world around him for the way he feels or for his situation. When someone tells you, "I'd be different if. . . ," then you know it's just an excuse.

But I can take you to places in this country and around the world where older people never talk about their old age unless they're counseling and guiding children. This is what grandparents should be doing, because they have the life experience, the compassion, the patience, and, more than parents, the capacity to allow children a great range in their development without boxing them in, since they are once removed from the child. Therefore, they are not dictating to the child, but guiding. It's always easier to guide than to dictate.

I think that we underutilize senior citizens in our society. We dump them and we shouldn't. Of course many dump themselves first, because they don't keep growing. Those that do grow, however, have wonderful lives.

WHEN IS CHANGE POSSIBLE?

Nothing ever changes for individuals unless someone first shows you it can change. When the runner Roger Bannister broke the four-minute mile, it was after years of competitive track during which no one could do it. Then, within six months after the record was broken, six other people did it. Once it was proven that it could be done, then everybody could do it.

It works the same way when you show that you can change the aging process, as we just did in a study. We've shown that anybody can do it. Now more people will try. But realize this: You can't do it if you're still connected to your old world view. You've got to separate yourself from the old paradigm, go into the void, and then be motivated by someone else who did it.

I think about a recent marathon. A woman was out there twenty-four hours later, still on the course. She didn't have any water. Nobody was helping her. She had to go through traffic. But she did it. Can you imagine people who heard about this, or saw it, and then said, "Gee whiz, I didn't think anyone could do that." Suddenly, someone else had altered their perception of the possible.

DO YOU THINK THAT PEOPLE ARE HEALTHY BY CHANCE?

They're not. To be truly—not just superficially—healthy, a person has to have worked at it. That's why when I talk about success at living, a large part of what I'm talking about is being healthy. That's a choice. To be healthy is to be successful because you cannot be healthy by accident. Health is a process you must address yourself to every day, mentally and physically. When you think a negative thought, your body responds with a disease process. A positive thought causes a healing process. There is no neutral place in life.

Society and traditional medicine have a superficial, overly simplified notion of health. The doctor says you're well because he or she can't find a classical disease. He neglects to ask whether you are functional or dysfunctional, under stress or not under stress. He fails to look at your blood chemistry to see if you have viruses or bacteria or parasites. Instead, he adheres to an overly simplistic model of health and disease. If you haven't gone over the threshold of a particular cholesterol measurement, for example, or weight, or blood pressure, the doctor says you are well. In reality, that's absurd. It takes you out of being responsible for the things you may be doing to your body that will soon result in disease.

Why wait until that full-blown classical disease strikes before you do anything positive for your health? Realize that you're unhealthy *before* the health crisis, take steps to reverse that, and you may avoid the crisis completely.

DO YOU COMPLAIN, BLAME, OR CHANGE?

People who change don't blame and complain. People who complain and blame don't change. Which are you?

Do you think anyone likes to hear you blame and complain? What is someone supposed to do with negativity when you give it to them? Are they supposed to say, "This feels good"? No. When you give others negativity in the form of gossip, anger, or blame, what can anyone do with it? Your negative energy only brings them down.

Nothing is going to change until you have no more energy or desire to blame. Then, you will begin looking for solutions.

It's exciting to be around people who are solution-oriented. They say, "I'm going to try this. What do you think?" Now you're engaged. They're asking you to be a part of a solution, and solutions are fun. Creative minds come together, and you're part of it. That's exciting. That's altogether different from blaming and complaining.

ARE YOU OPEN TO NEW INFORMATION?

I gave a lecture not long ago on the topic of mental health. Three other speakers were also there to present information. I spoke first, and discussed orthomolecular psychiatry and the role of nutrition in treating illnesses. The second speaker did not follow his prepared agenda. Instead he used his time to attack me. He said my claims were nonsense and pseudoscientific. When he was finished with his tirade, I once again addressed the audience. I asked, "Would you want to go to this man as a psychologist when he has just been so judgmental and paranoid about someone he has never met and a system he hasn't any idea of? How open is he going to be when you talk to him about your problems? He already has his mind made up."

Every day I meet educated, responsible people from different backgrounds. They are supposedly the best and the brightest in their fields. But often, I find them extraordinarily closed and fearful. They over-control their environment so that no new knowledge gets in. New information is a threat.

I did a series of shows on patient experiences. I interviewed people who had all recovered from so-called incurable illnesses. And it was remarkable what all of their stories had in common. Their doctor wasn't able to help them and told them they were going to die. They chose an alternative therapy. They were helped. Their lives were saved. They were cured. Then—and here's the interesting thing—they went back to their original physician— who did not want to know about their recovery! The doctors had no curiosity about what their patients had done to save their own lives.

You'd think these physicians would be intensely interested in every detail of their patients' recoveries. But no, they limit their reality to what they were taught. This allows them to maintain the status quo, and their power within the community as the ultimate authorities on health. It's as if they're horses wearing blinders, seeing only a small portion of what there is to be seen so they don't get off the path they're supposed to be on.

Why not see more, learn more, and get off the path if you have to? In the case of these doctors, it would help society, and it would also benefit them as individuals because when you're open to new information it helps your mind stay young. When you close yourself off from anything new, your mental processes fossilize.

HOW DO YOUR DELUSIONS AFFECT YOU?

People have delusions about what they might have been and what they could have done. Do not live with delusions; live with what you're willing to be. Otherwise you will sabotage your efforts by always setting goals that you cannot reach, then trying and failing, and finally feeling bad about yourself. Eventually, you won't try at all.

Try setting practical intermediate goals that come before the long-term ones. We often set only long-term goals, and when something goes wrong we say, "I shouldn't have tried it at all." Don't be like the artist who says, "I'm going to get my work into the Museum of Modern Art" and then gives up painting in disgust when MOMA doesn't accept his work. If he'd planned, instead, on having shows at the local library, and then at a neighborhood arts center, and then at a gallery, he could still be painting, and feeling a sense of accomplishment.

I've never met a person who is happy and successful with his or her life who hasn't failed many times before getting where he is. The key thing is that these people never feared getting up and trying again. And trying again and again after that if need be. Be realistic and don't allow your delusions to control you.

• • •

WHERE ARE YOU IN LIFE
VERSUS WHERE YOU NEED TO BE?

When training for a marathon, you may only be able to run one mile, when you need to go twenty-six. Getting there takes an awful lot of focus and determination. It means picturing yourself getting to the finish line, because before you can actually race the marathon, you have to do it in your mind.

Likewise, in other areas of your life, successfully becoming your real self means seeing who you need to be. Do not allow any distractions to interfere with that image.

You may find help if you pay attention to the following:

Your View of Self

This is the most important thing. What makes you different from other people? What stands out as unique, defining your character? Focus on manifesting your special qualities. And if in doing so you find you have to rebel against the norm, so much the better.

Anyone who knows me knows that I'm always advocating being a rebel; I think that's a key to living a really meaningful life. If you're never a rebel—if you try to fit in all the time—you're going to be suppressing your true nature. So rebel against what's expected if it doesn't fit in with who you are and what you feel. Speak up if racist jokes in your office offend you. Refuse to tip if service is unsatisfactory. Avoid people whose gossip makes you uncomfortable. If someone is rude to you, tell that person you don't appreciate it. You have a right to voice your feelings and opinions.

Your View of Life

Do you embrace life? Or can you appreciate only bits and pieces of it? Many people enjoy only parts of life. They cut themselves off from other sides of it because of prejudices and biases, limitations and fears.

Many of us look to our leaders for understanding. The more biased our leaders, the more closed off we become. So you have bits and pieces of reality that work, and a lot of reality that doesn't.

If you are rebellious you do not follow people just because they are your leaders. You follow whatever works. When something does not work, you do not have to accept it. If that means rejection by others, so be it. There are plenty of like-minded people out there waiting to fill the gap.

Your Age

How old would you be if you did not know how old you were? Biochemically, it is possible to reverse some aspects of the aging process. Foods, supplements, and exercise help you stay young. But the most important part of not aging on schedule is in your mind. Your mind holds the key to freedom. It allows you to be all the different things you want to be, when you want to be them. It lets you do the things you find important. Allowing yourself to be young, when everyone around you is growing older, is a rebellious action.

Your Emotional Age

Most of us become more serious as we get older, and we forget how to play. Play is important every day of our lives. But we get tied up in our problems, and do not make time to play. Even entertainment is solemn. We read serious novels, and go to sad movies that mirror the way we feel about our own lives. We watch someone being victimized on film because we ourselves feel victimized.

When you are too serious, you are boring and pretentious. You lose your sense of emotional balance and become hypercritical, obsessed, and perfectionistic. Academics tend to be boring. They generally are afraid of showing their human side for fear of not being taken seriously.

Make yourself younger emotionally by starting to play more. Begin by visualizing what that will be like. What kind of play would you like to put in your life? Don't be too serious, like most of the people around you. Be rebellious and take time to enjoy life.

Your Spiritual Life

Every great spiritual leader throughout history was a rebel. But we forget that and make religion ultra-conservative. These leaders followed the guidance of their own higher nature. This is what each and every one of us can do.

Once you know that you are guided by your higher self, then your insights change. You realize, for one thing, that nothing is permanent. Material things come and go. Life is fluid. The trouble is, mainstream belief systems would have us believe in permanency. In truth, everything changes all the time.

Once you realize this, you can go with the flow. You will not be caught up in thinking about the good old days. The good old days were never that good anyway. I was interviewing a person out in the bayous. We were looking out the window of a boat we were on when this person said, "I wonder what it would have been like in the good old days."

I said, "The good old days? I don't think so. First, if you had been sitting out there you would have been bitten by snakes, alligators, and phantom spiders. You would have had to wear clothes that were extraordinarily restricting and uncomfortable. You would have been in 110-degree heat with 100-percent humidity. And you would have been in petticoats and all kinds of clothes. There was no air conditioning, no running water, only water from a cistern. That would not have been a healthy way of living."

Even if you're reminiscing about "good old days" more recent than the ones I've just described, chances are your memory's editing out the more negative details. You might remember the 1950s, for instance, as a halcyon time when kids were free to play in the streets of their neighborhoods. On the other hand, if a child ever had a problem with an adult, such as a parent or teacher, it was always the authority figure who, was to be believed, and never the child. Children could be hit by adults with impunity then; in fact, it was expected that they would be. Sometimes these harsh realities get lost in the haze of nostalgia.

Your Career

Where do you need to be in your career? Where do you want to be? Once you determine the answers to these questions, seek to develop mastery. What you are doing is worth doing right.

Think of yourself as the recipient of someone else's work. Would you want to drive a car whose engine was not put in properly? Would you want the tires to fall off after twenty miles? If you were to go in for bypass surgery, would you care if the doctor was an expert or not?

I chose to strive toward a mastery of nutrition, and I still allow time to learn by studying several hours each day. Now, I've never mastered my field, and I don't believe anyone totally masters anything. But people are always capable of learning more; that's what mastery's about.

Mastery means going beyond what you already know. Since most people tend not to grow in their thinking, seeking mastery is going to make you stand out.

Your Anger

Anger is fine. It is a normal, healthy emotion. But it needs to be channeled constructively. Rather than hurt someone, or go into a depression, you can let anger motivate you to go out and do something positive. When I see something I feel is wrong, I try to change it. It may be something in the environment or something to do with nutrition or medicine. Whenever I see abuse going on, I respond to it, but never with wanton anger. It must be peaceful, positive, and creative anger.

Your Health

Where are you now and where do you want to be? If you really want to be as healthy as you can be, you may need to change an awful lot. You've got to have awareness and control of your body, mind, and spirit. It takes discipline.

Awhile ago I went to a restaurant with a few people. We were given a giant, healthy, wheat-free, dairy-free, yeast-free pizza that was made from spelt. I took one little piece to see how good it was in order to know whether or not to recommend the restaurant to others. I don't eat pizza, but I do recommend wholesome pizza to people who are learning to be more healthy and are on a transition diet. I noticed that a couple of people at the table could not stop eating. Or they chose not to stop.

When you look at people who have no discipline, it shows on their bodies. And it affects every area of their life. They always stop short. Remember, you cannot have dysfunction in one part of your life and manifest a completely integrated self in other parts of it. So taking care of your body means that you take care of other aspects of your life. It's a package deal.

When you look in the mirror, you should always see not just your present self, but the ideal self. Always envision yourself at your best no matter what you physically look like at the moment. See the trim body. See the ripples on the belly, the tightness on the legs, the strength in the arms. See someone who can run a marathon or mountain climb, who can roller skate or snorkel. As you see your ideal self, you will begin to do what it takes to get there. You'll do aerobics for conditioning; you'll lift weights for strength. Then, in six months to a year, you'll have that body.

If you really want to be youthful and healthy, you've got to work on it. It's not going to come naturally. Ask some of the top athletes in my running and walking club how it felt to go from being a slow to a fast runner. It was hard work! What got them through it was that they were joyfully committed to the process.

Getting healthy means overcoming people around you who try to discourage you. They kid you, but their attempts to restrain you are no joke. You hear, "Why aren't you eating this? I cooked this meat for you. Why don't you eat like a normal person?" Not complying with others' expectations takes strength.

Your Creative Self

When was the last time you allowed yourself to be creative? People are creative by nature—even people who aren't members of the energy type I call creative assertives—and so it's good for all of us to spend time every day in creative work. Let your imagination tell you what you want to create. You can create anything from original recipes to new furniture arrangements to different ways of living. Of course there's music, art, and writing too. Do something creative each day, not just occasionally.

Being creative yourself is different from supporting other creative people. It's fine to see a play, listen to a symphony, or go to an art gallery. But you need to express your innate creativity as well.

Your Fantasies

Many people in our society are too repressed to fantasize about anything. We need to fantasize about what we could be. If I had never allowed myself to fantasize, I would be working in a shovel factory, like everyone else in my family in West Virginia. I fantasized about coming to New York, and being able to write. I fantasized about being able to make a difference in people's lives. Many people I met along the way said that it was not possible. I did not have the education, background, or connections, as I was a blue collar kid out of a bean field in West Virginia.

Fantasize about what you want to be. Keep that fantasy alive and positive by focusing on it. Then you will get to where you want to be in your life.

DO YOU ALLOW PAST PAIN AND NEGATIVE
ENERGY TO INFLUENCE YOU NOW?

Many people live in their pain. They wallow in it. They carry it around like a merit badge on their chest. "I got fired from a job and I worked so hard." "I paid my taxes and they audited me." People brag about their pain. They keep bringing it up over and over again. I keep hearing about what didn't work in the past. Why don't people talk about something now? You live now. If it's dead, you bury it.

People who are dynamic, who have meaning and purpose, don't dwell in the past. You only need your past when you don't have a sense of self. That gives you an excuse. You try to convince other people why you are allowed to stay stuck, why you are allowed to have your depressions, why you are allowed to have your moods. Sure I can feel bad if I want to. Who couldn't? All of us have had things from our past that didn't work, that we didn't like, that didn't feel good, that were abusive. That's a part of the proving of life. For every marathon I've run that felt good, I've run one that felt bad. Does that mean I stop running marathons or blame marathons for my feeling bad? Of course not, as that would make no sense.

Everything that can cause a bad feeling can also strengthen us. Why not use the experience and say, "Yes, I had some bad moments there. I've learned something from them. I'm stronger because of them. Now I've got my life, and look what I'm doing with it." So thank your experience. That's the healthy way.

HOW DO YOU FEEL ABOUT YOUR BODY?

Think of your body. You probably spend a lot of time looking at it. If you are like most people, you are utterly obsessed with your body. You look in the mirror, for example, and notice that your hair is thinning and graying. All day long you think about your hair. What you think about your hair creates an emotion that creates your mood.

If you accept yourself, you will not allow negative emotions to adversely affect you. You won't stop going out and doing things because of the way you look. Some people don't care; others do. When you're in the business of your body, those things become very important. They're not really important but you make them important because you focus on them.

The way you feel at work on a particular day can be directly related to what you saw in the mirror that morning. Yet, you may not consciously connect those events. You look for something out there to justify why you're not feeling particularly well, or why you're being testy, or a little negative.

You can change this in several ways. First, you can allow yourself to accept what it is that you do see in the morning. You can then try to let the negative thoughts go. This isn't the same as prohibiting negative thoughts. It simply means you're not giving the ones that enter your mind any power.

Once you accept yourself, you can improve your body in a reasonable way. You can look in the mirror and say, "This is the body I've got right now. It's not ideal, but it's a starting point. From today on, everything I do will honor this body." Then you will take logical steps. Your diet will change and you will start exercising. Gradually, changes will occur, all as a result of accepting yourself, of thinking good thoughts about yourself and feeling healthy emotion.

ARE YOU ADDICTED TO ATTENTION, AFFECTION, OR ANY EXCESS?

Take a good look at anything you are addicted to. If you constantly need attention or affection, just like if you constantly need food, or alcohol, or cigarettes, you've got an addiction that will keep you from being who you are, and allowing real needs to be met. Yes, we have to eat and we crave closeness to others, but beyond certain levels, food and affection are not real needs. They're substitutes for something deeper and more essential.

If you need someone else to constantly confirm through affection that you're alright, it means you don't really trust that you are alright. It's best to get in touch with what is missing within yourself.

DESCRIBE YOUR SELF-LIMITING BEHAVIORS. WHEN AND HOW DO YOU USE THEM?

We frequently engage in self-limiting behaviors. We plan to lose weight but never start an exercise program or diet regimen. We make excuses for our actions by saying we're too busy or tired. Those excuses prevent us from taking actions that will help us reach our goals.

We need to start noticing when we act in self-limiting ways. We need to notice what we are doing and how we do it. Keeping a journal is useful for that. When we write we can explore our actions. And when we read our journals back after a time we can see patterns in our behavior. We can note such things as, "I was going to start my new diet today but didn't because. . . . " We can then ask ourselves why we acted in that way and what we choose to do instead. After awhile we will get in touch with what we need to do and make time for that. Only when we know the excuses we make can we banish them from our life. If we don't pay attention to them, they will continue to limit our potential.

WHAT PREOCCUPIES YOUR ENERGY?

Everything that happens in a day is either positive or negative. Try this for a week. Carry a notebook with you. Every time something positive happens, write it down. What was it? How did it happen? Who was involved? How did you respond? Do the same for negative things. You'll start seeing patterns in your experience, and in your behavior.

Look at the negative and ask yourself, "How can I change this and make it positive?" You can change it no matter what it is. I got out of a cab one day and later realized that I had left my prescription sunglasses there. I didn't like the fact that I had left them there because they were expensive. But I said to myself, "I'm not going to be angry at myself for having overlooked the fact that I took them off, talked to someone, distracted myself, and left." Now, every time I get into a cab, I look on that seat before I get out. I take a mental inventory. You can learn from your experiences and in that way make something positive out of something negative.

WHAT HAVE WE CREATED THAT IDENTIFIES WHO WE ARE?

We can't achieve personal excellence until we have something to show excellence through. Is it our body? Is it our mind? Is it something out there? What are we creating consistently on a day-to-day basis?

We generally think of ourselves as helpless and limited, so we align ourselves with groups, or "isms" (socialism, conservatism, environmentalism, or something else) with which we associate our image. As long as we are attached to a group, we feel we're doing something. I don't find that works. I've stopped being a part of groups or "isms" because everything I saw was contradictory. I would lecture on Earth Day about the environment and see people eating hamburgers and drinking sodas and leaving garbage and smoking. Rather than handle the contradictions I find in groups, I prefer to work on my own.

HOW ARE YOU TREATED WHEN YOU FAIL TO CONFORM TO YOUR PRESCRIBED ROLE?

When we veer from our prescribed roles, we're ostracized. We're the point of everyone's gossip. No one likes us. We're not being attacked because we've done anything wrong; we're being attacked because we've changed.

Showing ourselves as different from others is threatening. Before, when we and they looked in the mirror, we all looked the same. Now we look real and they look distorted and artificial. They never forgive us for showing them how utterly unnatural they look. That's the pain of change.

Once you change, you'll never want to look the old way again.

WHAT HAPPENS WHEN YOU'RE HAPPY? WHEN YOU'RE NOT?

Happy people have better perceptions, and are more optimistic and more open. That is, when you feel good, you allow things to happen. When you feel bad you close yourself off.

Think of the things you won't allow to happen to you when you feel bad. You'll say, "Don't touch me; I don't feel right." "I don't want to talk now." "I don't want to do anything." Remember, you feel bad because of something you tell yourself. Then you create the emotion to justify what you say. Now you won't do things. Feeling bad is limiting. Your world closes in and stops. It's not fun being around someone like that.

The people who feel bad stay gridlocked. The people who feel good go forward.

LIFE IS TRANSITIONAL.

Some transitions are voluntary. You change from a job you don't like to one that you do. You end a relationship that doesn't work and enter one that does. You get out of an abusive situation and into a healing one. Other changes are outside of your control. Right now, over 50 million baby boomers are realizing that they are no longer teenagers. People between forty and fifty-five are seeing wrinkles, gray hair, and bodies that are not what they used to be, and it is scaring them. They think of where their parents and aunts and uncles were at forty and fifty and remember them as being old. They were one step away from retirement and then death. Baby boomers don't feel ready for that. Nor should they.

As we go through transitions, we have to be honest about how we feel. Transitions are a time when we need to think about our direction. We can learn from our parents' mistakes. Just because they perceived themselves as old at forty doesn't mean we have to age prematurely. We don't have to kill ourselves by smoking and eating fatty foods. We don't have to retreat to Florida or end our days in a nursing home.

Pioneering a new path is not easy. In a sense, our parents had an easier time making transitions because they expected to get old and sick and to die at sixty-five. We don't believe that. We know that we can live to 120. We know that people can run marathons in their eighties. But we have to make choices if these things are going to happen.

Making these choices then becomes the issue. Are you going to take antioxidants? Which ones, and how much? Are you going to eat right? Exactly what foods are you going to cut out, and what are you going to eat more of? Are you going to exercise? How?

And why? Why are you going to make these changes? What is your life about at this stage? Transitional times are periods when you should ask yourself what meaning life has for you now and what action you need to take to fulfill that purpose.

If you are like most people, you will benefit from support during transitional times. Talking to others who understand what you are experiencing can help you in your change.

By the way, don't think that you will necessarily feel fearful, strange, or uncomfortable as you enter a new phase of your life. A transition can also be exhilarating. You will feel what your mind tells you to feel. If you expect an experience to be terrible, it will be. If you think it will be exciting, it will manifest in that way.

WHAT ABOUT DYING?

The thought of dying is difficult to accept in our culture because no one prepares us for it. This is unfortunate because death is an inevitable occurrence that is on most people's minds, young and old. Children fear their parents dying. The thought of their parents not being with them any longer is a terrifying one. Part of the transition from childhood to puberty to adulthood is being able to accept the parting of a loved one. But our culture doesn't help its children make these transitions.

The people who are least frightened by death are those people imbued with life. When you are fully living, you automatically honor death because you understand that it's a constant companion.

You can change the meaning of a word by changing how you respond to the word. You don't have to accept someone else's association with a word as your own. An example of this is people who have transcended the fear of death because they believe that they are spiritually immortal. There are multiple meanings you can give to words. Choose the ones that create the healthiest images in your mind. Replacing a negative thought with a positive one is healing.

NO ONE IS ESSENTIAL OR INDISPENSABLE. BUT THAT DOESN'T MEAN THAT PEOPLE'S LIVES ARE INSIGNIFICANT.

Everyone is ultimately disposable. That's the way life on this planet works. People don't like the idea of being impermanent, but no matter how important they are, every person and everything in life is. Everyone who ever lived was disposable. As important as Buddha or Christ were, they were impermanent too. They helped mankind, they gave people new insight, but ultimately they came and went. It's what they left afterwards that other people remember and treasure.

We remember people who live honestly and who earnestly seek to create. We love the honesty of expression in music, literature, poetry, and art. We also cherish people's contributions made on a more personal level, to their families and friends, and to their communities.

Create meaning in your life so that you are not forgotten after you leave. Then your life will not really be a disposable one. The memory of what you have left will be honored. In that way you will live forever.

Mistake Number Nine:
Thinking We Have to Age "On Schedule"

1. What activities did you enjoy as a child but no longer do because they seem inappropriate or embarrassing, or because you feel you're not good enough at them at an adult level? Examples: running, swimming, water painting, singing, planting seeds in milk-carton flower pots, jumping rope, bicycling, building tree houses.

Write them down._____

_____

Pick one, circle it (in crayon, if coloring was one of your favorite activities!), and start doing it again. It's okay if you feel you have to do it in private. Just be sure to get clearance from your health care provider for vigorous activities like rope jumping.

2. If you're not already doing so, start engaging in a half hour of aerobic activity several times a week. Be sure to have a physical examination before you begin.

3. People forget about posture. Make a concerted effort to improve yours. Think in terms of being a soldier, but one who is in the "at ease" mode. (Pacifists can picture themselves as ballet or modern dancers who are offstage!)

4. If you're not already doing so, arrange to spend a minimum of an hour outdoors daily.

5. Most people will advise you to think young to extend life. I would tell you the opposite—think old. Specifically, tomorrow, for the entire day, go about your regular activities, but imagine that you are 100 years old. If you are a reader who is 100 or over, be 130 mentally. I believe we have the potential to live several decades beyond 100, but we're going to have to change our mind-sets, along with our lifestyles, in order to do that.

How did you feel, "being" 100 or older?_____

_____

How did you feel the next day, being your chronological age?

_____

_____

Forgetting We've Reached a New Millennium

AFTER THE BIG ball finally fell on Times Square on December 31, 1999, a lot of the so-called "sophisticated" people breathed a sigh of relief. No more would we have to hear the endless prophecies about "the year 2000," because that time was finally here. The forecasting had been going on for about thirty years now, and all the hype was getting a little old. Plus on January first when we saw that the world was still functioning, we could forget the whole "Y2K millennium bug" thing. Also, there'd be no more silly hairsplitting about whether the new millennium really started in 2001 rather than 2000. Enough already!

Counting myself among the sophisticated people, I experienced all of these reactions. But on the other hand, counting myself among those still unsophisticated enough to feel excitement and joy, I did genuinely celebrate the new year. Whether or not we were one year short of the new millennium, our culture had reached a numerical milestone, and it was exciting. Many of us baby boomer types were concurrently marking half a century of being alive, and while we've seen some troubling trends during this span, there have also been welcome ones, as well as major expansions of society's consciousness, not to mention wonderful new inventions. Sometimes I'll be talking to people who don't seem to acknowledge anything new in the world in any way that goes beyond complaining, and I'll feel like shaking them by the shoulders and shouting, "We've reached a new millennium! Live like it!" What I want them to do is look around and see what today's society has to offer, and then pick and choose from these things in order to create a better life for themselves.

Take the Internet, for instance. Some people fear it's going to bring about the end of social interaction as we know it. But the advent of the Internet does not mean that we all have to become alienated Web-surfers who spend their lives clicking away in the loneliness of their own darkened rooms. You can do what I do and use this miraculous system not as a crutch or a hideout, but as a way of gaining entree into a whole range of information sources. I celebrate the fact that the Internet has given me instant access to the latest in the world's medical literature; it's made my work in the health and nutrition fields so much easier and more effective, and it's actually freed up some of my time for more social activities. There's no way I'm going to get sucked into the downside of the Internet; I simply never get involved in chat rooms, or time-wasting lists of jokes, or commercial come-ons. The choice is mine.

The other day I took the train from New York to Boston, something I hadn't done in a number of years. While the cityscapes of Connecticut and the red-tinged countryside of Rhode Island were familiar, some things that were going on in the railway car were definitely new. For instance, on both parts of the round trip there was seated near me a type that I have come to think of as the "nonstop cell-phone guy." This is the individual who makes call after call, during which process you find out all about his work life, social life, family life, medical problems and practitioners, sense of self-importance, and opinions on which stocks are hot. While some people find this type obnoxious, as a student of human nature I actually don't mind listening to them, and I marvel at the way that nonstop cell-phone guys have transformed the train into a virtual office, and have made not wasting a second of travel time into an art form.

People can now plug laptop computers into the railroad car wall and extend their office hours this way as well. Are those who do this neurotic workaholics? Some probably are, but who cares?

Personally, I think it's great that you can now spend your train time gazing out the window, reading a book, sleeping, or continuing to contribute to the gross national product, or your own personal product. The choice is yours, and that's a positive thing.

On the way back from Boston, I couldn't help overhearing—between the cell-phone guy's calls—some of the conversation between a young man and woman who had been strangers before they found themselves seated together on the train. There seemed to be some chemistry developing between them, and, although I couldn't see them, I could hear why: He was a Hugh Grant sound-alike whose accent and tentative, self-deprecating way were probably appealing to her, and, as for her, the young woman's obvious intelligence, sense of not overstepping polite bounds, and pleasant voice were probably appealing to him. I was rooting for them, and no doubt other passengers were too; they evoked much more sympathy than the cell-phone guy. I was saying mentally, "Would one of you please give the other their card or their phone number before you get off the train! Stop being so self-deprecating and polite!"

Ah, the age-old agony of two attractive strangers meeting on a public conveyance! What to do?

But then something happened that was not age-old. She gave him her e-mail address. She just slipped it casually into a sentence. And I thought, isn't e-mail a great invention? You used to have to hand a prospective date your card or write down your phone number, which can be intimidating challenges because they require actual physical action at a time when your hands may be liable to shake. Sure you could just state your phone number without writing it down, but seven digits strain the limit of memorizability, and if there's an area code involved, forget it. Now, with e-mail addresses, building a social life becomes easier. Since the addresses are often just a simple name *at* a probably familiar phrase *dot* a familiar syllable, you can easily finesse yours into a conversation and trust that the person will remember it. This approach seems less committal than the old way—when you had to get out a pen, and then find a piece of paper, procure something to lean on, and finally write the number down—so you somehow feel there's less at stake. Not to mention that the act of sending an e-mail itself has to be a whole lot easier, for those on the shy side, than making that first phone call or even mailing a letter. I'll bet those two train-mates did go on to make contact, and they might have had e-mail to thank.

Not all new developments in the railroad car were electronic. I looked up at the luggage rack, and flashed back to how things would have looked up there in the 1950s or 1960s. Then, luggage consisted almost totally of rigid, hard-sided pieces that were heavy and clumsy to maneuver. Getting them up and down from a luggage rack was a hassle, not to mention walking through stations or streets with them. Now, virtually all the luggage on the rack was soft-sided—much lighter and easier to manipulate than the valises of old. A lot of today's travel cases can be suspended on your back or slung over a shoulder, and many of the bigger pieces are now on wheels so you can glide them through stations or airports, with some designed to "piggyback" smaller pieces. The result is that you don't have to be as strong or as young as you used to be to travel easily on your own. Again, that's a good thing.

The seats on the train had improved too. I thought back to the time when all train seats were bench seats. Now, the train seats were individual affairs, like they are on airplanes, and you can recline yours if you want, or use a little drop-down table attached to the seat in front of you. True, there's not much legroom, but I'd still call the redesign progress.

WHERE WE ARE NOW

But are railway seats, or suitcases, or e-mail, or cell phones what's really important in life? Of course not. What's important are our attitudes. What do people generally feel about life? Toward others? Toward the world?

Again, I think things have changed for the better. Think back to the way things were in the 1950s. Today, there's a much wider range of acceptable behavior for people in various roles and of various groups. If you're a mother of young children, for instance, you can choose to stay at home all day taking care of your kids, a la June Cleaver, or you can have a full-time job. Fathers, too, can choose either of these options. You can be a member of a minority group and, if you've got the brains, expect to enter any university or occupation you want; being a WASP is no longer a requirement. If you're disabled, you can expect to participate in society in ways you couldn't years ago. If you've got any one of a multitude of physical or emotional problems, or are in any one of a multitude of challenging situations, you can join a support group, either in person or on line. No individual has to feel isolated any more. Some people take these realities for granted, but they are no small things for those who remember when the world was a more rigid place and everyone was expected to be "well-adjusted." What you had to adjust yourself to was the norm, and if you didn't, there was no "I'm okay—you're okay" attitude. It was more like "I'm okay—you're a sicko!" Society let you know it was displeased.

Today, there is much more of a possibility that you can depart from the American norm and feel fine about it. This is particularly true in our bigger cities. If your family life doesn't fit into the mom-dad-2.5 kids mold, you're no longer labeled a pervert. If your nutritional habits don't fit into the meat-potatoes-and dessert mold, you're no longer labeled a health nut. If your work history doesn't follow a steady climb up the ladder of one particular occupation, you're no longer called unstable. I'm not saying that the way things are today is perfect—far from it!—but, in general, we are a lot freer than we used to be.

The catch is this: If you're going to take advantage of society's liberalized attitudes and new freedoms, you have to liberalize your own attitudes toward yourself. It does no good to live in today's world of relaxed rules if you're still playing by yesterday's rigid ones. Are you? Exploring the following questions can help you decide, and help you see how you might improve your life in the years to come.

HOW DO WE EXPAND OUR BELIEF SYSTEM?

Early in life we become conditioned to believe in certain things. Those ideas and values shape our belief system. Everything we accept as true falls within the parameters of that belief system. At some point, though, we may feel compelled to go beyond what we've been told. Our consciousness wants to expand, and that expansion necessitates that we change our ideas and values.

As an example, consider the way we eat. Most of us are raised to eat meat and are taught to believe that meat-eating is both necessary and healthy. We may, however, get a glimmer of a feeling that consuming another animal species is wrong. That, in turn, may be confirmed by various sources of information—an article, perhaps, or a lecture. New values begin to form as we learn that man is not naturally carnivorous because our teeth are flat like those of other vegetarian animals, not sharp for tearing flesh, and that our intestines are longer than those of carnivores, making it difficult for us to digest meat properly. We begin to see how eating meat poses various health hazards—putrefaction in our long intestines sets the stage for colon cancer, for instance—so we start to perceive meat-eating as unhealthy, the opposite of what we had believed. Furthermore, we learn that great cruelty is involved, making the practice unethical, and that much land is destroyed for animal grazing purposes, making it environmentally destructive. These new ideas and values set the stage for our expanding consciousness, and may then result in life-changing actions, such as becoming vegetarian.

Growing in consciousness is not an easy task because as social beings we are influenced by those around us—family, peers, educators, co-workers, employers, and governments—and the collective groups that make up society tend by nature to be conservative. They are slow to change and sometimes even reactionary.

Look at the typical cardiologist. He or she has been trained in what is believed to be the best possible medical model for helping people with arteriosclerosis: balloon angioplasties, beta blockers, calcium blockers, and coronary bypass operations. All ideas about treatment are bounded by those beliefs. Therefore, hundreds of patients are handled the same way.

That doesn't mean that they are necessarily going to be helped, as we see people who die after undergoing a coronary bypass. People often don't recover in the long run because the operation doesn't change the underlying cause of the disease. Despite many failures, the doctor believes that there is nothing beyond what he or she knows to offer. Any suggestion otherwise is seen as quackery, as unproven, or as bad science.

Say a patient comes in and says, "Doctor, I was going to have a coronary bypass. You told me there was no other way. Then I read Dr. Dean Ornish's book and learned that with a vegetarian diet, relaxation techniques, supplements, and exercise, I could reverse arteriosclerosis. And you know something? It worked. Isn't that great?" Would this doctor be amazed at his patient's revelation or even curious to know more? Probably not. In fact, most doctors would flat-out reject the patient's experience because the medical profession, as a whole, is not open to new paradigms. They've been taught to value coronary bypass operations and medication, and hence, that is what they value.

This is not to say that doctors should be open to every single claim that is made. Obviously, many claims cannot be supported. However, in the case of Ornish's work, his large-group studies yielded statistically significant results vis-à-vis reversing arteriosclerosis, results that were published in peer-reviewed scientific journals. So there's no excuse for ignoring or dismissing his approach, as is so often done by mainstream physicians. I consider the outright rejection of Ornish's work to be a prime example of how belief systems can become so rigid that nothing, not even sound logic, can change them.

We live in a society that values conformity and obedience. So we value the individual who makes it a point to do what he or she has been told to do. We reward acceptance, and we reject those who challenge, or who "think outside the box."

Consider what it meant for Ornish to think outside the box. In a world unreceptive to change, that took courage. It also took dissatisfaction; he had to have been dissatisfied with the status quo in order to look for something new because, if what he had learned in medical school worked, he would have had no reason to look for another way.

People don't go beyond what works. There's no point to it. If you're living in peace, harmony, and bliss, you don't have to look for something else. You have everything. But if our systems, or our models of behavior are not working for us, then we have every right to expand our ideas and beliefs.

It's unfortunate that most of us remain limited in our thinking. Looking at our medical example, since the American medical world values drugs and surgery above all else, the only breakthroughs it is generally willing to embrace are those that fall within that model. When you go beyond the accepted paradigm, what you offer is rejected. You can discover a better way of helping cancer patients, a non-drug approach to helping hyperactive children, or a nutritional protocol for overcoming depression, and your ideas will automatically be turned down. Reason says they shouldn't be. Reason suggests that if doctors' primary interest is to help patients, and they find that there is a better way of doing something, one that is documented to work, they then have an ethical responsibility to try it. Based on their stated commitment to help other human beings, they should allow themselves to let go of their current consciousness and push it out to new perimeters.

Think about your own situation. What do you want to change?

Are you willing to look outside the box so that your consciousness can grow and transcend current limits?

ARE YOU LIMITED BY NOT KNOWING WHAT YOU REALLY NEED?

A lot of people know what they don't want, but they can't tell you what they do want. That's because, growing up, we heard a hundred no's for every yes. We were told what we couldn't do and what we couldn't have. We were taught to be pragmatic, and in the process no one invited us to explore and find out what we really wanted.

As a result, most people live limited lives. They have few new experiences. Their diets are limited, for example, and they almost never travel out of their own neighborhoods. Their lives are a series of limitations: "I did not do this." "I did not do that." "I didn't experience that." "I didn't taste that." "I didn't drink that." "I didn't go there." "I didn't speak with him." It's as if somehow they're supposed to be rewarded for all the things they didn't do.

Life should not be lived by exclusion. Life is meant to be inclusive. By this I mean that you include the things that resonate with the essential self. You won't know what that is until you know what you want and have the courage to go after it. The worst that can happen to us when we follow our desires, ambitions, and dreams is that we do not succeed. But at least we've tried. At least we've engaged in the process of going after what we want.

If you accept process as being important, then the goals are secondary to the very process that you were free enough to try. Why do you think that when people come out and do a marathon, every one of those people is considered a hero? The crowd doesn't applaud just the first five or ten runners. They applaud the person who comes in seven hours later—because that person tried.

WHEN YOU SET A GOAL, DO YOU ALLOW ITS ACHIEVEMENT TO NATURALLY EVOLVE, OR DO YOU SEEK IMMEDIATE PERFECTION?

Do you jeopardize your goals by wanting too much too soon? Setting unrealistic goals is a way of undermining yourself because when you don't achieve what you set out to do, you continue to feel bad about yourself. It's a way of perpetuating a poor self-image.

Realistic goals are ones that you can meet. Such goals are just slightly beyond your current threshold of comfort. You have to create some discomfort in order to grow, and every day that you go through discomfort is a day that you've grown.

DO YOU RESIST CHALLENGE?

How many times have you avoided challenge, not because it was unreasonable or destructive, but because you didn't want difficulty in your life? Have you noticed that the same types of confrontations appear again and again until you decide to take them on? That's because challenge precedes growth.

The road to growth is filled with adversity. For no project that I've ever undertaken in my life have I been able to go from an idea's conception to its completion without traveling through hills and valleys, without running into criticism and what seemed, at times, to be impossible obstructions. But then one day I was there, and I was stronger for it. I'd finally achieved my goal.

As an example of meeting challenge head-on, consider Ed Finkelstein. He experienced adversity when he chose to go against the advice of most medical professionals and avoid surgery for a clogged artery that was 90 percent blocked. He believed that he should try a more natural, alternative approach. Doctors and others tried to negate his idea, his body, his consciousness. Here was the adversity. What allowed him to continue with his idea, instead of falling back? "It made sense to me to go the natural way," Ed said, "and to follow a program of detoxification." Ed's beliefs were strong—he also had the unwavering support of his wife—and he chose to follow them.

As a result, Ed achieved success. To date, with a health program that includes a vegetarian diet, chelation therapy, vitamin C drips, and exercise, his arteries have de-occluded to almost 50 percent. He went from almost having to have a major heart operation to being voted outstanding athlete of the year in his age group. Ed is seventy-seven.

What kind of strength does it take to follow through on your convictions? Quite a bit. Imagine the average seventy-plus-year-old man being told that he needs to have an operation on his heart and not doing it. Imagine the courage it takes and the level of consciousness a person must have to embrace an alternative approach.

I am thankful for life's challenges, and try to work with them, not against them. Working with challenge is like running with the wind on your back. It supports you. On the other hand, resisting challenge is like trying to run into a storm. Everything is an effort far beyond what it should be. So ask yourself, what healthy challenges have you had that you've resisted?

DO YOU CHOOSE TO CHANGE OR DO YOU WAIT UNTIL YOU ARE FORCED INTO IT?

People rarely choose to change. Most of the time, when people change it's because they've encountered a crisis that forces them to.

This is unfortunate because the difference between choosing to change and being forced to change can be summed up in one word: control. You can control change that you choose, while you cannot as easily control change that's forced upon you. If you have prostate cancer, for example, your doctor will tell you that you must receive radioactive pellet implants or that you need surgery and chemotherapy. At that point, you don't have much control over your situation. But if you had gotten involved in the change process earlier, rather than waiting until your body degenerated into a state of crisis, you would have had more control. By thinking, "I want to help my prostate gland to not become cancerous. What in my diet can help? Can I use saw palmetto or some other alternative treatment?" you would have had more room to choose because you would not have been acting out of desperation.

We must stop waiting for things to happen that cause a breakdown. Do you want to be always in a reactive mode, waiting until something happens? Or do you want to have more control, through reasoning and early action? There's a big difference there, and it's up to you.

HOW DO YOU SOLVE PROBLEMS?

Big problems don't generally start out that way. They are an accumulation of smaller ones that were ignored or overlooked. Therefore, I do not believe that we should solve problems by going after big solutions. That never works. Rather, we should solve problems by constructive deconstruction.

Positive deconstruction of a problem—looking at it piece by piece—takes patience, but it always produces good results. For example, some people will say, "I want to lose weight, but I'm going to gain it all back," while others will say, "It took me twenty years to gain this much weight; it may take ten years to lose it, but I will."

If you have an interpersonal conflict, keep in mind that you can never end a conflict with only one person winning. Both people have to gain something from it before it's over. Otherwise, the conflict will continue. Always put yourself in the shoes of the other person, and ask yourself, "What does it feel like to be this person?

What can I hear through his ears and sense from his experience? If I were him, how would I want this conflict resolved? Once you understand what it's like to be the other person, you can change in a way where both of you gain something. Suspend judgment and listen to what the other person is saying. Then see if that gives you greater clarity regarding his or her point of view.

When you do respond, instead of answering in a threatening way, or in a manner that shows you are trying to correct the person, simply say, "I want to first clarify things to see if I understand what you're saying." Then repeat back to her (or him) what you think she said, so she can confirm whether or not that's what was meant. Now if the person responds, "Yes, that's what I said. You heard me right," you might say, "Okay, I can understand that from your point of view. How would you like me to respond to it?" You are now giving the person an option. You're not trying to correct, embarrass, or degrade. You're trying to resolve something. Once you ask for the other person's input, you take the sting out of the person's initial inflammatory response. You've listened. You haven't judged. You've shown that even if you disagree with someone, you can still feel what she is feeling. You've repeated the other person's view back, and now you're asking that person what she wants from you. Thus, communication is open. This is action/reaction. Your actions help shape the reactions you will receive. That's how, at least initially, steps are taken to deconstruct a problem.

WHEN THERE'S CONFLICT, DO YOU THINK BEFORE YOU ACT?

Recently, the press reported a murder prompted by "snow rage" when a Philadelphia man shot and killed a neighbor during an argument over where he was shoveling snow. This is an extreme example of acting before you think, although unfortunately not a scarce enough one in the modern world. All of us experience conflict. And often we don't deal with it appropriately. As a result, we victimize others and ourselves.

You run the risk of overreacting when there's too little time between an action and a reaction. A reaction is instantaneous; it happens in a millisecond. But before we react, there's a brief period of time when we can still get out. We can use that moment to ask ourselves, "What really caused this incident to happen? Why did he do that? What should I do now that will be in my best interest in the long run?"

How do you react in conflict? When something happens to set you off do you respond within the bounds of reason? Do you take the time to consider what happened before you act on it? Or do you react before considering what the consequence of your action will be?

Do not allow your mood to determine how you view your circumstance. Since moods change, there's a good chance you'll soon view what happened differently. Recognize when you are feeling stressed or angry, and tell yourself, "I'm not in the best mood right now. I really shouldn't be dealing with this. Let me think about this tomorrow."

And remember this: Once you react, you can no longer undo your action. Think about the results that may follow. Otherwise, like the man who killed his neighbor over some snow, you may spend a lifetime in prison thinking about what you did.

WHAT ARE YOUR BAD HABITS?

All of us shortchange ourselves in some way with patterns of living we fall into. We procrastinate, for example, clutter up our lives, or lack self-discipline. It's difficult to change, no matter how much we want to, until we look at the deeper meaning behind our actions.

Look at procrastination. When we truly love what we are doing, we can't begin it soon enough. When we procrastinate, on the other hand, we are putting off responsibility, and that stems from being involved in something we do not love. A habit of procrastination, then, can be an indicator that we're working solely out of a sense of obligation.

Or are you a habitual "clutterbug?" When we live in clutter we are making an excuse for not getting things done. Clutter keeps us from seeing what our lives would be like if we had organization. It prevents us from completing a job. That's because too much stuff gets in the way, and we lose our focus. Clutter may also mean that we're afraid of criticism, either self-criticism or criticism from others. To prevent that, we engage in a lot of little projects without finishing anything. By keeping our lives cluttered, we also keep ourselves busy, and we feel important. "Look at how much stuff is on my desk. I've got no time to do anything else. It'll take twenty lifetimes to get through this stuff!"

Life functions better when there is organization. Accept that you've been disorganized, and realize that clutter is an extension of your mental disarray. Start saying, "Today I organize," and change a little each day. Once you get organized, you will manage your time better. Go into your desk and take care of loose ends by filing papers and throwing things away. Pay your bills, and keep them up to date. Then, at any given moment, you will be able to get to whatever you need. You will have more room to grow. You will have the time to return to your dreams and incorporate those things into your life that give you joy. That will free you and allow you to ultimately feel better about yourself.

Another area of concern for many people is discipline, or their lack thereof. It takes discipline to accomplish and learn. When we discipline ourselves it shows that we believe we are deserving. Conversely, not disciplining yourself might be your roundabout way of saying that you don't feel you deserve success.

Have you ever sabotaged something in your life because you felt you didn't deserve it? When we don't truly believe that we should have success, love, happiness, and acceptance, we ruin our chances of attaining it. I've seen people betray each other and end relationships for no good reason. I'll ask, "Why did you ruin your relationship? Why did you lie and cheat?" They answer that they don't know. They're pushing away love that they feel they don't deserve.

ARE YOU UNREALISTIC ABOUT WHAT A RELATIONSHIP CAN PROVIDE?

When we can't figure out a purpose for our life we feel incomplete, and we seek fulfillment through another person. But unless we have a clear sense of self, we only complicate our life by bringing dysfunction into the relationship. No one else is going to compensate for that sense of lack, despite what lyrics to popular songs may tell us.

Maybe you recognize this pattern. In the beginning, both of you are on your best behavior, and your faults stay hidden. Everything seems nice and easy.

"Oh, you like poetry?"

"Yes, and walks by the ocean."

"And nice music?"

"Oh, yes. Are you into that too?"

"Yeah. And, cotton clothes?"

"Yeah."

And you think, "This is what I've been missing in my life." So, you let the person in. Once he or she is there, you feel really happy about it. You think, "This is a good package."

A few months later, a "big, hairy ape" greets you at the door. You ask, "Who are you?"

He says, "I'm the past."

"What's in the trunk?"

"That's all my garbage."

"You're bringing in seven truckloads?"

"Well, we couldn't bring it in the first day, not on the first date."

"I don't want it."

But you've already committed to it.

We weren't paying attention. Our needs were so great that as long as anyone had something we thought would make us feel better about who we are, we believed that the external circumstance would rebalance the internal emptiness. But it never has, and it never will. When do you finally learn? You must learn about growing and not seeking perfection in a relationship.

When you seek perfection in another, you become ultra-critical of both your partner and yourself. You see your reflection in others. What you see in them you also see in yourself. If you see that you're weak, you're going to abhor anything that represents weakness in another person. You're going to pick another person to pieces because he or she is not perfect. And since no one is, of course, you're never going to be happy.

Looking at this from a man's perspective, we men have got to stop thinking that women must be perfect in order for us to be interested in them. The average woman doesn't look like the average man expects her to look. We glamorize artificial beauty. An example is a poster I see at bus stops that features pouting women with big, fat lips—hard, angry faces with sixteen tons of silicone staring at you. Women, too, have got to stop thinking that they must reach a certain level of perfection before they're going to be interesting to look at. We are both wrong because we are in conflict with reality.

Whatever happened to natural beauty? Look at a natural nose. Nothing is wrong with it. Now look at these little, artificial, ski-slope noses. Something is wrong with them—you carry on a conversation looking up someone's nose! We have artificial standards, and we expect perfection; we want our partner to be happy, and smiling, and sexy all the time. But that's just not the way things are in the real world. Perhaps we forget this because we've let so many unreal, media-generated images fill our consciousness.

ARE YOU AFRAID TO FORMULATE
YOUR OWN TASTES?

Don't be. Be authentic in your reactions to things, people, and experiences, and you'll get so much more out of life.

I remember the time I was on the island of Jamaica to see about opening a rejuvenation center. It was late at night and I needed a place to stay, so I asked the cab driver to recommend a hotel. The hotel he suggested was a place called Club Hedonism. I had never heard of it, but I took his advice and checked in. It was beautiful, with a big lobby.

I decided to take a swim and took a walk to the beach, where I saw four seated women. To my astonishment, they were all naked. We said hello, and I kept walking. I walked closer to the beach, noticing that everybody was nude. There had to be 150 nude people. I thought to myself, "This is strange." After my swim, I was resting under a palm tree watching all the fun everyone was having. Some people recognized me. In fact, a couple twenty feet away from me stopped having sex on the beach to ask me a nutrition question. Again I thought, "This is very strange. I've never been asked a nutrition question by people who were having sex."

As it turned out, none of the nudists at that hotel tried to pressure me into being one of them, and we were all able to have a peaceful, happy experience in our own ways. So I actually enjoyed my stay at Club Hedonism, not that it's ever on the list of places to stay that "people in the know" will give you if you're planning on visiting Jamaica. And that's precisely my point, and the truth that was reinforced for me by this experience. The opinion of others should not influence me. I want to judge my own experiences. I will decide what I like and don't like. I don't need someone else to tell me what I should do and should not do. Many people were later astonished when they learned I went to Club Hedonism. But I was open to the experience, and it was a positive one. As I explained to those who later raised their eyebrows, "It was just some people. They were friendly. They didn't force me to undress and swim with them. I was myself. I wasn't offended by the experience, because I chose not to be." That's a choice, you see. I can choose to let something be what it is, and I can even enjoy it.

ARE YOUR EXPECTATIONS REALISTIC?

Swami Muktananda, a wise man from the East, once said, "Expect nothing, and you will never be disappointed." The problem is, people generally expect more—they expect to receive in proportion to what they give, and that is not always what happens. As an example, you may have the consciousness that allows for compassion. You may be able to listen to others and understand them. But that doesn't mean that those others will have the same capacity to offer compassion in return. You can't expect another person to be just like you. So don't blame others if they're unable to give you what you've given them. If you have to give 90 percent in order to receive 10 percent, that's still balanced if that's all the other person has to give you in return. They gave what they could. That's their ability level. It's rare that you're going to find someone who is able to give equally. Accept that, and you will truly be compassionate and caring.

DO YOU FEEL THAT SOMETHING IS MISSING FROM YOUR LIFE?

Most of us want to be someplace other than where we are. We move around thinking that the next place we inhabit is going to be better than this one. We would be happier if only we lived in the city, in the country, in the mountains, by the ocean, closer to people, further away from civilization. But every place we go becomes just one more place we want to get away from. We look in the mirror, and we don't like what we see. We look at the people we're with, and we don't like them either. We look at our job, and we see the imperfections. We never seem to be happy with who we are or what we have.

The happy person is balanced. And balanced people appreciate what they have. This is one of the most important things I have learned about life, and why I insist: Stop always thinking that there's someone or something missing from your life. And if you think that someone out there has the answer—Krishnamurti, Tony Robbins, Deepak Chopra, or Gary Null—you're wrong. We don't have the answers for you. The best we can do is offer some questions.

I grew up with very little. But I never lived a day when I didn't enjoy my life. That's because I valued whatever I had. Where I grew up, there were the very rich, the middle class, and the poor. My family was right at the point between middle class and poor.

When there was a soapbox derby, the first in our town, I joined it. One of the other kids told me that I couldn't. When I asked him why, he responded that I didn't have any money, or a sponsor. Everyone else in the race had sponsors to afford them sleek little racers. My attitude was, "So?"

I searched and found all kinds of stuff at an old used car place with which to build my racer. My vehicle turned out to be a big contraption, several times bigger than all the others, and it was pretty slow. In fact, I had time to wave to everybody I knew as I was racing, which was kind of neat. When everyone else had finished the race, I was still going, and waving. I came in dead last, but I did it, and it was fun. I didn't think, "Poor me." No, I just enjoyed what I had.

What happened to simple living, where less can be more? We're a society that wants to take advantage of every millisecond. We artificially stimulate ourselves, creating manic schedules, and then we get angry because we have no time left for ourselves, our families, or our friends. Essential needs are not being met—only artificial demands—and as a result we are kept in constant conflict. We think, "There's no time to do anything. I'd love to rest, I'd love to meditate, I'd love to juice, I'd love to just go for a walk in the park. I don't have time because I have to make money because I've got to pay for this big house, and this fancy car, and this whole lifestyle." Most of us need less stimulation, fewer complications, less ambition. That's why, sometimes, you have to say no to opportunity. You have to intentionally slow down the engine that propels you.

ARE YOUR CHOICES OF A MATE, FRIENDS, CAREER, AND LIVING ENVIRONMENT AN EXTENSION OF YOUR VALUES?

We select people, places, and possessions. They just don't drop into our lives. We need to make conscious choices about the people we allow into our lives, as well as the work we choose, and our living environment.

The most intimate of these—the person we choose to spend our life with—should have closely matched values and beliefs. You don't want to spend most of your time with someone whose values are contrary to yours. Otherwise, there will be constant conflict. Unfortunately, in our society we are not always honest about what our real values are. Nor are we always careful about selecting someone who shares our views. We don't necessarily try to truly know each other, but rather base the relationship on physical attraction and outward personality. Only later do we find out that our deeper values don't mesh.

We have no right to tell someone to change his or her values for us. Nor should we change our values to accommodate someone else. In the best-case scenario, we can learn to appreciate another's point of view, but we don't want to change who we basically are. When we do, we end up living in conflict. Conflict leads to crisis, and crisis, if it becomes a chronic state, generates disease.

Choose the people in your life carefully. Be honest about who you are and look for honesty in return. Finding someone with similar values will keep you together naturally. You won't have that feeling of being artificial, of compromising every single time you're with someone. All those little compromises add up, and, one day, something insignificant, of no relevance, becomes that final one thousandth compromise. You just can't take it anymore, and everything falls apart. That's why it's important, when seeking a relationship, or friends, or a career, or a place to live, to consider common values at the outset.

DO YOU LIVE CONSCIOUSLY?

Living consciously means living spiritually, and that means paying attention to people in need. Most of us consider ourselves good people, but our actions prove otherwise. I see this manifested in small ways. Every Sunday, I help people who want to run or walk in a marathon. I observe the people I've helped train and notice which ones offer to assist new people in the group. Many don't care. They go off on their own to work out. It's amazing how quickly people forget what it felt like to be the new person who needed help. All they can think about is themselves. People do this all the time in every area of their lives.

We see this same selfishness magnified in our society at large. For example, a recent report found the United States government guilty of withholding vital information from thousands of workers in the nuclear weapons industry. People's jobs were making them deathly ill. Although thousands of employees were developing various cancers, when any attempt was made to get compensation, the response was blunt: "Take a hike." Not admitting responsibility kept the government clear of any lawsuits.

On a global scale, selfishness is manifested as multinational corporations exploiting every inch of the planet. In Africa and

Asia, where massive poverty exists as a result of corporate inter-vention, do Fortune 500 companies give even a small portion of their income back to provide proper wells for water? Do they plant trees where they've devastated the environment through deforestation? Do they build medical facilities so that people can receive drugs to counter malaria and tuberculosis? Usually not one penny is spent on such efforts.

The heads of these corporations are respected, religious people who give large donations to their churches and synagogues. But they are not spiritual, nor even decent. Wall Street and the media may look up to these folks, but I don't. You're only decent if you help other human beings. Who cares about how much money you have? A person can sell cocaine and make just as much.

In our society as a whole, the super-rich are admired and emu-lated. Millions of baby boomers and their children work fifty-plus hours a week to get richer, even the ones who have more money than they could ever spend. Young men on Wall Street earning $800,000 a year are snorting their money away on cocaine. They don't know what to do with it all, yet they can never get enough.

DO YOU BELIEVE THAT YOU WERE MEANT FOR MORE?

Do you ever feel as though something more should be happening with your life? Do you feel as though you were meant to be on this earth for some special reason other than going to work at some nine-to-five job?

This is not to put down all "regular," workaday jobs. It's really not a question of what you're doing, but rather of how you're relat-ing to what you're doing. You could be working for years as a sub-way token clerk, taking great pride in your efficiency and the courtesy with which you treat the public. If that's the case, then you are living a meaningful life. But if what you are currently doing lacks meaning for you, it's time to start seeking something new. And what better place to look than in the dreams that you had as a child, when anything was possible. Then, you weren't closed off from your heart and soul, the things that inspired and moved you. Rediscover those dreams that you put on hold, perhaps in order to be more practical, or to follow other people's notions of what you should be. Reclaiming lost innocence will renew meaning in your own life.

Honor what gives you the greatest love and joy, and you will find yourself doing what you were meant to do. It may not be what you thought you should do, and it may not be what you were trained to do. You may have to retrain yourself to learn something completely new. But so what? It won't be that hard because you'll probably be learning material that you are really interested in. Whatever you do, if you feel good about it, you will find the work relatively effortless and feel that you have found your life's work.

Now the key to change begins with what I call constructive disengagement. This means that if you've been living other people's dreams but not your own, you should deconstruct the life you've been living so that you can reconstruct the life you should be living. You, alone, are the only one who can do that. In most instances, it is better not to seek advice from others. You know what you want and, in many cases, other people will try to stop you from changing. They are afraid, and perhaps jealous. The fear comes from a feeling that a change may separate you from them. In reality, this may or may not be the case; in fact, you may actually grow closer.

I'm not suggesting that you make a radical change where you wake up tomorrow and suddenly quit your job. It may take months, or even years. Plan your changes. Organize them. Make change a purpose and function of your life, and watch the joy come back into it. Your eyes will sparkle when you talk. You'll almost always sound positive, because when you love who you are and what you are doing, you're always looking at the positives in life.

DO YOU LOVE WHAT YOU'RE DOING?

How often do you hear someone say, "I love what I'm doing"? More often, people say, "I need to be doing what I'm doing. I've got responsibilities—a family, a mortgage, car payments and other bills. I can't do what I love."

I believe that, to the contrary, you absolutely can love what you do, and that it is your responsibility to do so. You can prosper at what you love to do and find fulfillment in the process, making your life easier, more satisfying, and meaningful. When you do something you truly love you are choosing to live your dream, and that's exciting. By living your own dream, the work you do becomes an extension of who you are as a person.

Unfortunately, most people today have opted to live someone else's dream. Their dream becomes finding happiness through wealth, and they have a lot of big, flashy stuff to prove it. Sometimes it seems as if all you hear people talk about is what they have and how much they paid for it: "Look at how much money I saved, paying $35,000 for that $40,000 car. Boy, that was a good buy." People parade around with what they think justifies their life, but it's really only a substitution for fulfillment. It becomes like trying to find substance in a shadow. Embrace it, and nothing's there.

DO THE STRONG OPINIONS OF OTHERS OVERSHADOW YOUR OWN JUDGMENT?

Can you remember a time when someone in a position of authority made a statement about you, and you accepted it unquestioningly?

It may have been something positive, but most probably it was not. Perhaps one of your parents implied that you were stupid. Maybe, in exasperation, your father said, "Here, let me do it," as if you could never do anything right.

In our society, this happens frequently, and it's one of the reasons we carry around such enormous feelings of conflict. The negative words we hear in childhood stay with us into adulthood. That's why so many people never seem to be able to speak up on their own behalf.

The other day on my radio program, I asked people to call in to talk about positive results with alternative therapies. A woman responded, saying that as a result of a healthy lifestyle she had lost twenty-five pounds. Now she had more energy than she had had in years. She was sleeping two-and-a-half hours less per night, and reorganizing her life. She now had time for everything, whereas before she had always been too tired to do much of anything. In the process, her skin improved and her hormones rejuvenated. She was, in effect, de-aging.

This caller related an incident that had occurred at a social function at Princeton University. During a conversation with a friend about renewed health due to a change in lifestyle, other people overheard and became interested in what she had to say. A woman who worked in public health science at the university suggested that she was all wrong. She even asked the caller about the last time she had had a mammogram. The caller replied that she didn't need to have mammograms because she was healthy. She expressed her belief, based on statistics, that mammography increases the likelihood of getting disease, that over time more women die as a result of having mammograms than are cured from having cancer discovered. She was also told that she, as an older woman, should be getting estrogen replacement therapy, to which she replied, "Why should I? I'm eating phytochemical-rich vegetables and fruits and grains. My body is rebalancing its own hormone levels. I don't need a synthetic hormone in my body." She responded to every single point that this public health official was making.

Afterwards, she looked at the woman challenging her and thought, (but wisely did not say) "This is a fat, pasty-faced, angry woman." She then realized that, a year earlier, she couldn't have stood up for herself as she had just done. Then, the circumstance of being faced with an authority figure telling her what she should be doing would have been stronger than her own reality and her own sense of presence. Now, she had the strength to remain true to her own convictions.

Do you allow other people to control the way you live your life? Do their thoughts dominate your own? Focus on becoming stronger in all areas of life.

DO YOU SET A GOAL BUT THINK CONTRARY THOUGHTS?

Perhaps you think, "I'm going to be happy, healthy, and prosperous." Those are noble goals. Then you turn around and think negative thoughts. "I'm miserable, constantly sick, and spending money faster than I can earn it." You allow those thoughts to dominate your consciousness and bring you down. Even though you want one thing, you're allowing another to dominate your life because you give power to it by thinking about it.

Thoughts have a life of their own. Think a negative thought, and ten to twenty seconds later you will feel a negative emotion. Think about being victimized, and you will start to feel angry, depressed, and hurt. That, in turn, will perpetuate more negative thoughts and more negative emotions. Before long you will have created a monster. At first it's unreal, but then it rips your throat out. You end up a victim to a thought that you created. And then you blame it all on outer circumstances.

Stop the thoughts that are contrary to the ideals that you would like to be living. Ask yourself, "Where am I going with this?" If you don't like where your thoughts are taking you, turn them off. Replace them with healthier thoughts. You have that ability. Focus on a goal or purpose, and then keep your thoughts consistent with that.

How do you perceive your mistakes?

Learn from a mistake, and you grow stronger. Ignore it, and you don't learn a thing; you stand still or fall behind. Anything worth accomplishing is a growing experience, one in which you must learn from your mistakes. Consider the process of learning an instrument. You don't master the violin by walking away from it for six months and then picking it up again at some distant time in the future. You've got to practice daily, making mistakes along the way, playing the same piece over and over until you memorize the notes and develop the feeling you wish to express. Much work is involved. That's true of all accomplishments.

How do you react to pain and loss?

Pain and loss will either damage or purify you. To give an example, someone I know is a naturally motivating speaker. Fifteen years ago, when I first met this person and befriended him, I suggested that he find work encouraging people to stay focused on their health regimens. Instead, he went into network marketing, which was big at that time, and he did very well. Once, in fact, he threw a big business party at Studio 54, and the place was mobbed.

But, despite his outward success, I sensed that he could do better by serving those in real need. I spoke to him, saying, "These are not the people who really need your help; they're already self-motivated. The folks who need you are the ones who are confused and depressed, the people who don't know what to do with their lives. You should be motivating them, but not to sell a product. Rather, you should get them to make basic lifestyle changes." I felt that he had a choice between inspiring people to improve their health, or merely motivating them to make money. At that time he chose to go the money route.

One year later he was broke and in debt, with massive lawsuits because his company was a pyramid that had crashed. All the people who had gotten into it had lost money, and he couldn't show his face anywhere. I was at my ranch in Texas when he called to say that he was in the middle of a crisis. He came to see me, and we walked around the lake, talking for hours. Then I asked him to just sit and watch the swans swimming by.

After about an hour, when he had finished sighing and crying about his problems, I said to him, "There are two ways to look at what happened to you. You can choose to see it as damaging to your reputation and to your economic situation. Or you can choose to see it as a purification. You created a tragedy because you needed that experience. You needed to see the excesses of an unbridled ego. You needed to see that freedom used irresponsibly is a misapplied gift. When you acted on that with no sense of contrition you crashed and burned. Now, look at that crashing and burning as purification. Was it a purification through pain? Yes. With suffering? Yes, yours and others. But now you're purified. You've learned. You could write a book on what you learned about the greed syndrome of the 1980s. Or you could go into therapy for the next fifteen years, blaming everyone who didn't stop you. Which do you want to do? You can commit yourself to only one choice. Which will it be?" He sat and watched the swans as I left.

Later that day we had a workshop. About 100 people attended. I asked each person to talk about the worst thing that had ever happened to him. There were some really harrowing stories, but in the end each person had survived to become stronger for his or her experience. They had become purified as a result of their crises. This gave my friend the impetus to choose purification as well. Today he is no longer greedy. Rather, he is a spiritual, giving person. He doesn't abuse his gift, but rather uses it to help people. That's what I mean when I say that pain and loss can either damage or purify you.

Think about the pain and loss in your life and realize that how you perceive your problems is all-important. When a problem arises, view it as an opportunity to explore what happened and to make a change. See your experiences as opportunities for purification, and you will be stronger for it.

WHEN YOU NO LONGER HAVE ANYONE ELSE TO BE RESPONSIBLE FOR, WILL YOU FINALLY FOCUS ON YOUR OWN LIFE?

Quite often people tell me that they cannot do anything for themselves because they have no time. All their energy is spent taking care of everyone else.

At some point, however, people reach an age and position at which they have more time to spend on themselves. But many people don't; rather, they make mantras out of past excuses, repeating over and over in their heads, "I cannot be responsible for myself. There is someone else I must be responsible for."

Difficulty doing things for yourself is often based on fear. You were always afraid that if you were to tell people what you needed they would reject you for it. It became easier to figure out what someone else wanted from you, and to center your life around that, than to actually go after what you wanted for yourself. Once you understand that, being true to yourself becomes easier.

DO YOU VALUE YOUR TIME OR MERELY EXIST?

Should any day be disposable? Saturday or Sunday perhaps? Should any hour be expendable? The answer is no. We should see all of our time as valuable. Because all of it is.

So many of us drift through time rather than living life fully. By working at something that we do not love, for example, we are simply marking time. We're unhappy at our job, but it pays the rent, so we stay there, all the while wishing it were Friday when it's only Monday. We remain in unfulfilling relationships because we feel insecure by ourselves, and afraid that there is no one else out there for us. We live someplace because we don't want the hassle of starting anew. We keep gossipy, negative people as friends because we don't want to take the time to look for more supportive people. Each time we settle, we compromise our time and keep ourselves from living fully.

How can we maximize each moment? Begin by sitting quietly and thinking about the good moments in your life. Then consider the experiences that leave you feeling unfulfilled. Where are you compromising? What do you need from your work and relationships that is lacking? Dare to dream, be open and positive, use affirmations, and expect the best.

WHAT DO YOU WANT TO EXPERIENCE
BEFORE YOU DIE?

By becoming increasingly conscious of our finite time on this planet, we are more apt to start living the way we want, to procrastinate less, and to make our lives happen now.

In today's fast-paced world, many of us have lost touch with what is truly important. When I meet people I often ask, "Do you have a hobby?" I learn that very few do. What is the importance of a hobby? Hobbies allow us to create, to experiment, and to master a skill that has nothing to do with our occupation. There was a time when almost everybody in America enjoyed a hobby. By contrast, few people have them today. Americans have become increasingly passive, squandering precious free time watching television or playing computer games.

Passivity is detrimental to our health. Too little thinking and a lack of creativity result in degeneration of the brain, since neurons die sooner when left unchallenged. Hobbies enhance creativity, and by so doing, they help us stay younger. We need to get back to them.

We also tend to fall short in the amount of face-to-face time we spend with family and friends. What is the purpose of a friendship if you're not going to engage in it? Nor do we give ourselves enough time to expand our minds. We don't read books or visit new places on our vacation. Everything takes a back seat to work—specifically to the work done only for the sake of making more money.

I am not preaching poverty, but I am asking you to take a closer look at your values. Does the quest for money dominate your life, and, if so, to what extent? Does that take away from time you could be learning, growing, experiencing, and sharing with family and friends?

Finally, if you ask yourself only one of the myriad questions we pose in this book, ask this one: What is the meaning of this day?

Each reader's answer to this question will be unique. But I believe you'll find that your purpose is more than just to keep busy, to work "on automatic," or to be responsible for things that have nothing to do with you as a human being. Make each day meaningful. Discover a purpose for why you are here on this earth—and then act on it.

Mistake Number Ten:
Forgetting We've Reached a New Millennium

1. Have you been keeping journals? Choose an old one at random and read through it. If you haven't already, begin keeping a journal.

2. Survey your home and write down all the objects you can find that did not exist twenty years ago._____

_____

_____

3. Spend half a day in a good library reading the magazines of fifty years ago, particularly general-interest and women's magazines.

4. List two alternative careers that you could conceivably pursue.

_____   _____

List three fantasy careers you might dream of pursuing.

_____

_____

_____

Evaluate what it would take to go into each of these fields.

5. The calendar reaches turning points when it hits zeros, but people reach turning points at all sorts of unique times. When did you last reach a personal turning point? When do you next anticipate one?

PART II

EIGHT LESSONS EVERY BABY BOOMER SHOULD LEARN

Connect!

W HY DO WE have so many self-empowerment books, lectures, workshops, and, in my own case, sleep-away detoxification weeks, when people come together because they want to change and feel better? Something's missing, but people don't know what it is. They just have some vague irritation from life not feeling as complete as it should.

They should feel complete, they think, because of the commitment they've made up to this point. And it's true that a lot of people have made very strong commitments. Everyone makes a commitment in a different area. For some it's just trying to be a good, honest person. For others it's a commitment to spiritual values, sometimes associated with a religion or some form of community service. Or it may encompass being a caregiver to individuals in need.

Other people commit themselves to trying to understand the psychodynamics of life. If you come from a highly analytical background, you tend to try to figure out your problems. You think, "If I do x, I'll get y as an effect." You know that if you smoke, there's the likelihood that you're going to end up getting emphysema or lung cancer. But sometimes you can't predict effects. What about the people who don't smoke and get lung cancer, for example? And what about the vegetarians who get heart disease? What about the kind souls who never get a break? And what about the mean, conniving folks who succeed fabulously? Take a look at some of the world's most powerful people. Look at the more established families and the respected celebrities. They're not necessarily nice people. It doesn't always hold that because you do good deeds you're going to be rewarded in this lifetime.

What's more, if you look back in history at the people most admired today—Christ, Mohammed, Confucius, and Buddha, for instance—you might wonder whether they would be accepted in modern times. Would they be among our policy makers and opinion leaders? Would they be at the helm of institutions? Would they be a part of the establishment or the anti-establishment? Would they be in the mainstream, or part of the counter-culture? Indeed, in their own time, they were considered outsiders. These individuals, though esteemed today, were clearly set aside in their time and never given the reverence or respect they deserved. Spinoza, Euripides, Sophocles—all the great minds throughout history were never part of any mainstream movement. I find that noteworthy.

The same could be said about Hippocrates, the father of medicine. It is my belief that today Hippocrates would be considered a quack because he said, "Let food be your medicine and medicine your food." Try saying to a doctor, "I want my food to be a part of my healing program." The typical doctor would say, "Nonsense, food can't heal you. It may prevent some diseases of nutritional deficiency, such as scurvy, beri-beri, or pellagra, but it's not going to have an impact on your cancer in any way." So where would Hippocrates be? Do you think he'd go over well with your local HMO? The very people who give an oath of allegiance to Hippocrates would stone him intellectually.

Though they come from diverse backgrounds, what unites Hippocrates and these other revered individuals is their connection to universal truth. And what connects us to them is our recognition of what they represent. The rest is forgotten. Do you remember Walt Whitman's critics? No. Do you remember the critics of the great philosopher Spinoza, who threw dishwater on him as he walked on the streets of his town? No, but you remember him. The throngs of critics are forgotten; it's as if they never existed. But those people who chose to connect their truth with a universal truth have lasted throughout time.

So it's not surprising that there have been movements over the past forty years to try to help us feel connected. And there have been some good ones. In the 1960s and 1970s there were George Leonard and Michael Murphy at Esalen. Those were exciting times—in the west there was the political radicalism of Berkeley and the bold new lifestyle of Haight-Ashbury; in the east people could plug into Woodstock and then go to The Farm, that unique place in Tennessee that was one of the first co-ops, where people could live close to nature and grow organic food. They felt good about that experience. And then other seekers of connection started going off to India. From America and Europe people flocked to every Indian guru who came down the pike promising enlightenment, something that would illuminate our situation.

Then we wake up one day, and we're in a new millennium. We've had Life Spring and the Sterling Group; we've had dozens and dozens of movements. But where's the enlightenment? We've had all of the very expensive guru retreats, but where's the change?

I travel all over the United States. Recently I was out in San Francisco lecturing in a gentrified community where most of the audience were baby boomers. Many had gone through the different movements, and most of them had worked very hard at trying to prove their self-value. They had their families, they provided for them, and they were successful. Yet, they weren't happy.

Something isn't right. Something is missing. And people are trying to figure out what it is. *If I work this hard, and I am this dedicated, shouldn't I feel more connected?* And so I see that even where it all began there's almost nothing left. People who need real security go into more orthodox movements because orthodox movements don't wash away. Orthodox movements don't start today and end tomorrow. Many feel that the movements that are most stable, that give a person the most sense of connection, are the ones that last. Hence, whether they work or not, at least they're a good place to park yourself until you figure out who you are. They give you a sense of meaning because they take meaning from the larger paradigm that you're a part of.

Visualize it this way. See yourself as a wonderful, multicolored light bulb meant to radiate at all different frequencies. Know that, like everyone else, you are unique, because no two lights are the same. All are capable of giving a sense of completeness. Know that nothing is so dense that the light of your illumination could not penetrate it. Hence all of life is transparent, and through that transparency you see the essential part of yourself and every other illuminated soul.

Then one day you begin to flicker and go out. You can't even see your way to the next week or day. You're floundering in the darkness and you've lost your way. But you do see a variety of outlets that have nice signs. They appeal to you, "Plug into us! We are the enlightened ones!" Some of these are called vegetarianism, fasting, macrobiotics, Judaism, Catholicism, and Islam, plus there are a thousand other belief systems, all of which have some reality, some truth, and some value. All promise completeness. "We are all you will ever need," they tell you.

People like simplicity. They don't like to struggle with their issues. They want help, and they're quick to say, "Alright, if I give you my total loyalty, if it's you I'm going to plug into, will you give me all the answers I need to make my life meaningful?" "Yes, of course we will. We have the knowledge, the scholars, the history, the charismatic leaders." So people obey without challenge. And one day they wake up with the old sense of emptiness again.

If this happens to you, you may then choose to put your energy into your work. This seems to make sense at first because work provides us with recognition, which boosts our self-esteem. It gives us our sense of who we are. Most important, it gives us a connection. The harder you work, the more you achieve, and the more connected you seem to be. But it's not always the right connection. You could be connected to insider trading, cheating, lying, and other practices that cause people great harm.

The question arises that if we have all these people who are so successful in our culture—so rich, and so accomplished—why haven't they connected with something that gives them a sense of completeness so that they can slow down, simplify their lives, and start looking at what they've actually achieved? Why can't they deconstruct the toxic, reconstruct the positive, and then share it with others who can benefit from their efforts? Isn't the purpose of being connected to be able to make choices from a place of security and confidence rather than insecurity and fear? Shouldn't connection free you from acting out of self-contempt? When you are connected you should no longer feel the need to abuse the body, mind, and spirit because you're no longer confused about who you are and what you should do with this wonderful thing called life.

One day it occurred to me what was missing. Visualize yourself in a coma. You have a hundred life-support systems going into you, each one feeding you something else to keep you alive. Through that, you're told you have meaning because you're alive. Well, how many people do you know, possibly including yourself, who are being kept alive by being figuratively hooked up like this to outside systems? You are alive, but you're not functioning at an optimal level because you're not independent. You're not autonomous. You're not taking the appropriate risks necessary to reveal the uniqueness of your being.

In our society we don't want people to fail, but we don't want them to succeed if that means challenging the status quo. So what we do is give people very specific ideas of how they can succeed. They're allowed to succeed as long as they honor what we're telling them from inside that connection. "You're connected now," we tell them. "You've got current coming in, information coming through, inspiration, motivation." But what if this connection is not real to you? What if it's not matching your needs? Yes, you do go out there, take on big challenges, and perform the way you're supposed to. But you're doing it in the wrong way for the wrong reasons. You end up succeeding, but success is not the issue. We have tens of millions of Americans who are successful, yet incomplete and unhappy.

I say we've got to start disconnecting all of these lifelines. At some point, we have to disconnect every single support system connected to our being. We must stand on our own and regain a sense of completeness in order to become illuminated on our own. Then, and only then, when we're completely self-sufficient, will we feel connected to our inner creativity. That will open us up to a wonderful, mystical experience. We will automatically connect to the blissful energy of life.

We've all had moments when we've been truly connected to life. Perhaps it was watching a beautiful sunset, when we experienced the wonder of it rather than analyzed it or tried to figure it out. Later, we may try to recreate that experience, but nothing's ever the same twice. That's because no two moments are ever the same, and we're never in the same place in the universe that we were one millisecond before. Yet our tendency, when we do touch something that is blissful, is to try to capture it. We try to immortalize it. In a sense we can do that by allowing it to penetrate every cell of our being. Once in our cells, the memory of that experience is indelibly with us. All we have to do is simply think and we re-experience it. The thing is, we can't keep creating it anew.

Most of our lives we remember the best experience we've had, and we yearn for it again. We look to see if it will happen once more, but it rarely does. The good news is that we can have a myriad of peak experiences if we're not fixated on making any of them carbon copies of the others. Think of playing with your pet cat or dog, petting him. He's bonding with you. Pets give you their unconditional love every moment. Or think about when you're playing with your baby, and she's happy, and you're happy. You've connected then. Watching a waterfall you feel connected. When you're making love and having happy sex, you're connecting.

It's my belief that we can connect every single day of our lives.

We need not have any disposable days or moments. And it's important to remember that we need not depend on other people to make us feel complete and connected. How many times in your life have you looked for someone else to connect with, because you didn't feel on your own that you had any of that magnificent illumination? You thought that connecting with the right partner was what you needed to feel complete. So you searched for the right person to connect with and compared resumes. "Well, they've got this, and so do I. Hey, that's good. They're this, and I'm that. That's good, too." You went to connect, and it missed, and you thought, "Well, okay, so it's not a perfect connection, but it's close. So, let's make believe it's a connection." Ah! There's the danger. Why? In a society that says life isn't perfect so take what you can get and be happy with that, you end up sacrificing your essential self. To expect someone else to complete you will always result in disappointment. Maybe two good people not blaming each other comes close, but don't expect to feel completely fulfilled. What you will probably find instead is that you're sharing your life with someone you wouldn't normally have in it.

Say it's someone who has a sarcastic nature. Would you go out and look for such a person? Would you say, "Hey, Sue, I need sarcasm today. I want to spend eight hours with you to experience your sarcasm"? I don't think so. But what about when you're in a relationship in which you accept that quality from someone? Many of us have accepted negativity within a relationship because we believed we were getting something else that we considered important. We needed the relationship because we did not feel complete in ourselves, and what you don't feel complete about in yourself you think you can attain from someone else. Even if it's a mismatch, you're still going to think, "This is better than nothing."

Think of how many times in life you've accepted something that wasn't the real thing. At some later point you realize that you've adapted to something that's not a connection. It's not a great job, but it pays the bills. It's not a perfect relationship—

there's no happiness, joy, or passion—but you're with someone. But why be with someone? What's the purpose of a relationship except to wake up each day with a sense of complete passion, that eagerness to share the energy of the other person?

There are plenty of good people, but if you go out not knowing what you are looking for, you're not going to find them. If you don't know what you want in someone, how are you going to ask for it? If you don't know what kind of career you want, how are you going to know how to train for one? Often, because of this self-knowledge gap, we take on what we've been told should be our goals. But what if those are not what we truly need? What if our needs are unique and different? And what if what we're taught to believe in can't fulfill all our needs? We generally say, "What I cannot fulfill within my beliefs I dismiss, because I don't want to start asking questions about my own belief system."

That's because if you're unique and different from the norm, and start asking questions, you're considered a problem. So first, you're warned. Then you're punished. Then they try to make you normal, like you were before you started questioning. You see, you're allowed to ask questions provided you don't challenge the answers. But if you pose a challenge there is little patience for you the next time you decide to ask a question. "Uhhuh. Uhhuh. Well, Alice, I'm not going to answer you this time because you're a trouble-maker." But that's not a fair assessment of the situation. Alice is simply trying to figure out why my answers to her don't meet her needs.

Now if Alice were to incorporate my answers into her belief system, assuming that whatever I say, whatever I teach, is going to fulfill her, and it doesn't fulfill her, then it's not Alice that's the problem. She's taken on my concept of how to live, how to think, how to be, and how to relate, and it's not working for her. It's not connecting with her.

She then has to separate from me in order to find out who she is, and what she needs. And that's scary because it's so easy in our society to run out and become a part of something. Everybody likes to belong. We love connecting. But what if we connect to the wrong things? Think of all the things in your life you've connected to that you wish you hadn't. What we have to do is disconnect from everything in order to reconnect with what is essential. We need to do it right, not superficially. That way we can reconnect to our essential self.

TO WHOM AND TO WHAT
DO YOU FEEL CONNECTED?

Make a list of whom and what you feel connected to. There are people and things that promote health. They keep you in balance, and you need to feel harmonious on every level—mentally, spiritually, and physically.

When you're feeling connected you're moving rhythmically throughout life. When you're not, you feel limited, and that stifles your creativity. When you're out of harmony with your true nature, you're prone to becoming tense and angry, with a limited repertoire of reaction. Look at a person who becomes enraged, and the limited number of constructive outlets he or she uses. By contrast, when you feel connected you are more relaxed and have a greater capacity to understand the options available to you. When you make a choice, not from fear but from the enlightened inner self, the likelihood is that that choice will be better and easier to honor.

Of course, sometimes you may be connecting with problematic influences. For instance, what if you're connected to addictive substances, such as drugs, caffeine, fast foods, or sugar? What if you're connected to negative people? I was speaking with a person recently who told me, "Everyone with a complaint comes to me." I responded, "That tells me less about the people coming to you than it tells me about you. Why would they choose to complain to you? Do you complain too?" Actually, I knew that this person was a chronic complainer. It made perfect sense that others who always blame and whine would be attracted to this person, as like attracts like. Would you complain to a person who is happy and positive, or to one who is going to be empathetic? You would choose the person who encourages and accepts you. It's a way of identifying and, again, connecting. But how healthy is that?

RECOGNIZE THAT ALL OF OUR ACTIONS AND BEHAVIORS—BOTH POSITIVE AND NEGATIVE—GIVE US SOMETHING.

We tend to think that if we're a drug addict, an alcoholic, a glutton, or a compulsive gambler, that that isn't us. But it is. Realize that everything you do—whether it's sticking a needle in your arm or coke up your nose, or betting on the stocks that are about to rise—is you. You are all these things.

Don't just take responsibility for the things that work in your life and make you proud. Also take responsibility for the failures. Both took effort. In fact, it takes more effort and a stronger mindset to do something that's destructive. That's because with destructive actions you have to rationalize what you are doing, or lie to yourself about it. You might say, "That was the last time. I'll never do that again." But you know deep down that you're going to engage in the same behavior over and over again. When you repeatedly do the same thing you start to rationalize why you are doing it, excuse yourself for it, and then go on and engage in it. Think of all the energy that goes into that.

So don't deny your connection to your negative behaviors. You are connected to them. Own them. Don't dismiss them as diseases, as something that merely happened to you. Your actions are not diseases. No, to make them diseases is to make them nouns, and to make them nouns is to make them something that befell you. Then you can say you caught this alcoholism or drug addiction, and that they're not your fault.

Well, they *are* your responsibility. And if we're ever going to grow, we have to start growing at the level where we take responsibility for what we do. Realize that you have choices and that there are consequences to the choices that you make. Don't blame the world.

Everything you do you do for a reason. If you are an alcoholic or a drug addict you are gaining something from the experience. You don't have to face painful realities. You don't have to feel; you become numb, anesthetized to what you couldn't deal with. The high you get is a substitution for something essential that you need but are not getting.

What I'm saying is, as long as we're meeting our essential needs, we're not going to do anything self-destructive. So connect with your essential needs. Connect with that which is blissful, and you will no longer do anything destructive.

The fact that so many individuals engage in unhealthy activities demonstrates how disconnected we are today. In America alone, millions engage in drinking, smoking, taking drugs, gambling, overeating, and pornography. More money is made from these pastimes than Microsoft earns, and Microsoft is the number one company in America. If we were positively connected, we wouldn't be doing these things. Feeling content, we would not need these forms of sublimation. But we do. And these socially acceptable sublimations are taken for granted. They have become the norm so that people no longer say, "That's wrong."

As for connecting with the wrong people, what do you get from remaining in a bad relationship? You get the certainty of being in a relationship. Plus you may think that you don't deserve a good relationship. How many times do people who don't believe that they deserve better select someone who gives them exactly what they think they deserve? And if you think that all men are bastards because your mother told you they were, you may want to prove that your mother was right.

So we don't always admit that we're gaining something from a dysfunctional activity. We like to think, rather, that we get nothing out of it, that it's nothing but a problem. You may not like to

273

acknowledge what you get from it, but you do get something from it; otherwise, you would have dropped it and gotten out.

DISCONNECT; THEN CONNECT.

I believe we should be working on our weaknesses rather than our strengths. Our strengths are self-evident. Our strengths are there. They're not going to go anywhere. You're not going to lose your strengths. You've mastered them. I believe that through the normal course of living, by simple repetition, we will continue to honor our strengths, but our weaknesses are a different matter.

Honor your weaknesses by being open about them. Don't hide them. Whatever your weaknesses, they're yours. The only way to change and get rid of them is to face each and every one of them and see how it impacts upon your life. Then constructively disengage from it by understanding how you use it, how it impacts you, and how it manifests. Affirm, "I no longer am choosing this connection. I choose something better." What's nice about disconnecting from something negative is that it leaves you room to connect with something that's essential. So you're disconnecting and reconnecting. Have what you want to connect with ready. Then shift your energy and don't go back. Remember, what you've disconnected from has no power over you. It's a memory without the power. So stop thinking that that live wire can electrocute you. It can't. It's not in your life. It doesn't have the contact. It's a dead line. You're no longer allowing it to hurt you.

My friend Martin Feldman is a doctor who went to Yale and Columbia, graduating magna cum laude. For a time he was a successful, orthodox, straight-laced physician who connected with the values of mainstream medicine. But somewhere along the line he questioned whether or not those values were helping people. That's when he realized that they did not contain all the answers.

At that point he decided to honor the orthodox way but not be limited to it. He would use other modalities as well. The moment he made that decision he started to disconnect from some of his orthodox views on how to treat patients, and to connect with some alternatives that helped his patients get better.

Did any of his colleagues find this to be of interest? No. Did they welcome his enlightened insights? No. They didn't attack him, but they did not honor him either. Would he go back and reconnect with previous values just because more money and prestige were involved? The answer to that is no. He knows what not to reconnect to. Yet others in the field still don't know that because they haven't severed old connections.

You've got to disconnect to see the power something has over you. When I have sleep-away detox programs, there are no phones, no newspapers, no radios, and no televisions. All day long people are involved in yoga, meditation, exercise, juicing, lecturing, and counseling. After about a week, they start to feel more at ease. They connect with nature, paying attention to the birds and animals. By the second week they are practically in a state of bliss. Everything becomes so easy and effortless.

They've disconnected from the anxiety produced by daily fixes of coffee, sugar, negative news, and fast schedules. At first, disconnecting produces anxiety, because it is a challenge, and challenges are met with resistance. Why do we resist challenge? It's because we're afraid of what the results of embracing the challenge might mean. What if we embraced a challenge and we actually were to become the person we were meant to be? What if we were to realize our dreams? It would mean that much of what we were doing up until that point wasn't in our best interest.

We don't want to feel guilt about having wasted life. We'd rather continue with, "I don't want to. . . ." It's like the gambler who loses a hundred dollars and then ten thousand more to win back the hundred. If you have not lived the life you should have lived up until this point, don't be foolish enough to continue living that way. No—surrender that, embrace the life you should have, and forgive yourself for what you did.

DO YOUR CONNECTIONS
PROVIDE YOU BALANCE?

Spiritually. Are you provided with a spiritual connection? If so, you'll know it because you'll have a love for all humanity. You will not fear people of other religions, races, or cultures. You'll look and see grace in every human being. You'll honor all people. You'll take time every day to see what you can do to help another person.

Emotionally. Are you able to share without dominating? Can you share a full range of emotions? We've got a ten-octave emotional capacity, but we only use a few of those octaves. Stretch yourself emotionally. Allow vulnerability. Express what you feel.

Physically. In general, we're a society of physical wrecks. We spend $1.5 trillion on disease yearly. If we were connected to what is essential, would we abuse ourselves the way we do? Would we smoke and drink and eat ourselves into oblivion? Not at all. We should honor our bodies as temples. We should feed the body as if it were our best friend. Just as you wouldn't give a sick person something to make her sicker, you should never put anything into your body that would bring harm to it. There should never be a question of making the wrong choice, because you should be dealing with life-enhancing substances only. And, of course, you should be exercising your body, working all muscle groups because the body works as a complete unit.

Interpersonally. Do you listen to what people have to say? Are you patient? Are you compassionate? Are you nurturing? And are you giving—not in a codependent way, but in a thoughtful way?

IS YOUR NONCONNECTION REAL OR PERCEIVED?

Sometimes we feel disconnected because we're suffering an altered state of consciousness. Depression is an altered state of consciousness. Fear is another. Insecurity alters our consciousness as well. If we suffer from depression, fear, or insecurity we will think we're disconnected when we may in fact be completely connected. It's just that we haven't allowed the connection to be felt. We've numbed ourselves.

We may have people who love us. We may have all the things we need to give us that sense of completeness, and yet we're not engaging it. All around us we can have beauty and harmony. But in an altered state we don't appreciate what we have, or allow ourselves to be open to it. For example, some people call New York an ugly city. If you want to see the ugliness in New York you can, but you can also see its beauty. Are you looking for the beauty? My point is that what you're not looking for, you won't find. What you don't believe is there, you won't see. If a doctor says there's no proof nutrition helps disease—case closed—then no amount of evidence will ever prove it to him. But if he says, "I'm interested. Show me that nutrition will help disease, and I will have an open mind," that's another story. That doctor will see and embrace the truth, because he has opened himself to the possibility. You will find things that you're open to. But anything you're closed to, you cannot find.

We have to question our assumption that something cannot exist because we can't see it or feel it or recreate it scientifically. The existence of reality supersedes scientific proof of it. Science can't prove religion or God. We can't even prove that life exists in the sense of a pure energy. We can prove that a person is alive or dead, but we can't recreate the energy that caused that life when the energy has gone and the person is dead. And because doctors can't, they don't usually see the body as a life force. They see it just as a collection of working organs, systems, and glands. They see 100

trillion pieces and no whole. That's a remarkable sense of discon-
nection. Imagine if the medical community connected to what life
really is, and hence understood that disease is an imbalance of life.

ARE YOU AFRAID TO SEEK HELP?

Many people are reluctant to acknowledge that they could use help,
particularly if they're educated, and especially if they've been somewhat successful. They refuse to see any of the weaknesses and limitations that are causing them to feel disconnected or incomplete as people. Generally, the more powerful you become, the less you want to
acknowledge your own weaknesses, and, in fact, the more contempt
you develop for those weaknesses. What you feel contemptuous of you
never embrace, and what you do not embrace is going to remain.
That's why we see people in positions of power, who should know better, do stupid things. Once they're caught, we wonder, "Why did they
do it? They had so much to lose over something so stupid!"

They didn't like the fact that they were that powerful and that
successful and yet, still had weaknesses. They knew they did, but
others didn't know, and they didn't want others to find out. So
they didn't reach out.

If we reach out to those we can trust, to people who are compassionate and helpful, then we can grow into the healthy, balanced people we should be. Don't remain in contempt of any
weakness you have. Realize that we all have weaknesses, and that
there's nothing wrong with seeking help.

DO YOU PUT YOUR RELATIONSHIP
FIRST OR LAST?

If you put your relationship first, you are wise. This allows you to
connect. If you put your relationship last, which people frequent-

ly do in our society because they've crammed too many other things into their lives, they lose. People frequently sacrifice their relationships at the altar of busywork. They figure, "I've got this relationship. It doesn't have the passion anymore, and it's no longer sexual. Everything's kind of perfunctory and obligatory, but it's not bad. I mean it's not great, but it's not bad, so we'll put it on the back burner because other things are more important."

No, they're not. Consider that what you don't nourish, what you don't feed energy into, dies. So everything that you want to connect with you should feed energy into. To do that, you need time and space, which is one of the reasons you have to unclutter your life. Stop focusing on so many activities. We are a society that prides ourselves on how much we can get done. We do too many things, equating a hectic lifestyle with a productive one. The problem is, the more we try to do, the less importance we place on the essential aspects of our lives, such as our relationships.

Find a good balance in your life. Adopt a comfortable rhythm, one that keeps your pace unhectic, but focused.

PUT YOUR EMOTIONAL, CREATIVE, PHYSICAL, CULTURAL, AND SPIRITUAL LIFE ON HOLD FOR A MOMENT.

Look at each of these parts of life and ask, "Am I balanced here?" If you're not in balance, then seek to be. To create balance you need time and attention. That facilitates nurturing. You need to nurture these different areas of life to connect with them. And when you do connect, you no longer make decisions that negate the values you are connected to. In other words, you will never act to reinforce those things that are opposite to what you're honoring.

For instance, if you're connected to your spiritual self, you won't do unspiritual things. You're not going to commit a crime, and you're not going to lie or deceive. If you're connected with your physical side, you're not going to do bad things to your body. You won't make decisions that go against the positive connections you've made.

That's why it's so important to understand your connections. What you're connected to you will honor. What you're not connected to you will not honor.

ARE YOU REASONABLY DISCIPLINED?

Discipline can work to our benefit or against us. If we're disciplined, we can grow. But if that discipline is excessive, we won't. We need a certain amount of discipline in order to accomplish tasks, and we do need structure. If our life is chaotic and filled with clutter we will be unable to get much done.

Stop and clean up everything in your life. Put nonessentials on hold, and do a thorough housecleaning of your life. As you unclutter, think in terms of creating a loose structure that leaves you feeling comfortable, not constrained. It's within structure that systems can be created, and systems allow us to function at the detail level of life.

The details are what ultimately will create less or more of a problem. If you don't have the details taken care of, problems will arise. For instance, if you don't maintain your car, and check it every 2000 miles, you could end up burning out your engine. If you don't weed your garden at least weekly, it might turn into an overgrown mess. Think about this: Do you tend to have a lot of things in your home that are broken because you didn't pay attention to them? Everything you own in life has to be serviced. That includes relationships. So unclutter, restructure, refocus, and allow into your life only what you can honestly and properly maintain.

EVEN A DESTRUCTIVE HABIT HAS A BENEFIT.

What is the benefit of a destructive habit? A destructive habit supports your weakness. If you don't feel as though you deserve success, then you keep sabotaging yourself. Does the following sound familiar? After much effort, you finally get to a place where you can succeed, but then you sabotage your own success. People sabotage themselves all the time because they don't believe they deserve success. Part of their mind says yes, but their weakness says no, and guess which side wins!

It's important to remember that you can never grow further than your weakest point. So we have to stop, get out of denial, face our weaknesses, and realize we've gained something from them but that we don't want them anymore. We want a different, real, type of gain.

IF YOU FEEL YOU ARE BEING TESTED AND JUDGED, WILL YOU BE AS OPEN AS IF YOU ARE SIMPLY EXPLORING OR INDULGING YOUR CURIOSITY?

Have you ever been given something to do and you thought it was a test? You may have become defensive, or even hostile. We don't generally like the thought that we're being tested and challenged. But what if you didn't take that attitude? What if you said, "I'm going to do things because I'm a curious human being. I'm like the little boy who jumps up every day, runs to the window, looks out, and says, "Wow! I can't wait to get out there! What a wonderful place to explore."

So we want to go out and we want to start exploring life, and to explore life we've got to get out of the house. To get out of the house, we have to recognize the door, the opportunity to walk out that door, and our right to go out and explore life. We have to stop thinking about what we haven't done or can't do. We have to start focusing on what we can do. Pay attention to all the wonderful things you can do with your life if you're willing to put yourself out there to try things, to experience, and to explore. Try the many different things that as a kid you loved to do, but as an adult you were afraid to do because you might not do them right, or you might be tested. "I'm not going to be tested on it, so I'm not going to do it! You won't know if I succeed or fail. I'm adamant! I'm defiant."

It is in our defiance, and in our fear, that we limit ourselves. "When I tried something earlier in life, I was judged by my father, and I didn't like how it felt, so I'm never going to be judged by my father again. I'm never going to allow *anyone*—for the rest of my life—to *ever* judge me, so I'll never do anything. As long as I never do anything, I can never be judged. I'll never fail—because I'll never try to succeed. I'll show them! No one will ever criticize me again for failing, and I'll stay in a kind of never, never coma support system. I'll never be strong enough to survive on my own completely—intellectually, emotionally, or spiritually. I'll need everyone else's input and everyone else identifying who I am as a person."

WHERE'S YOUR SELF-VALUE?

In this society, your self-value is generally in what you achieve, what you possess, your status, and how you obey, in the images you continually see in your mind. But maybe you're looking in the wrong places. What about the value of a sense of connecting eternally to all the things that are essential to us? These are things that do not complicate our lives, but rather harmonize with it.

Take a moment to slow down and reflect upon how valuable this moment is to you. Guard the moment, be present for it, and be conscious of it. Then at least you're aware that you're a life force. As a life force all you have to do is extend yourself and make yourself vulnerable to what you truly believe in. Allow nothing else to interfere with that energy. You have to allow energy in before it comes in. If you don't want an energy that would disconnect you and move you away from what's essential, you have a right to say no to it.

If you begin to live like this, you will find that, one day, every day begins to take on the beauty of a sunset. You will find that every day, from morning till night, no matter what you're doing, you're doing it with a sense of inner peace and inner calm. That's because you will now be functioning from a simple framework of values and intentions of your own design.

Live Consciously

LETTING OTHERS CONTROL your life, as we discussed in the first chapter of this book, is a common—but big—mistake. The opposite of that is consciously directing your own life. When you get into the conscious living habit it suddenly becomes a lot easier to achieve goals, be they in the areas of health, intellectual activity, or interpersonal relations.

ARE YOU READY FOR TRUE, HEALTHY CHANGE?

Most people say that they want to be healthy. They don't want a diseased heart, cancer, arthritis, or depression. But few, in actuality, work toward making their health goal a reality. Over 90 percent of the people who listen to my radio program don't work toward actualizing any of the health goals I mention. I recently finished a hair study, for example. For a year and a half, I helped people reverse balding, graying, and thinning. Seven people demonstrated their new, thicker hair. These people found, after following their new protocol, that some of their facial wrinkles were gone, and several types of maladies had disappeared or were improved as well.

The thing was, 140 people had started the protocol, and only seven finished. That's a really small percentage. Why did so few finish? It was due to the unwillingness of most to follow through and truly change. Lots of people say they want to be healthy, but they are not willing to undertake the change necessary. Learn to do what you say, and you will be in balance.

Stop the games; stop deceiving yourself. There are 100 million people—that's over one third of the American population—who are chronically ill. And that number is actually an understatement because it's based on the assumption that you're only ill at the point of a disease diagnosis. It does not take into account that you could be close to death but not yet manifesting symptoms. It may take twenty years, for example, for enough tumor cells to develop and show up on an x-ray or mammogram. So at the time of diagnosis, you're at the end stage of a healing crisis, not the beginning. Your arteries could be 90 percent occluded before you find any symptoms of angina or anything else. It might take forty years for the occlusion to get that bad. You think you've caught it early when really you've identified the disease at its end stage. These pre-symptomatic people aren't counted in that 100 million. They comprise an additional 100 million.

Add to that the 50 million young people who are in the beginning stages of processing disease, and you'll bring the proportion of American people who are processing disease up to 90 percent. Take 100 ten-year-olds at random, and you'll find that 50 percent of them already have the beginnings of coronary heart disease, arthritis, and the losses of smell, hearing, and taste that come from an overstimulated lifestyle. If you are a baby boomer, you can see a sharp contrast between a child's lifestyle today and how things were for you when you grew up. You didn't grow up exclusively on a junk food diet. You probably ate junk a couple of times a week, but it wasn't the main course. You probably exercised daily. Today, children are constantly eating junk foods. Many are total couch potatoes. Also, they live in an overly stimulated, toxic environment. Their lives are more polluted than was the case for those of us who grew up in an earlier era.

The 90 percent of Americans who are processing disease contribute to a 1.3-trillion-dollar disease budget. And we're increasing our health care costs at almost 13 percent per year. Medicine, in fact, constitutes the greatest single increase in our gross national product. What we spend in the medical arena is six times the defense budget; in fact, it's more than all our food, education, and military spending combined. Next year it will be $1.5 trillion, and within ten years $2 trillion will be spent on disease.

The problem is that, much of that money is ill-spent because it is not used for prevention. Improvements in heart disease rates, for instance, are due to lifestyle improvements, not to medicine. The same could be said for cancer. People are making changes in their habits that are helping them prevent the disease, and prevention is really the only factor that reverses disease rates.

Because most Americans are not willing to change their lifestyle, you only have a tiny percentage of the population that is truly healthy. A person is not healthy by accident; we have to work on health. We also have to work on disease. They're both processes based upon the choices we make. The trouble is, that the consequences of poor choices are frequently delayed, causing many people to miss the connection.

When do we finally change? Most of us wait until we lose it all. Most of us don't pay attention to the warning signs along the way, and have to hit rock bottom before being forced to change. That's not the best motivation.

Breaking old patterns of behavior takes courage and introspection. You've got to stop thinking about every distraction that comes your way. Otherwise you've got a thousand exits along your path, and you keep searching for the exit signs instead of going forward.

WHY DO WE MAKE WRONG CHOICES WHEN WE'RE SMART ENOUGH TO KNOW THE RIGHT ONES?

We need to be conscious about what may happen as a result of a choice that we make. Think of the times you made choices without forethought; you simply reacted.

Before you can make a healthy choice you've got to love yourself and you have to be working toward self-actualization. You've got to love who you are changing for. How in the world can you heal yourself if you don't first love yourself?

A prime reason that you get sick and angry is that you become filled with self-loathing. When deep down you despise yourself, nothing you do ever makes you feel complete. The opposite is true when you feel good about who you are. Then you don't need anything more. You don't need another car, more money, more stocks, more vacations, or a more beautiful partner. You feel complete just by waking up each day. You're happy to be alive, and you smile at the adventure each new day brings. That's when you know that you're going to make the right choice by doing something positive. That's when you are ready for true, healing change.

I have seen very few people make constructive changes after they lose it all. Why do you think so many people go all through 12-step programs and yet never succeed at being happy? They do get off the particular substance they were addicted to, but they now believe that they're addicts for life. I would start with the notion that you're not an addict. You made some wrong choices, and now you're willing to make right ones. You will no longer choose to drink or take drugs. Instead, you will concentrate on mastering your life.

Stop blaming everything outside of yourself for why you became an addict, an overeater, or a gambler. You didn't have to do any of it. It was a choice. In a moment of utter confusion about why you were so incomplete when you had done so much and worked so hard to be whole, you felt angry with yourself. You felt that you needed a break from the responsibility of living. And what was that break? An addiction. Alcohol or drugs would take away the pain. It was like being so stressed out that you wanted to go into a deep sleep and wake up two years from now when the problems were over. But life doesn't give you that possibility. Therefore, every day we have to get up and realize that the storm will pass, leaving a rainbow on the other side. Unfortunately, most of us can't get past the dark storm. We need the drugs, the alcohol, the smoking, the gambling, the overeating, the compulsive working, or the abusive relationships to distract us. Of course these distractions merely keep us from feeling bad for a moment. Wrong choices always produce side effects, and to avoid the awful feeling of withdrawal, we have to keep taking a substance again and again. After awhile, we lose sight of what it was that we were trying to do before we made the original wrong choice. Then the repeated wrong choices become a pattern of behavior.

Perhaps you think that you won't be able to deal with your rage unless you go to those 12-step meetings. I don't agree. In my observation, people in those meetings will think nothing of smoking, drinking ten cups of coffee, and being angry at the world. And I find something terribly wrong with that: it allows for the replacement of one addiction with another. Have you ever noticed that when people finally realize they are no longer addicted to something, they immediately shift their focus to something else? They shift from one crisis to another. They never stand up and say, "Hey, I'm off alcohol. I feel great. Thank you all very much for helping me. I'm going on with my life. I respect the fact that you've helped me through a crucial time, but I don't need you now. I don't need to be in this movement. I don't need to be told every day that I'm incomplete and diseased. I'm not; I'm complete and well."

We endorse 12-step programs, thinking that we're doing a service by convincing people that they've got a disease. We tell people that alcoholism is in their genes. It is not. We tell people that they're genetically predisposed to being crack cocaine addicts. That's not true either. Soon they'll be telling us that it's in our genes to be a shoplifter.

It's hard, sometimes, at the 12-step meetings to find people who are interested in anything outside of themselves. "Pay attention to me!" everyone's saying. "Over here. Me, me, me, me, me, me! Listen to my story!" It's common to find a total selfishness, a lack of caring for anything or anyone else. That one's own needs are being met is all that counts. I've known people in alcohol programs, some of them quite close to me. I've watched as they gave up alcohol but remained addictive in their behavior, never taking any appropriate risks that would help them to grow. Out of fear of backsliding, they depended on people in the group to "bring them up" each day. That becomes an unhealthy, codependent relationship. It becomes almost like a cult.

So, when are we ready for true, healthy change? We're ready when we are self-loving and self-actualizing. That enables us to go forward with our lives because we will be doing it out of love, not desperation, out of self-acceptance, not self-pity.

WHAT HAPPENS WHEN OUR TRUE NATURE CONFLICTS WITH OUR EFFORTS AT IMPROVEMENT?

Perhaps you follow a program of self-improvement. Although you enter the program with great anticipation, within days you start to feel a lot of resistance. That could be because the program is not well-suited to your real nature. Perhaps you're a creative person, and the program emphasizes strictness and organization. That's not your style, and having to change drastically from what is naturally comfortable could seriously disrupt your creativity and, thus, your happiness. The "one-size-fits-all" approach does not work when it comes to self-improvement. This is particularly evident to me on those days when I have people call in to my radio show and describe how they've made positive changes in their lives. Everyone's calling in with success stories, but what stands out is that each person's way of arriving at success is totally unique.

Yet our societal tendency is to want to treat all people the same way. Everybody is supposed to look, dress, act, and behave alike. We're supposed to conform to an artificial standard, and then when it doesn't feel good we get angry at ourselves for being out of control. We see a psychiatrist or psychologist, and he or she tries to make us "normal" again. But what's normal? Is it to be like everybody else, to be obedient to authority, not to question, and not to criticize? Is it to think like everybody else? Recently, I spoke with two journalists for a special program called *Reevaluation of AIDS*. I spoke about Peter Duesberg's theory challenging the mainstream dogma that says HIV causes AIDS. Duesberg is honoring who he really is and how he really thinks, but the journalists were not open to any of that. They were speaking from a controlled, reactionary mind, while Duesberg was speaking from an individual mind.

Have you ever worked hard at perfecting something that wasn't at all related to who you really are? You may have gotten it perfect, but you didn't feel good about it. That's because you gave up too much of yourself in the process.

WHY DO WE WORK SO HARD AND SO LONG? WHAT IS THE PURPOSE OF OUR WORK?

Most of us work to prove our value to others because our self-esteem is largely based upon other people's responses to us. So the recognition factor is important. One wonders, would sports people play their games in the same way if there was no audience to acknowledge them? What if we had anonymous sports where the ego was not recognized, just the performance? What if politicians could never take credit for anything that they did? What if you had to share the credit for achievements with others?

In our society, we reward a highly competitive person who wins at all costs. Look at the people who head the Fortune 500 companies. Society looks up to those who have made the most money and suggests that they are unique. The idea is that we should respect their opinions just because they're so rich and powerful. But we never think to ask about how they did it. Was their money earned ethically? What side effects occurred because of what they did? How many people lost their jobs or their pensions because of these "leaders'" machinations?

Think of what happens to those men and women who are sought out because of all the power and money they have. Money and power become their opiate, and there is never enough. One man now has close to $50 billion. He's the wealthiest man in the world. Do you know what you could do with $50 billion? You could create sustainable agriculture. You could wipe away the mortgages of struggling farmers and help them set up organic farming projects with greenhouses that support local economies. You could change the current practice of raising one monocrop per year with pesticides and herbicides and do no-tilling farming. You could set up self-sustaining retirement communities throughout the United States where residents could grow their own food, create their own crafts, and have their own consulting services. You could have a complete program to get these people healthy again. You could do a world of good.

But none of that is being done. Throwing some money into a foundation that no one ever pays attention to never gets results. Generally, the number of dollars given is the amount that's tax-deductible.

I wonder what that Fortune 500 CEO would feel like if he had to start over from nothing. What if he were to wake up one morning and be like the average person? In my opinion, if you can't feel good about being like the average person, then you're living an artificial existence. I believe, also, that we do no one a service by excessively praising his achievements. All we do is motivate that person to work harder. There's a danger in this. About twenty million Americans are super-high-level achievers. These people are often extremely sad. They have everything money can buy, but no comfort of the spirit.

Why, then, do we work so hard and so long? We work hard because we feel that as long as we continue to accomplish and achieve we will be acknowledged for that achievement and accomplishment. People will be proud of us. Our egos will, therefore, be satisfied.

ARE YOU CONSCIOUS ABOUT THE WAY YOU CONFRONT ANGER?

One of the hardest times to remember to respond consciously—rather than to simply react—is when you are met with anger, particularly when the anger is unexpected, or misplaced.

Some time ago I worked with a group of about twenty-five people from Washington, D.C. All we did together was talk about behavior modification, and we touched upon this issue. I had a restaurant at the time, and after our meeting they went to my restaurant for dinner. I met them there a few minutes later.

Four of them were standing outside, and one person said to me, "Your manager is not treating us right. She's angry." I asked why, and was told, "She's just arbitrary." And I responded, "You learned nothing. If I saw that someone was having a rough time I would feel compassion, and I would try to honor that person by saying, 'I understand that you're having a rough time right now. How can I help you? What can I do to make this problem easier to deal with?' By doing that you're giving them no place to go with their anger. They'll then try to explain their anger, and you can then explain how that makes sense and suggest working with it. Then it's all gone. It's dissipated. And in the process you've become part of the solution, rather than part of the problem."

But they had learned nothing. When you see a person's having a rough time and getting angry, don't get upset with her (or him). Instead, try to understand. Show her that you care about how she is feeling. Let her know that you'd like her to feel better. Let her know that you're willing to do whatever it takes to help her feel better. Let the person know that you're willing to work with her to find a solution. Suddenly that person can't be angry with you since you've surrendered the need to challenge her (or his) ego. You've used your ability to respond consciously to improve, rather than worsen, the situation.

Honor Your Life

D O YOU HONOR your life? Many of us never even think in those terms. We may work day to day at jobs we abhor just to make enough money to survive. We focus on our problems, which, at times, appear to overwhelm us—ill health, relationship issues, dissatisfaction at work—and lose sight of our higher purpose.

It's important to take a periodic break from our daily routine to assess where we are and where we want to be in our life process. The following questions have been designed with that purpose in mind. They will give you the opportunity to step back from your situation so that you can become objective and anxiety-free. That will enable you to think about where you are in your journey and what your next steps should be.

DOES FEAR MOTIVATE YOUR DECISIONS?

I grew up in a small town in West Virginia where the mindset was to put in your thirty years with the fire department, or the school system, or wherever your secure job was, and then retire. At seventeen, people were already talking about retirement. The assumption was that, without a totally dependable job you would be insecure. In fact, most folks seemed to believe that only when you retired would you be fully secure!

This is a philosophy of life based on fear. If your choices are based on fear, where is the joy and spontaneity of life? Where is there room for appropriate risk-taking? How is it possible to wake up each day feeling that this is a wonderful life?

With fear as a big factor, life becomes controlled and predictable. If you can't control something, you don't do it. Think of the things in life that you have not experienced because you could not control the outcome. Think of a place you haven't visited that you would love to see. How that could expand your world! Think of the people you haven't spoken to because you were afraid of criticism. That fear may be due to a time in the past when someone expected perfection from you. Now, to feel a greater sense of security, you do only what you know you won't fail at. You try to please everyone so that no one can say you're not a nice person. At the end of the day, when you have not done anything of importance to you—you have not made time for meditation, for hobbies, or for quality reading that's just for you, nor have you allowed yourself time for a leisurely dinner or an evening stroll—you have lived a day that does not honor your spiritual, emotional, physical, and mental needs.

Every choice, then, is of paramount importance. Choose wisely to create a life that honors your essence. Focus on what you want to achieve. Begin by understanding who you are. Each person has his or her own unique energy. Some are creative, some are leaders, others work well behind the scenes to support a cause. Get in touch with who you are. Honor that.

When you set a goal for yourself ask yourself whether this is something you want to achieve or whether it is simply expected of you. Notice the difference. I do what I feel I need to do—share, communicate, challenge. I've spent my life trying to honor my gift. Everyone has a gift. What is yours? Don't let fear stop you from using it in a positive way that honors who you are.

ARE YOU ENJOYING LIFE?

One way to determine whether or not you honor your life is to judge how you feel. Are you happy in your relationships? At work? By yourself? Lots of people spend eight or more hours working at jobs that bore them. They're just putting in time. Nor are they happy in their relationships. They stay with a partner to keep from feeling alone rather than for the joy of experiencing life together.

As a result of their disenchantment, people either exhibit anger or they repress it, often channeling it into unhealthy habits like drugs, alcohol, gambling, overwork, or gossip. Others develop an unpleasant attitude. They're sharp and sarcastic, quick to retort. Or they walk around trying to dominate their environment.

Consider the quality of your life. If your work honors you, you will look forward to waking up each morning to begin it, and each day's energy will be well spent. When you are happy in your relationships, your heart will be warmer, your mind fuller, and your spirit more complete.

HAVE YOU DECONSTRUCTED
YOUR FRIENDSHIPS LATELY?

What constitutes friendship? The answer to that question is different for each individual, but it's important to ask it, and to be honest with yourself. Is a friend someone you're going to actually see and do things with, or is it someone you will speak to occasionally on the phone? When you were growing up a friend was someone you spent time with, and generally a lot of time. Do you have that same dynamic with your friends now? Should you? You need to determine what you are looking for in a friendship and then take the time to ask yourself, "Who are my friends? What do they mean in my life? Do they meet my needs for friendship? And what am I to them? What are they getting from me?" Deconstruct your friendships—i.e., determine what you need—and then reconstruct your friendships so that you can get what you want from them.

As a result, your life is going to change. For instance, you used to consider your bowling partner, Charlie, your friend, but now you realize that he was always putting people down. By deconstructing the relationship, you realize that he is not what you want in a friend anymore because you don't want to hear someone putting other people down. So you tear your friendship apart, analyze it, and then reel it back up. When you build back up there's a whole lot less of what was there. You're not going to listen to racist statements any more, you've decided. You're also excluding sexist statements. You're excluding gossipy statements, and so you're going to have to go to Charlie and say, "I'd still like you to be my friend, but I have changed. I'm not the same person that I was before. Here's what I'd like you to consider changing if you want to be my friend." Charlie will say either, "I'm not going to change for you," or, "You know something? No one ever told me that. I'm glad that you had the honesty to tell me something about myself that allowed me to see my blind spots. Thank you for caring enough to be that honest."

You've presented choices, and you don't know what's going to happen. But if you now know what you need to have a whole and balanced friendship, then you have a responsibility to focus upon what you want, to put your energy into it and say, "This is what I need." Of course, Charlie may use this opportunity to deconstruct the friendship as well. He might come back and tell you things about *you* that have started to bother *him*. "You're sometimes arrogant," he may say. Or, "Every time we get together, you're late. I feel like you think your time is more valuable than mine." If you can discuss all these issues with Charlie in an open way, you'll probably end up with a more meaningful friendship than if the two of you had just left everything status quo.

ARE YOU PROCESS-ORIENTED, OR RESULTS-ORIENTED?

We're a highly competitive society that likes only winners. So we have NBA champs, Super Bowl champs, and boxing champs. We even compete in our personal relationships. In fact, almost everything we do is a form of competition, and most of it is very unhealthy. All this competition is not meant to improve us. It's not meant to help promote inner development. It's just the way we've been conditioned to act. We pride ourselves on beating people, and categorize others as being either winners or losers. The losers are sad and dejected, while the winners are wonderful. But this is all just a game. People shouldn't take it that seriously. As with baseball, in life you'll win one season and lose the next. It's not all that significant. We just make it seem so.

Most of us deny the importance of process. In this fast-paced world, the end is all-important, as opposed to the means of getting there. Think of all the money made at the expense of other people's suffering. Look at junk bonds, at pesticides, at silicon breast implants, at the land mines that cause an injury every ten seconds. We don't stop to think of the consequences of what we create; rather, we fast-forward in our minds to the results.

What if, instead of being motivated just by what we have to gain, we were focused on the process of getting there? We would be less concerned about achievement and more centered on growing, learning, and being aware of each moment. The process of living would become as important—and in some instances, more important—than the goals achieved. That would improve the quality of our lives. We would be able, for example, to take a day off from work to spend time with our children, instead of working all hours, nonstop.

Ask yourself how much of your unhappiness is the result of being too focused on goals and results. Shift your focus to the process of life. That's where your energy should be. Then, no matter what you achieve, you will be able to accept it. Look at a marathon. No one in the crowd remembers anyone's names other than those of the first one or two to cross the finish line. Yet everybody who finished the marathon, all 29,994 people, did it for the enjoyment of the process. They didn't have to win for the race to be worthwhile.

Similarly, losing weight is a process of learning to change habits and, therefore, feel better about yourself. So it doesn't make sense to beat yourself up for not losing the magical number of pounds you think you ought to lose. If you're focused on the end result only, you're going to try any drastic means to get there—diet pills, fad diets, liposuction, stomach stapling—and never learn a thing. In fact, the all-too-common yo-yo phenomenon will result in your gaining everything back that you've lost, plus more. So it's better to focus on the process of becoming healthy. Of course you'll have a goal and you'll want results, but that should not be your main concern. Rather, your focus should be on the process of feeling better each day. That way, every moment counts.

Do you take credit for your successes?

I'm a big believer in giving yourself credit for every single thing that you do. This means that ten, twenty, or thirty times a day, take one second to stop and say, "I'm doing the right thing." And say, "I'm happy with myself."

When you become your own support system you don't rely on the approval of others. That's because you build inner confidence. A friend could make a negative remark, for example. Without the habit of self-encouragement you might feel bad about yourself or angry at the other person. But when you have given yourself approval all along, you don't take the negative comment to heart.

ARE YOU REALISTIC ABOUT GOALS?

There are a lot of options to choose from in the world; it's up to you to make the choices that are right for you. I recommend setting a daily goal to make better choices. Then set a weekly goal, and then one for the year. As we've stressed, you've got to keep your goals realistic; if you overreach you'll soon be self-sabotaging and ditching the whole effort. Also, remember that the journey is as important as the end point. That said, here are some hints for making your goals happen.

Prepare an outline of what you want to change and achieve.

To make a goal realistic, you've got to see it in black and white. I create boards and write down the projects I plan to complete. The boards keep me focused. That way I am more likely to achieve what I set out to do. Keeping focused will help you when resistance sets in. Whenever you go in a new direction, there is a part of you that says you shouldn't change. You may hear, "You can't change that. That's not right." Remember, you are making changes for you.

Do your homework.

It's one thing to know that you want to be out of a bad situation. It's another to know how to go about doing it. Unless you're prepared, you may be jumping out of the frying pan and into the fire. Don't be compulsive; prepare for change. That's an important part of mastering life. You wouldn't walk on stage to perform a piano concerto without years of preparation. Mastery takes time.

Someone recently complained to me, saying, "Gary, I don't want to live in Brooklyn anymore. My family lived there, my family's family lived there, and everybody expects me to live there too. But I want to live in a place that's not congested, not crime-ridden, not filled with prejudice. I want to get more out of life." This person was ready to just pick up and leave. I suggested doing some homework first: "Why don't you travel to different places on weekends? Stay within a reasonable traveling distance. Then take a four-day weekend each month and go someplace farther." The person did this, traveling throughout the United States, and finally settling in the beautiful town of Boulder, Colorado. That city supports this person's lifestyle with its health-minded orientation.

Another example is a schoolteacher I know from the Bronx who retired at forty-six. This man had always been enamored of the arts and languages. I suggested visiting Barcelona, Spain, and visiting Italy as well. I thought he should see what life was like in the Mediterranean. Now he lives in a beautiful home in Spain, and couldn't be happier. With his pension he is able to afford a villa, a cook, two gardeners, and a driver. He's only twenty minutes from the capital, yet he has thirty-one acres of land, which includes an olive grove. He makes his own olive oil. He sent me a video telling me of everything going on and he said it's just heaven. He is able to grow his own flowers and make his own flower arrangements, which brings him great joy. When you're from the Bronx you generally don't go out and hand-pick flower arrangements!

By the way, with these two examples I don't mean to put down New York's outer boroughs. There are plenty of great, livable neighborhoods in them; the point here is that these two people were looking for a drastic change from what they had, and in order to successfully follow through on that, they had to do their homework.

Do yours if you're contemplating a similar change. Don't be impulsive. Don't just quit and take off. Prepare for a transition. Prepare yourself mentally, and then prepare the resources you will need to make that transition.

Prepare yourself mentally for the challenge.

I was recently counseling a terminally ill person who was told that he was going to die because of liver cancer that had metastasized. His cancer is very advanced and he is taking pain medication for it. He asked me for a protocol to follow. I told him that the very first thing he should do is prepare himself mentally for the challenge so that every thought is on doing something positive. I advised him not to make the fear of the disease all-important in his life. Being overwhelmed takes up all of one's energy. He needed to take back the energy to regain control of his life.

I could see that there was a sense of optimism and joy on his face after our talk. He had come to me with a slumped posture, but he left with a surge of energy. That's important. Each day we have to feel that our challenges are going to be supported by our passions.

Remember that passion is what drives you.
It's what keeps you going day in and day out. Look at Ralph Nader, Michael Jacobson, Sydney Wolf, or other people who have lived their lives in a committed way. Many thousands of people have daydreamed about being one of Nader's Raiders and making a difference, but they didn't have the passion to follow through for any length of time. They worked at a cause for a week and then stopped. I've had so many individuals come to my office to help me with projects or issues. Often they begin with great interest and enthusiasm, but a day or two later I won't see them again. They have no passion.

Unfortunately, much of our life these days is filled up with junk, and we tolerate it. That weighs us down and buries our real passion. So you have to choose. Either put your energy into what is essential to you, or waste your time on nonessentials. When the nonessential has replaced the essential in your life, it's as if you're at a meal but you're perpetually eating the after-dinner mint and skipping the main course. All you get is a little taste in the mouth for two or three seconds.

How many doctors are living nonessential lives because they no longer believe they can cure anyone? How many teachers are living nonessential lives because they can no longer teach anyone?

Many people are going through the motions every day to earn a salary, but they aren't making a difference. You look in their eyes, and you see coal dust where once there was a crystallized diamond. The spark is gone. We get burned out from leading nonessential lives. And then we think that's all there is.

Begin with small changes.

I don't believe in the big-change concept, at least not for most people. Many people think they are going to change suddenly, but that approach generally doesn't work. To realize this you have only to look at the 100 million overweight Americans who diet every day; yes, they do lose weight, but only to gain it back.

Now picture yourself losing weight on a small-lifestyle-change plan, rather than on a strict, artificial diet. You're not gaining it back, because you aren't dieting. You've uncluttered your life and you are not focused upon what is nonessential; your health is your number-one priority. Before, eating was important to you for all the wrong reasons. You ate for comfort, to feel good when life was stressful. Now, when you eat, you eat for the right reasons. You've made dietary changes involving juicing, taking nutritional supplements, and cleansing. You're certainly not starving yourself. What a difference there is in that approach! You are working on yourself, making all the small changes necessary for a healthy life, rather than expecting miracles. And it's working.

Accept that you cannot control all results.

A major frustration most people have is their inability to control outcomes. What we can control is our ability to do the things we know how to do well. We therefore keep doing the same things over and over and over again. But that makes for a boring, tedious life. The idea is to do new things, even though you won't succeed at first. That's how you learn. Attempting the new can create wonderful experiences for you.

Now I'm not saying that you're going to like every new experience. What I am saying, though, is that you should not prejudge any experience based on your fear of not being able to control it. Do things simply for the joy of doing them. You'll find that you enjoy certain new experiences, which you can then spend more time on. Otherwise life becomes boring. The average person follows the same routine constantly during his or her whole life. Most people could live the rest of their lives by pressing a button that says "repeat." I find that appalling, don't you?

Look at your gains even when the results are not what you wanted.

There's a gain in everything. Accept that and realize that you can feel good about what you are doing even when you are not getting what you want from it. You can still feel good for having done it. To give an example, I was leading a national championship race recently and feeling really good. Then I developed cramps, and I couldn't work them out. I had the choice to either stop, as other athletes frequently do in such a situation, or just continue and enjoy the race. I chose the latter course. Even though I didn't achieve a personal best, I experienced joy in the process of racing. There was something to be gained—finishing something that I had started and savoring the activity of it. That's how we have to look at life. We are not going to win at everything we do. But we can always benefit from the experience.

Be flexible.

As I write this, I am in the process of looking to purchase or rent an office space to create a holistic medical center because I counsel so many people who need quality medical care. I can't give them medical treatment; they have to search for doctors on their own. Often the doctors they find do not follow my suggestions. Sometimes their egos get in the way of true service, and they charge outrageous prices. So I'm trying to set up a center where truly holistic, humane practitioners can work.

Anyway, every time I find an office I begin to reformulate what

I will do in that office depending upon various factors. For example, one space is 4000 square feet, while another one spans 6000. One is uptown while another is downtown. I am constantly reformulating ideas. I'll probably see dozens of spaces before I find the right one. But if I don't keep myself flexible, I may pass one by that truly meets my needs. That will leave me feeling forever frustrated as I continually look for the "perfect" space.

Think long-term. Be patient in your journey. There's no stopwatch that you have to abide by. Give yourself time, hold to your higher ideals, and be flexible. Before choosing my ranch in Texas, I looked at hundreds of ranches throughout the United States. Brokers were constantly sending me videos. The process, from start to finish, took four years. Finally, I found land that I turned into a beautiful place. The same process was true for my ranch in Florida. I looked at numerous places; many of them looked good. But I wouldn't have been able to do as much with them as I was able to do with the one I finally chose. It took patience.

So be patient, be flexible, and reformulate your ideas. If one of your ideas doesn't work, rework it, modify it, mold it until it's usable. Sometimes we're too rigid, and that works against us.

Stop focusing on your limitations. See your positive attributes.

Don't accept your imperfections as limitations. All of us are imperfect. Look closely at anybody, and you will see his or her imperfections. We try our best to hide our imperfections. We use cosmetics. We use haircuts. We use clothes. We use language. We use everything we can. We use our mastery of something to hide the imperfections of what we have not mastered, but all of us are living embodiments of imperfection.

That's okay. There is no perfection in life. There's only process, and we've all begun a process. If I don't blame myself or beat myself up for what I'm not, then I can accept what I am. And if I can accept what I am, then I can grow. If I'm always angry about what I've never achieved, then I will deny the virtue of what I am at this moment. And if I deny my basic virtue, then how in the world can I be complete or self-loving?

Never fear being introspective.

If you're introspective you're going inside to resolve your conflict instead of outside. The only thing you can fear from that is meeting the real self and being angry that you didn't embrace that self long ago. That's where forgiveness comes in. Stop comparing yourself with others. People in this society tend to say, "At this age I should be this, and I should have that." You can't. You are who you are, and you're at where you're at, and that's where you've got to start the process. Don't look at someone else and say, "They must be happier, or better, smarter, or wiser." You don't know what anyone else says to himself with his own inner voice.

I've had the chance to counsel some very famous, powerful, and successful people. On the human level, not one of them has any more going on than anyone else. Take those people outside of their areas of expertise and power, and they're just like everybody else. That's one of the reasons celebrities want to be away from everyone who is, so-called, common. They don't want you to realize how close you are to them. They want to make you feel that they're unique—when they're not.

Yes, there's a lot of room between where you are now versus perfection. But don't overvalue perfection, and don't undervalue where you are. You've survived and learned a lot. Give yourself credit for that.

Determine Your Focus

D O YOU OFTEN start a project only to realize somewhere down the line that you're never going to finish it? Perhaps every time you go to work on a project some other priority keeps you from completing it. This happens to a lot of people, from what I hear. The question is, when do we stop all the distractions and make time for personal accomplishments? At some point you need to decide, "Okay, this is my life. I've spent all my energy dealing with everyone else's needs but my own. From this day on my needs count. Today I will focus on taking care of me." Otherwise, what happens is you take care of all your responsibilities, your whole to-do list, and you are not included. It's a sad thing when you're not on your own to-do list because you feel guilty about giving yourself any time at all. If you find yourself in that situation, it's time to reassess what you're doing with your days.

And your nights. Look up at the buildings on Wall Street any night, and you will notice that the lights stay on. The people inside are not cleaning people. They are workers seeking love through material success. They're trying to buy love. They're buying a boarding school for their kids, the right dress for their wives, an expensive suit for their husbands. They're paying with sixteen-hour workdays.

You pay a price for such success. When you consistently over-work, your life is out of balance. Inevitably, it will begin to crumble. All the apologies—"It's going to get better," and "When I just get this amount of money we can then buy this and do that," or

307

"We bought so much that I've got to work this hard to pay for it"—will not make up for the irreplaceable time that is lost. I don't know about you, but I'd rather live in a modest apartment with a person I love, knowing that I'll have quality time with that person, than live in a mansion with a virtual stranger.

WHERE IS YOUR FOCUS— ON MATERIAL SUCCESS, OR ON TIME SPENT WITH THE PEOPLE YOU LOVE?

The smart person is the one who knows how to say no to opportunity in order to have time for self, family, and friends. Fostering these relationships is truly what's important. Otherwise, you're going to get that call that your mother, your father, your brother, or someone else close to you is dead, and you'll regret the paucity of time you made for that person.

You may rationalize that you were too busy because you had so many bills to take care of. That's because we Americans have a constant need to spend. We certainly buy things we don't need. How about making the choice to buy nothing that is not essential for six months? Buy only what you need to live; make no purchases simply to satisfy a whim, or for convenience. You probably don't need more clothes. You certainly don't need toys and gadgets. We try to make things replace time spent with people. But deep down we all know how well that works!

DO YOU EXPECT PERFECTION?

There is no perfection, only a thousand honest mistakes made in the process of mastering life. When I think of the concept of perfection, what comes to mind is the dancing of Fred Astaire and Ginger Rogers; the way they move together seems to me as close to perfection as it gets. But how many times did they have to practice to get each step right? They worked on a single dance for weeks. Yet all we see is the perfection. Seeing only the end result, we can come to believe that everything about us should be instantly perfect.

What if we didn't look to others as role models of perfection? What if, instead, we just worked on mastering our own lives moment to moment? We could say, "I'm going to do it until I do it right."

But we get discouraged so quickly. We listen to others, who instead of encouraging us, often serve to remind us that we are not that good. We shouldn't be so quick to ask for people's opinions because, often, the people we rely on are the ones who are envious of us, who don't want us to change for the better. I never ask anyone's opinion about anything. It's not because I think I know it all—I do not—it's because I trust my own feelings. I'm the one who has to experience those feelings, and I don't want to walk around with someone else's feelings in my head. I don't want to be living someone else's experience. What do his feelings have to do with me?

Have there been times that people gave you the wrong advice but you took it because you thought they knew better than you? You probably weren't too happy later on. The fact is, all of us are biased. There's no guarantee that others have any more insight than you, especially when it comes to your life. You have the biggest stake in your decisions, while others are only marginally interested. So look to yourself for answers. Don't be afraid of making mistakes. Do what you believe is right, and learn from your own experiences.

DO YOU AVOID CHANGE?

What happens when you feel you are going to lose something important? Does the expectation fill you with anxiety or regret?

One of the reasons many of us don't make needed changes is we want our lives to remain forever the same. That's because we don't like the way it feels to lose something. I have a radically different view than that of most people, a view I'd like you to consider. It might open you up.

I grew up in a small town where you were supposed to live in the same house forever and ever. You would inherit your house from your parents, who had inherited it from your grandparents. You were supposed to have only one job, and retire after thirty years. People who shifted from one job to another were considered irresponsible. Friends were supposed to be the same throughout life. I attended my high school reunion a few years ago and, sure enough, that's how many of my former schoolmates had lived.

What if you thought of everything as just a passage? We discussed this briefly when talking about mistake number three, planning for the future, the idea being that whatever you're doing is just going to be done for a period of time, and then it ends. Everything in life is a passage. Look in the mirror today and you'll see the passages occurring physically. Look at the people in your life today versus twenty years ago, and think of how many passages you've gone through. And yet you want one person for life, one home for life, one job for life, when it doesn't necessarily work that way.

Begin to become more realistic about what your needs are, and try to fulfill those needs in a segment of time, recognizing that when those needs are met and that segment of time ends, there may be an end. That will enable you to either renegotiate a new beginning or create a new direction altogether. You have the right to change course. You have the right to go on several paths if you wish. You need not follow one path.

Recognizing these realities, I live my life through passages. I will work on a project for six months or so. During that time, I'll focus my attention in a certain direction. There will be a complete commitment on my part. But then the project will end, leaving me the right to redirect myself. I built a beautiful ranch in Texas. After ten years, I sold it. It was time for that passage to end. The experience taught me valuable lessons as it brought both pleasure and pain. But there came a time when the project no longer met my needs, and I let it go. I didn't think about whether I was selling it in an up market or a down market, or whether I would lose or make money. I thought about my having reached the end of something, so I surrendered the need for the ranch in order to make room for the next choice in my life.

Similarly, I had a radio show down south that I eventually gave up when I no longer needed the experience. I also had a healing center for four years that I gave up when I was ready for my life to take a different turn.

Even friends are passages. Some people play an important role in your life for a period of time. Then one or both of you move in a different direction. You may meet again or not, and it's not a matter of that being good or bad. It's a matter of people making choices about where they want to put their time and energy. I don't want someone calling me once a year to say, "I was just thinking of you." People are either in your life or they're not. If I can't communicate with someone on a regular basis, then I don't want that person in my life. I don't believe in acquaintances bumping into each other and everyone making excuses for why they haven't spoken. Friends are people you befriend. If I'm in a relationship with someone, I'm going to spend quality time with that person.

Consider redirecting your life from this moment on, focusing on what is really important to you. By honoring your essence a lot of things could change.

HOW DOES A SECURE PERSON PERCEIVE LOSS DIFFERENTLY FROM AN INSECURE PERSON?

If you're not making changes because you're afraid of losing something, ask yourself, "How would I feel about losing this if I were more secure in myself?" When you are insecure in yourself you are going to do everything possible to avoid change. You will procrastinate, deny—even lie—to hold on to what you have. But when you are more secure, you will realize that what you need to let go of is no longer essential to you. By holding on, you put a lot of energy into staying stuck. You will keep a toxic job because it pays the bills rather than let go and find work that honors you. Because you're afraid to go to bed alone at night you'll settle for a mate whom you don't even like.

What I'm saying is that most of the things we fear losing we shouldn't even have to begin with. Rather than nurture, they imprison. Unless you break free, how are you going to seek joy? How are you going to find happiness?

DO YOU LET CRITICS
DESTROY YOUR SELF-IMAGE?

We don't like to have anyone challenge our picture of ourself, and that's quite understandable because it undermines our pride. For instance, we do something that we think is right, and someone becomes nitpicky about it. Have you ever been around people who, instead of praising you for what you've done right, try to condemn you for some aspect of what you've done that they don't like?

You should be happy about the efforts that you've made and respect the fact that it is better to have tried something than not to have tried. Don't let someone pick apart what you've accomplished. Tell them you don't like what they're doing.

People are very open about showing us our flaws. But do they show us theirs? The next time someone starts to criticize you, you might say, "Okay, before you criticize me, tell me what's wrong with you. Tell me what you don't like about yourself." See how quiet they become.

For many people it's easy to come up with criticism but difficult to acknowledge the good. There is a Quaker statement I wish more people would adhere to: *Don't speak unless you can improve upon the silence.*

CAN YOU LET GO OF YOUR EGO?

The ego distorts judgment. It is the ego that says, "We must have power and control," and any choice that's made from that mindset is a distorted choice because ego misconstrues everything. Think of the distortion of the ego when it comes to making money. How much money does a person have to make before he or she can finally find happiness? There will never be enough. To the contrary, much is sacrificed in the search for all that money. A person will give up time with friends and family, and forfeit other essentials. Because of ego, the nonessentials are constantly nourished. But since there is no finite stomach in this ego, it's a bottomless pit. There is always the need for more money, more power, and more control.

One day you might wonder why you are so unhappy: "Hold on a second. Haven't I been doing this for years? I've got all this money and every material possession that money can buy. Why am I not happy?" Of course you're likely to look for answers in the same wrong places, thinking, "Maybe another deal will make me happy. Perhaps more money is what I need."

As numerous rich people will attest, money is not the solution. We have thirty million highly affluent people in this country. All these people have millions of dollars, and most of them are not happy because their ego has denied them the chance to change what doesn't work in their life. They're not willing to deconstruct the ego. Hence, they can't deconstruct their life. And if they can't deconstruct their life, then nothing is going to change. They will continue to just want more and never feel filled.

DO YOU HAVE TO FAIL
BEFORE YOU CAN SUCCEED?

I have a friend who was a successful writer of fiction. He was not making a lot of money, but ten of his books were published. He was a very funny, creative guy.

One day he received a major contract and wrote a big-selling book. My friend moved from his nice, little apartment to a big, expensive co-op. I saw a lot less of him. When I asked what was going on, he said he had more responsibilities and less time to hang out. Over the next five years I saw him less and less. Then I didn't see him at all.

Ten years passed. Then, walking down Broadway one day, I saw my friend on a street corner selling books. He acknowledged me and talked to me about what he was doing. He would get books that people didn't want anymore and sell paperbacks for ten cents and hardcovers for twenty-five cents. I asked what had happened to his royalties, and he told me that they had all dried up. He had gotten so stressed from having to support his lifestyle that he was no longer able to write. After a year of success he was living in debt and lost everything. That caused him to become depressed. He moved to the country and became a schoolbus driver. Upon returning to New York he vowed to never again do anything that would get him stressed enough to lose his appreciation for each day of life.

Now he doesn't make a lot of money, but he doesn't need a lot either. He lives a much simpler life. "My lifestyle is back to where it was fifteen years ago, Gary," he said to me. When I asked him why he hadn't called he said that he had been embarrassed about the change. "I was the big shot. I used to rib you about never working for money. I thought you were stupid."

He was referring to some of the conversations we used to have. He and other friends used to wonder why I had turned down opportunities to do Tang commercials, and preferred to remain broke. I lived off very little in those days rather than choose to sell my name. My friend said, "My God, do you realize what you could have gotten for your name? Yet you always managed to have fun, and you never talked about money. It wasn't important to you. But it was to me. I realized I was insecure about who I was. Now I'm happy."

We resumed our friendship. He's a wonderful human being who had to fail before he could succeed at life. There's no reason you have to fail before you can succeed, if you don't let yourself be run by your ego.

DO YOUR THOUGHTS KEEP YOU FROM BELIEVING IN THE POSSIBILITY OF CHANGE?

How many times do you make negative statements to yourself that prevent you from believing you can ever change? One problem is that, if no one has been an example of change, then you don't even have a role model. For instance, most senior citizens get high blood pressure or dementia. They accept their fate, believing that that's supposed to happen. Everyone around them, including their doctor, believes it's supposed to happen, which reinforces their own belief. What they believe will then occur.

You can surrender your thoughts of weakness and limitation. To do so, you must acknowledge what they are and look at the power that they have had on your life. You must make a list of the things in your life that do not work, that limit you, that you fear. And you must say, "These are the things that I do not like about myself. I'm no longer going to avoid and deny them. I'm going to resolve them." Only then can you change.

One day you will wake up and think, "I'm glad I worked on myself because the very things that were keeping me from fulfillment and completeness in my own life are no longer there. Now I feel good all the time."

Go against the norm and say, "I will not age prematurely; I will not become diseased." It takes courage to be a unique person. We need to have more people who are willing to stand apart and say, "This is my life. I'm going to choose to live it, from this point forward, as I believe it should be lived." You can then create your own beliefs, focus on those, and leave out the ones that keep you from growing.

LESSON 5.

Stop Blaming Others

WHAT'S KEEPING YOU stuck in old patterns? Maybe it's the blame mentality. I believe it's time that we stop seeing ourselves as a society of victims. It's time that we stopped blaming our dysfunctional backgrounds—"If my mother had treated me right" . . . "If I'd have been breast-fed" . . . "If my father had thrown me in the air and given me kisses." This is nonsense. Stop blaming your mother and father and others. Accept responsibility for the choices you make.

It is only after you stop blaming other people that you can start making changes in your life. Once you're willing to forego the blame mentality that's so pervasive in this country, you can go on to change from unhappy to happy, unhealthy to healthy, being biased to being unbiased, and your life will begin to turn around. You will be opening the door to unlimited possibilities. Remember, you're the only problem you have, and you're the only treatment you have. You're the solution if you simply allow yourself to be.

CAN YOU CLOSE THE DOOR ON THE PAST?

You must learn to free yourself from issues with others that happened in the past. Everything in life must have closure. We like to leave the door open all the time because we suspect that we may need something from our past, even it it's only a way of negative-

317

ly responding. We keep the door open, and stuff keeps oozing in. Just when you're about to think, "Isn't life good?" you suddenly remember, "It would be good, but that person lied to me, and I didn't like it."

But that was four months ago. You can't change the fact that the person lied to you. Understand the lesson from what happened, and close the door. There's a time we must close things in order to open something else. Otherwise, we won't ever move forward. You've got to get to where you can say it's okay for things to end so that other things can begin.

HOW DO YOU JUSTIFY YOUR ANGER?

Most people justify their anger by blaming others for how they feel. If you were anywhere in the south in the 1920s up to the 1960s, and you, as a person of color, went into a "whites-only" restaurant, the patrons and owners would have taken offense. You might have been beaten or even killed. The act would have been justified with cries of, "He deserved it!" stemming from their fears and insecurities, because your action was a threat to their power. Anger is often an inappropriate reaction to what a person cannot resolve in himself. So someone else gets blamed. We have personal conflicts, and we have wars because of this. It's all so foolish and so destructive.

Sometimes we blame our circumstances for our anger, our sense of helplessness, our insecurity, and our fear. You may think, "Gary, you'd be depressed and angry too if you were a poor, struggling artist in New York City. You don't know what it's like to be living on Avenue A, not being able to get a showing, and having nobody respect your work." To this I'd say, "Hold on. This is your choice. Rather than blaming people who have not acknowledged your work and blaming the galleries that haven't exhibited your art, you could say, 'This is not the only city in the world where I can do and exhibit my work. There are other places that are less congested, less hostile, less frantic. I can go to Sedona in Arizona; I can go to Taos or Albuquerque in New Mexico. There are plenty of art colonies in the United States that are less expensive, less polluted, and more conducive to an enjoyable life.' Do you really need to be acknowledged to the point of perpetual anxiety? How are you going to do good work when you're always anxious and depressed? You're justifying your depression and anger by creating stressful circumstances."

You see, it's a chain of events. Unrealistic expectations create fear, and that then creates pressure and anxiety. Then you begin to sublimate that anxiety. That is, rather than feel that intolerable sense of anxiety you may gamble or overeat; you may become cynical, mean-spirited, or perpetually busy. You may become a chronic caregiver or someone who takes inappropriate risks. Or you may simply go overboard with anger. Show me someone who is inappropriately angry, and I'll show you someone who will be forever hostile. That hostility runs deep, percolating up like a septic system that is overflowing. A little percolation in the soil is a sign that down below there's a big, toxic septic system that has to drain.

Sometimes we project our anger. That's why a lot of people love violent sports. Wrestling, for instance, channels all the frustrations as we watch the wrestlers be excessively violent in an almost cartoonish way. For a moment it works, but since it does not resolve any issues, the angry feeling soon surfaces again.

I'm convinced that if we were to revive public executions, they would be most popular. People would want to watch them on television. Historically, some of the most popular events ever were public executions. Large groups would assemble in a carnival-like atmosphere to watch someone being killed. The more gruesome the method—burning at the stake, the guillotine, public hangings—the better. Actually, watching death by guillotine was not that popular—it was too quick. People wanted to watch as much

319

suffering as a person could endure. It was a kind of sick catharsis that is actually not so different from the experience of watching certain of today's TV talk shows.

CHALLENGE SOMEONE'S BELIEFS, AND OTHERS WHO ADHERE TO THOSE BELIEFS WILL ALSO FEEL THREATENED.

Everyone believes they have a direct stake in the outcome of a conflict. To give an example, picture an oncologist specializing in chemotherapy for breast cancer. An educated woman comes to his office and says, "I've looked at the scientific literature, and I can't find where there's improvement in five-year survival using chemotherapy aggressively, moderately, or not at all. In fact, Dr. Harden Jones, a leading medical biostatistician, found that there was no difference. I would rather not have that used because it's going to be immunosuppressive. I'd rather have a strong immune system and deal with my cancer by rebalancing my body chemistry and detoxifying."

By the time she's gotten that far into the conversation, the doctor has already felt threatened. This person is saying, basically, "Doctor, your knowledge is neither sacred to me, nor is it the only knowledge." What generally happens is that doctors will band together and say, "We have these people who think they know something about their own bodies. Haven't they gotten it straight that they're diseased and we're the cure? They're here for us to treat them."

The doctors form a circle around this one physician to make sure there are no more personal challenges. They begin to issue statements that it is irresponsible to start taking control of your health unless you do so with the direct instructions of a physician. Now the medical society comes out, as does the larger AMA, and suggests that the best treatment for breast cancer is chemotherapy. At no point do they suggest that you can prevent this disease; instead, they state that breast cancer is genetic.

You may say, "Doctor, if breast cancer is genetic, then how is it that people can prevent breast cancer by changing their diet, their behavior, and the amount of unnatural hormones taken in?" They'll retort that those are anomalies. "Well, how can a whole nation be an anomaly?" you may argue. "Japan's women have 400 percent less breast cancer than America's women. Are you saying that Japan is an anomaly? It doesn't make sense. And how about all the women in China? Chinese women have substantially less breast cancer than American women."

The entire medical and scientific community together closes ranks. They have their legislators protecting them. They have their publicists guaranteeing that their image will not be tainted. So when you ask one question you are going up against a whole institutionalized belief system. That's hard to change.

But if you can't change the system, instead of being frustrated and then becoming apathetic and angry, realize that what you can do is change yourself. You can think, I'm not going to take vaccines. I'm not going to get a coronary bypass operation. I'm not going to take Ritalin or Prozac. I'm not going to have electroconvulsive therapy. By doing that, you, an individual, move from the blaming mode to the self-empowering mode. You take a negative and make it a positive.

DO YOU KNOW HOW TO END A CONFLICT WITH MUTUAL GAIN, NOT BLAME?

Often conflicts occur when we decide we just won't take anymore. Picture yourself in a relationship. Initially, you're compatible because you haven't gone far enough into each other's psyches to see what's really there. You've gone as far as the tactile sensations and the feelings that come with that. After awhile you've done some further exploring; there's nothing new there. Now you decide to take some chances, and go into the person's mind to see what's there. And whoa, it's a 3000-foot-deep pit. You didn't know what you'd be stepping into. At some point, all the good things you thought you'd love to live with forever become the things that you wouldn't want to live with tomorrow.

Now you've got a problem. You may not realize it, but it's the weaknesses within anything that we are associated with that will create chronic anxiety. If we don't feel that we can change it, and if we've accepted it, even though it's toxic, then what are we doing to ourselves? We're taking on the other person's energy. Each day waking up, instead of feeling good, we're thinking, "I've got this to deal with, and it isn't changing." Every day it's the same, and it wears you down to where you no longer have patience. You can no longer make excuses for it.

You'd think people would deal with the problem right then and there. But no, that would mean closure. That would mean saying, "Okay, this is over. Thank you. I've learned. I forgive. I'm going on. It's closed. I'm not doing that again." One problem is that, in a way, you lived through someone else, and you were tolerating someone else's limitations because you didn't see the strength within yourself to do for yourself what the other person was supposed to be doing for you. One day you wake up and see that what they were supposed to do for you they weren't really doing very well anyhow, and you could do it better yourself. You don't want to admit you made a mistake, though. So you hang on, figuring that, somehow, things will change. The person apologizes. He or she doesn't want to be out of your life. But it doesn't do any good, because the person doesn't change. Everything stays the same, and you're still living with frustration.

There's a time for closure, a time to go on, a time when the conflict has got to stop. And conflicts do not stop until you realize that there must be something to be gained for both people in ending the conflict. You're never able to end a conflict with closure as long as one of you gains and the other loses (or both of you lose) because people resent losing. What you have to do to successfully end conflicts is create a way that you can show that both you and the other person win.

That's the first rule in mediation: Show that both people have something to gain that's greater than what they're going to lose. If they don't feel they're going to gain anything there's no purpose in ending the conflict. It can keep going on forever. Look at parts of the world where conflicts have gone on for hundreds of years. On the other hand, make both parties winners, and the conflict will have a chance of ending. So, if you can show the other person in your unhappy relationship that you no longer want to be there, and that there's a way he or she too can benefit by no longer being in that situation, then you have the capacity to separate. That's the approach you should take if you need to.

IF YOU COULD CONTROL A CONFLICT, WHAT OUTCOME WOULD YOU CHOOSE?

Think of a conflict in which you felt angry. What if you could control the outcome? Would you seek an outcome that benefited only you? Or would you also be considerate of the other person? If you say you'd be considerate, that's the spiritual answer. You can't make decisions based on your anger because that hurts the other party. And then that doesn't really end the conflict, does it? You've got to separate the egos to fuse the false beliefs to end the conflict.

If I can show an orthodox doctor that he has something to gain by at least examining an issue from the holistic viewpoint, then he's going to be less likely to perceive me as a threat than if he thinks he has something to lose by engaging in what I want to share with him. As I write this I'll soon be filming a new PBS documentary. I'm going to have a room full of mainstream doctors there. I didn't have to have those people participate. I chose to. And I'm not having them there to attack them. I'm going to give them an opportunity to learn what women who have healed from major diseases can teach them about the healing process. All the women who will be featured have recovered from major diseases that mainstream medicine had no answers for, such as so-called "terminal" cancers.

Some doctors will come in peace. They will realize that they have something to gain. Maybe one or two of the group that comes will go home with new ideas. Is it worth it to have one or two out of forty people grow? It is when you consider that those one or two might offer something to their patients that saves a life. We're never going to have en masse change anyway. So when you seek to control the outcome of a conflict, always consider the needs of the other person as well as your own.

ARE YOU OPEN TO EVERYONE, OR ONLY TO THOSE WHO REMIND YOU OF YOU?

One of the difficulties we have in this society is making friends with strangers, opening up to people of different backgrounds and beliefs. It's because we talk a different language. We have different ways of doing things. And we tend to want to stay around people who remind us of us.

At my sleepaway detox programs I ask people to refrain from talking about themselves and telling people what they do. I don't want people associating because of some extrinsic characteristic they have in common—a career, a religion, economic status, or education. I want people to like each other for what they're sharing as human beings. We should judge each other by the openness and warmth of our heart, our humility, our humanity, our joy and humor, the things that are endearing, not the superficial qualities, such as status and education. Those are inconsequential.

Whenever you meet someone, instead of looking at him or her as Catholic, Jewish, Arab, Jain, Buddhist, white, or black, why not just look at him as a human being? Then start seeing what it is that that person can share with you that broadens your perspective. Don't look at what you have in common. Look at what is unique. Then try to understand how the uniqueness of that person's beliefs and values could inspire or broaden your own. If all you do is seek the comfort of people with whom you have things in common, you will never grow.

There's value in all beliefs and you can find something to learn from everyone. But we have to be open to that truth. I'm not afraid to go into the house of a person who is an atheist or an orthodox religious person. I'm interested in both their perspectives. It's not that I have to become like them. But I want to know what it's like to be them. Only by listening to what a person is saying nonjudgmentally—meaning I'm going to be there in the moment and just listen—can I understand that person. Sometimes I'll disagree with a person's beliefs, but I will not have judged that person prematurely. And I certainly will never start off saying," I cannot associate with you because you're this, that, or the other thing." The first rule in my book is to suspend judgment.

Forget the Excuses

WHEN I COUNSEL someone, I can usually tell within the first ten minutes whether or not he or she is going to make any of the life-enhancing changes I suggest. I have a very easy way of telling. It's not whether I see that person taking notes or hear him asking intelligent questions. It has zero to do with the person's educational achievement or social status. And it doesn't have to do with his current level of energy, or even of optimism. It's whether or not I hear excuses.

"I would, but I . . ."
"I was going to, but I couldn't because . . ."
"There might not be enough time . . ."
"Gary, I don't know anything about juicers . . ."

I've heard them all. And when I hear things like this, I know that person is a lost cause. So I'll try to wind up our meeting as soon as possible, because I don't like wasting time. On the other hand, if I don't hear excuses, I'll talk to that individual for hours if need be. The person could be very sick, fatigued, or dejected, but if he's not surrounding himself with a barricade of excuses, I know there's hope for beneficial change.

WHAT ARE SOME OF THE MOST COMMON EXCUSES PEOPLE MAKE?

I have too much to do.

I've never seen a person who couldn't find the time to do something that was truly important if he or she got rid of the unnecessary things in his life. As we discussed in the section on mistake number seven, trying to do too much, we ritualize the unnecessary and it becomes routine. For instance, do you really need to towel-dry, rather than air-dry, your dishes? To keep a hundred knick-knacks that you then have to dust? To belong to a dozen organizations even though some of their meetings are boring and useless? To subscribe to magazines whose main purposes are to advertise and to spread gossip? To engage in extended pointless phone conversations? Breaking wasteful habits, then, is one of the first steps you need to take to make time for what you really want to do.

I'm afraid I won't be able to do it.

People fear that failure will make them appear ridiculous and irresponsible, and that keeps them from setting challenging goals. They say to themselves, "I would try it, but I'm afraid of failure. If I fail, my husband [or wife, friend, or whatever] will think less of me." If we could just get more unconditional support from our family and friends, it would be wonderful, but to be realistic, that doesn't always happen, and we can't wait for it to.

My way of responding to people who say they're afraid is to say to them, "You're afraid of what?"

"I'm afraid of failing," they respond.

"What's the worst thing that could happen to you if you do fail?" I say. "I'm still going to like you. In fact, I respect people who try and fail, as opposed to not trying at all. And you're going to learn something by trying. Take a look at the Fortune 500 corporations this year, last year, and the year before. See how many of them failed, made adjustments and changes as a result of their failures, and today are healthier because of it. What if the CEO's, the board, the stockholders, and the employees didn't want to acknowledge that they'd failed? They would have lost even more. So they all learned lessons and came out ahead."

Consider the person who looks in the mirror and says, "My God, look how out of shape I am; I feel terrible." But rather than change, the person says, "I'll disguise it by wearing baggy clothes. And I'm going to stay away from places where people might see how out of shape I am." Compare that to the person who says, "I don't like what I see, but it's where I'm at. I'm going to start here. I'll begin by saying this is the worst that it is, and then every single day, I'm going to get better." In other words, if you look at the bad part of your life as being the beginning, then every step is a move toward growth. You're improving with every effort. Every effort makes you stronger and brings you up.

That mitigates the fear of failing. It works because it gives people confidence that they're not being judged based upon their perfection level, but upon their effort and upon whether they're moving in the right direction. You might say to yourself, "How would I rate myself today on effort, using a score of one to 100? Did I achieve any of my short-term goals?" Breaking a big goal down into smaller ones is always a smart strategy.

And when someone else starts to make excuses, starts to go back to their old patterns, you can be there as a supportive influence. You know what it's like not to try. You know how depressing it can feel. An altogether different experience happens when you're consistent in your effort. I've never met anyone who truly failed as long as they were learning through the process. Even an athlete who comes in dead last is not a loser. After all, that person learned more by completing the race than the millions of people who didn't race at all. I, therefore, never have anything but praise for people who make an honest effort. It is the effort that is paramount. Goal-reaching is secondary.

If it can't be done perfectly, then it shouldn't be done at all.

This excuse makes no sense when you think about it, since there is no true perfection, and only an ideal. And note: One of the most dangerous people to be around is the perfectionist. He or she makes sure everyone notices how hard he's worked, how much he's tried, and how critical he is of himself. The perfectionist overloads everyone with responsibility, including himself. He's the last to work at night and the first to begin in the morning. Perfectionists love the idea of extra responsibility on their shoulders because then everyone will admire them.

The reality is that John is addicted to approval. So he takes on responsibilities to displace everything else in his life that he's hiding from—his insecurity, his fear that he's not enough, his need to be self-critical and hypercritical of others. The result is that John doesn't have a life beyond his responsibilities.

DO YOU MAKE EXCUSES FOR STAYING PUT WHEN IT'S TIME TO MOVE?

I mean this literally here. Perhaps you've outgrown your personal space. You may have a new perception of what you would like it to be like. What can you do to overcome obstacles that get in the way of your visions? Many people use excuses to keep from making changes. But you don't have to live in unsatisfactory surroundings; there are always creative solutions.

A friend of mine who was living in the New York suburbs wanted to move to Manhattan to be closer to work. The person looked all over the upper west side and upper east side, but to no avail. The high cost of tiny rat-trap apartments was frustrating. Then I suggested going to Manhattan's warehouse district, getting an old loft, and fixing it up. Several months later, my friend found such a space, and it was fantastic, with 2500 square feet for all of $700 a month. It took some work to sand and paint the floors, but after everything was done, the space looked magnificent. Had these quarters been in a more fashionable area, they would have cost around $6000 a month!

By choosing to look in a low-demand area, rather than making excuses for not moving at all or paying an outrageous rent, this person found the ideal personal space. All it took was a little creative thinking, and, yes, some work.

WHAT ARE THE RESULTS OF
SELFISHNESS AND GOSSIP?

Let's say you have an exciting idea that you feel strongly about. Ideally, someone in your life supports you, which helps you turn your idea into a reality. But if no one is there to support you, you may need to explore why. Perhaps you have been insensitive and uncaring, even reprehensible, toward others. Then it's easy to see why people could not care less about your success. If you've been conceited and selfish, you have not earned their interest. If you want people to be interested in you, you need to show an interest in them. If you want people to care for you, you must care for them.

Our society has grown selfish. Many of us have become too self-absorbed to care about anyone but ourselves. That's the reason we frequently don't get support when we need it. It's not because we don't have good ideas. It's because we haven't given our unconditional support to others.

Unconditional is the key. Many baby boomers, particularly the more affluent ones, have not done a whole lot for anyone that wasn't highly conditional. Now they want to evolve. They think it's that easy: "Oh, I'm enlightened now," they say. "I'm evolved." To this I would reply, "Look at all the damage you've done. Are you going to go back and undo the damage? You've got to undo what you've done if you want to go forward. You can't just walk away from all the things you've left, assuming they don't matter. They may not matter now to you, but what about the people they do matter to?"

This year, I ended a friendship with a man who betrayed my confidences. I'm a very private person. If I were dating someone, you would never know it because I don't talk about it. It's no one's business. Being in the public eye, I want to avoid the criticism and nastiness that inevitably comes from people who are jealous. Anyway, one of my friends who was having a rough time in his life betrayed my confidences and made some untrue and negative comments that I found out about. When I confronted him about what I had heard, he lied. I told him, "There are two things wrong with this. First, you lied, and second, you betrayed a confidence. I don't want anything more to do with you."

He became angry at the rejection. Then some weeks later this person came to me and said, "I realize that what I did was wrong. I was really wrong. I shouldn't have done that, but, quite frankly, my life wasn't working, and I felt jealous. Every time I saw the good things that were happening to you, I thought, 'Why in the world do good things happen to Gary? What's he got that I don't have? My life's going down the tubes, and his isn't.' I was jealous of you, so I said a lot of things I shouldn't have said. But I understand all of that now. Let's let bygones be bygones, and resume our friendship."

When I was a child I could fight with someone—sometimes over the stupidest thing—and always become friends again. Fifteen minutes after a fight, I could be having lunch with my opponent. We'd forget what had happened. It wasn't important. But that was a physical fight, over simpler things, and it was different. In this situation, what I said was, "Think of every person who you lied to about me who then passed it on to someone else, who then passed it on to someone else. If you've told ten people something negative about me, I can assure you that five to six hundred people now think something negative about me that's untrue. Can you undo all that? Can you call up every person and say, 'I lied. I was jealous. I was envious. My life was a mess, and I turned around and hurt my friend'? If you can undo all the damage you've done, then you can come back and talk to me about being friends. Until then, don't call me."

Of course this person doesn't want to make a single call to rectify what he's done, because suddenly his ego would be on the line. He'd have to show humility. I wouldn't allow that individual back in my life again. You see, I have a standard: I don't allow people to abuse me and then come back into my life.

I've noticed over the years that people are consistent. You will never find someone who betrays one person who wouldn't betray anybody. You'll never find a person who hates blacks or Jews who doesn't hate everybody. And never ever trust a gossip. If he talks about someone else to you, you can be sure that he's doing the same to you behind your back. When you're talking about someone behind his or her back, you're dishonoring that person. Now, if you talk to someone's face, at least that person knows what you feel. The person has a chance to accept or reject it. At least you've been honest. But when you're talking behind someone's back, that's dishonest. It lacks courage. Remember, gossip is not about the person being talked about. Gossip is about the people who need to perpetuate it. The lesson, then, is for us. It's about having the spiritual and emotional strength to maintain our sense of confidence and self no matter who likes or dislikes us for whatever reason. You can't go around and make the world like you, but you certainly don't need to engage in any behavior that would denigrate anyone else.

I once tried a social experiment. During a weekend on spirituality and stress management at my farm, I wanted to prove to a psychologist that you could take an average group of nice people and make them into nasty, bitter, angry people in an hour or two. So the first night I gave a lecture that got people focusing on negatives. Afterwards, two friends who were there started spreading rumors about other people. Before the evening was up, the place was teeming with rage. Yet, not a single person tried to stop what was happening. No one chose to extricate himself and say, "This is not right."

At midnight, I called everyone together for another workshop to explain what the first workshop had been about. I said, "Isn't it interesting how easy it was to draw you into a negative action? We created a monster out of two people here, and all of you participated in their gossip—all of you." I said, "Could you imagine what you would do in your day-to-day lives?" It was a harsh reality for these people. "You tricked us," they said.

"Yes, I tricked you. It was to prove a point. I may have tricked you, but I didn't put those negative thoughts in your mind. You did. You manifested the bitterness. You accused other people. You verbally beat them up. All I did was feed your imagination, and you went for it. Now think of every politician who puts someone else down in order to get elected. Think of the media that criticize, isolate, and separate in order to control people and enhance their interests. Think of the extreme right-wingers. Think of all the others who pit one group against another. People buy into it."

What if you were a person who had the courage to say, "Hold on a second. I don't buy any of this negativity. Do not dishonor me with negativity. I will not accept it." The bad feeling would stop with you. The emotional passions around you could be aflame, but you would remain cool. That's why you should never be a part of the negative consensus.

A rule of life is this: If it wouldn't feel good being on the other end of what you're sharing, don't share it. Simply say, "Don't share it with me." No one I know would ever tell me something that's negative about others. They know I wouldn't hear it. They know I'd say, "If you've got a problem with someone, go to him or her with it. And if you don't have the courage, then the problem's not with the other person. It's with you."

WHERE DOES CONDITIONED BEHAVIOR ORIGINATE?

Much of our behavior originates in our youth. Children are innocent and honest until they're conditioned by expectations and by punishment and reward. Love and privileges are withheld unless children are seen as becoming exactly what the adults they're depending upon expect them to be. At first, their conformity helps them survive. They're little, vulnerable people who need food, shelter, and love from adults. Their dependency is healthy and natural. When an adult does not honor the child with unconditional love and kindness, the child will immediately adapt to whatever he or she is being told is necessary.

The child grows into an adult, and now his conditioned behaviors are no longer necessary. But he cannot break the patterns. He's not even aware of his behaviors any more, as they have become a natural part of his way of emoting and communicating.

You break patterns of unwanted behavior by identifying the behavior you want to eliminate. You can begin to do this by consistently writing in a journal. Look at how and why you used these behaviors in the past. You may see that, at first, you engaged in certain behaviors simply in order to survive. But now that you're an adult, they've become counterproductive. That is to say, they're in conflict with your own best interests.

Continue the unwanted behavior patterns, and you will continue the conflicts. Break the patterns, and you will break the conflicts. Every time you eat ice cream or pizza when you are anxious or lonely, for instance, you're continuing the process that allows for body toxicity. You are continuing to accept the pattern of food equating to comfort. Change that. Do something else. When you feel unhappy or uncomfortable, call someone to talk about it. Find a means of creative expression—writing, dancing, painting—that transforms your dissatisfaction into a feeling of joy and peace. You'd be amazed at how well that works. Take up meditation and yoga, and learn breathing techniques that overcome stress instantaneously. Join a group that offers support to help you get through your addictions. By taking these kinds of positive steps, you'll be developing new, healthy behavior patterns. And that's a much better alternative to simply making excuses for why you're stuck with the old, unhealthy ones.

Empower Yourself

WHAT IS BLISS? If you are like most Westerners, it is an abstract concept that has little to do with the realities of everyday life. Easterners would have a better understanding of bliss because it is an acceptable state of being in their culture.

Think about what is keeping you from becoming blissful. Perhaps it's all about undoing. I mean, consider how becoming healthy is not about taking a lot of supplements, but rather about eliminating toxins; i.e., if you refrain from smoking, alcohol, sugar, processed foods, meat, and fluoridated water you're bound to be more sound than someone with unhealthy habits who takes supplements to compensate. Starting from that concept I took a look at bliss and asked some questions: Why isn't bliss a natural state? Could it be that we are carrying around toxic ideas that prevent us from achieving it? And could we empower ourselves to achieve bliss by letting go of those ideas?

Here's what I came up with.

WE SUFFER FROM THE EMPTINESS OF NOT CONNECTING WITH OUR REAL SELVES BECAUSE WE'VE BEEN FAITHFUL TO THE IDEA OF PERMANENCE.

We all can agree that life is impermanent. Yet, that's not what we are taught. Our problems begin when we are children and no one discusses death. Children may lose a pet—their turtle, dog, or cat—or a grandparent may die, and no one discusses what this means. They know they've lost someone dear to them, but they're not connecting to what's really happened. There's sorrow, but soon afterwards they become reabsorbed into the daily routines of life.

The older we get, the more that issue resonates in our mind. We know we will die. But we choose not to think about it. Even people close to death will have a difficult time talking about it with their loved ones. We don't want it to happen, and we fear the inevitable, so we won't talk about it.

Since we find this issue difficult to deal with, we live each day as if we have an unlimited amount of time. We strive for permanence, desiring a permanent home, a permanent relationship, a permanent job. Indeed, up until the 1970s, men, at least, assumed that they would have the same job for life. Any man who changed jobs was considered irresponsible. People would ask, "What's wrong with him?" There's a scene in Tennessee Williams's *The Glass Menagerie*, set in the 1940s, that highlights this state of mind. The mother and son have an intense conflict over the son's dissatisfaction with factory work. The son perceives his dead-end job as worthless, while the mother thinks her son shiftless and irresponsible. This is how life was.

In recent times, people are confronted with the idea of impermanence. Millions of Americans have lost jobs because of downsizing. If you are one of those people you begin to think, "Wait a second. I gave you everything. Why am I not staying in this job forever?"

The reality is we know in our hearts that nothing will ever remain the same. We know that our world will change, and that it must. The deepest pool will stagnate if there is no movement. And we know that our muscles will atrophy unless we move them. We know that brain cells will die if we fail to think and challenge them. Yet the last thing that most people want, once they're comfortable in what they're doing, is discomfort, and change is uncomfortable. That's why so many people know they could do better—know they should change—but won't. It's too uncomfortable.

One of the problems with the paradigm of permanence is that you know in your heart it's not true. But you've already given your loyalty to that belief. Hence, you are living a conflicted existence, and that creates emptiness. On the other hand, when you live in the moment, and you accept the moment as not being permanent, then you don't feel betrayed.

ARE YOU HEMMED IN BY THE "CIRCLE OF THE KNOWN?"

For years I have tried to communicate with physicians about what I've learned from my experiences helping people. Unfortunately, some physicians are not open to listening to new ideas, even if they are based on repeated observation of cause-and-effect relationships. And unfortunately, most people take physicians' pronouncements as immutable law, because doctors are part of the circle of the known.

For instance, if your physician said to you that your arthritis had nothing to do with diet, you would probably believe it. Fair enough. But if you came to me, and I helped you to change your diet, and your arthritis went away, you would probably *still* believe your doctor. Why? For years, that was something I could never figure out. Why would you deny your own reality? Because that's what often happened—again and again. Someone would come to me, I'd give him advice, he would take it, and he'd see a change. He'd go back to his doctor and say, "Doc, I no longer have arthritis. I gave up dairy, wheat, meat, and sugar. I started taking glucosamine sulfate, vitamin C, silica, and chondroitin sulfate. I feel great." The doctor would respond, "It's nonsense. It's quackery." The person would then side with the doctor and follow his advice. The arthritis would return.

Occasionally, I'll meet these people and say, "How are you doing?" "Oh, I've still got the arthritis." I'd question, "Weren't you over your arthritis?" "I was, but it came back." "How did that happen?" "I don't know." "Did you stay on your diet?" "My doctor says it's quackery."

I'd wonder what was missing. And what had been missing when I sent out 100,000 mailings to physicians listing thousands of peer-reviewed journal articles showing the healing benefits of nutrients, and received only 300 responses back? Doctors *say* show us by our gold standard, prove to us that you have information derived from quality research done at a reputable school, such as Harvard, and published in a peer-reviewed medical journal. Show us randomized, double-blind, controlled studies. If the information is proven, we'll take it.

But they weren't taking any of it, and I realized, here's where the circle of the known comes into play. If the information hasn't come out of the circle of the known, if it hasn't emanated from the authority figures who are artificially removed from the average person by the assumption of power, then it's ignored. There's a clear distinction between those who are in a position of authority and everyone else. The latter always have to go to those higher up for answers. So in matters of faith, for example, you have to go to a priest, rabbi, or minister. They have to be the intermediaries. You can't go directly inside yourself because you wouldn't know how to believe, or what to believe. We are taught not to turn to our own hearts and minds for answers. And, in general, we obey.

As long as you're obedient, you're rewarded with acceptance. If you challenge, you're first warned, then chastised, and then threatened, excluded, and finally punished. It happens in a sequential order. It happens to every single U.S. doctor who has come forward to say, "If the point is to help my patient, and I've done everything that my education said I should do, and my patient's not getting better, then my education is what's at fault, and the protocols I'm supposed to follow from that education are not helping the patient. If the object is to help my patient, I must, with all due respect, go outside the circle of the known, to a circle of the unknown, and find something else I can bring back in." That's not tolerated. In fact, so great is the fear of contaminating the ideology, the power, and the control, that you can be excluded—thrown out of medicine—if you go outside the circle of the known. At one time, if you communicated with a chiropractor, you could lose your license. The AMA was that tough.

When you have generation after generation growing up and learning the same ritual, then the ritual is almost congenital. It's as if it's bred into you. You don't even question it anymore. You accept that, "This is my position in society. I'm better than you because I'm this or I'm that. Therefore, you must always defer to me." Look at movie stars. Nothing they do is real. It's all play; it's all image. And yet, if you're in line at a restaurant, they'll always get ahead of you. If you're waiting for a movie, they'll go in front of you.

We should ask why. "What did you do to have the right to go ahead of me?" The answer, of course, is nothing. Since we are all equal as human beings, we should all have enough respect to wait our turn. Not the power people, though. Power people assume that they are better because they are different. And what makes them different? Illusion. One aspect of being an arbiter of the circle of the known is that you never want to get too close to the people you are advising. If you do they'll see how impermanent and how common you really are. You're not really that much different than they are, but you've got to give them the impression that you are.

I once counseled a very famous actor, one of the most famous in the world. I was helping him to dry out and detoxify. This was about the tenth time he had gone off the wagon. Anyway, I remember asking him, "Why do you live in Hollywood? I have a friend who lives there, a producer. When I visit, all the people I meet at his house are superficial."

340

He didn't dispute that observation, but this is how he explained why he lived in Hollywood. "If I lived in the average neighborhood, where I'd be just as happy, people would see me walking down the street. They would talk with me, listen to me, and think, 'You're no different than I am. Then why are you so rich? Why are you so famous?' Look Gary; look at what I do each day. I do the same thing everybody else does until I have to go to work. Then they see me up on a screen. I don't put the words in my mouth. The screenwriter does. I just act them out. In all other areas, I'm just like everyone else." And that's the way it is with him. He was at least honest about it.

Now here's what's interesting. Famous people need you to recognize them, but they don't want to associate with you. They don't like you, but they need you. Without you they don't exist because power and success are illusions; Someone needs to give them to you.

You also need someone to give you authority. And once you have authority you have power because power always accompanies authority. The average person has power but has never used it. The average person says, "If I've got cancer the only thing I can do is ask the doctor in the group." I might respond, "You know, there are many ways of dealing with cancer." The average person will say, "They told me I had to have my breast removed if I had the gene that causes cancer," or "I'm supposed to start chemotherapy." And I'll say, "But wait, are you aware that outside of that are known ways of preventing and treating breast cancer alternatively? There are a lot of people who have done it." And the average person will say, "I can't do that, because I won't belong." Belonging is the single greatest need of the average person. We abhor the discomfort of being cast away.

Physicians and scientists, just like the rest of us, want to belong too. Unfortunately there's only a certain amount of tolerance that will be allowed before the doctor who uses an alternative therapy is punished and excluded, no matter what his or her former position.

In our society, we managed to destroy the greatest scientist of this century. The Louis Pasteur of this century was a man named Andrew Ivy. He was the dean of academic affairs at the University of Illinois. He was a great scientist who had 2000 citations in the scientific literature. But he supported an alternative cancer therapy, which, although it worked, was competition for the status quo. It was destroyed, and he was destroyed. People didn't come to his defense. People inside the circle of the known won't; once you're attacked, everybody backs off.

WHAT KIND OF DECISIONS DO YOU FIND DIFFICULT?

Some examples are money decisions, decisions about what to buy, how much to spend, and how much to save, and decisions about sex and relationships. There are consequences to everything we do and don't do. Our decisions are almost always directly associated with how we're going to be perceived by those around us. That's why many people have an incessant need to confess everything to everybody.

There's a basic rule in life: There are no secrets. Never tell anyone anything that you don't want everyone else to know, because no one's going to keep a confidence. Yet, people say, "You can trust me." Wrong. People are not trustworthy. Nor are they confident—that's why we keep asking other people if what we've done is right. Then when we do something wrong, we try to get others to agree that it really wasn't our fault, or that it's okay. It's interesting that you can do something wrong within the known and get away with it. Do it outside of the known, though, and they don't have any sympathy or compassion for you. "Oh, you're way out there. You made your choice; now suffer with it." There's very little understanding.

It's also interesting how no one in alternative movements—the nutrition movement, the women's movement, or the environmental movement, for example—has ever really been given a forum that would allow them to change the policy and direction inside the circle of the known. That's why when I come up with something that I consider important, and I investigate it, write about it, broadcast it, and share it, nothing happens. For years, it was frustrating. Then I realized that that was also true for Ralph Nader and other alternative thinkers. Nothing happens. And when one of the alternative people runs for president, even though they're intellectually, philosophically, practically, and politically so much wiser than the mainstream candidates—the Tweedle Dums and Tweedle Dees who have no integrity—they haven't sold out to the lobbyists, and so they get nowhere.

We all know that whoever's got the most money buys himself an office. But the masses never use their power to change that. They're like Pavlovian dogs, understanding only punishment and reward. Comfort is more important as a reward than the pain of truth. So universal truths and the capacity to change will never be factors for the mainstream group. Outside, I and others are looking in and saying, "Wake up, wake up! Look at what they're doing in the name of democracy. There's tyranny and fascism. Wake up! Your rights are at stake."

People are just walking around like zombies. But then one day you get let into the circle of the known by accident. In my case the accident was getting hooked up with PBS. They didn't think anything of it. "Oh, he's just going to talk about nutrition," they said. Suddenly PBS had the biggest turnout in their history. It wasn't the policy-makers who called in. It was the masses who had been given no direction on what they knew was right because their doctors and scientists weren't going to say, "Do this, do that, exclude this, exclude that." They'd never done it. They never would; there are too many controls. But I could do it because I had been invited into the circle of the known, and given a position of authority. Suddenly thousands of people called in and responded. It was a revolution right under the radar screen.

Now it's easier to get the people who have made those changes to make more changes. Once you start giving people permission to make changes—e.g., "You don't have to eat meat, and you don't have to eat white bread, and you don't have to eat sugar"—they start feeling better, and they're going to trust that. Now, if they heard me say I recommend those changes on WBAI, they wouldn't do anything about it. But when they hear me say it on PBS, they will. That's because I've been invited into the circle of the known.

DO YOU DOWNPLAY WHAT YOU ARE ABLE TO OFFER?

Never make apologies for what you can offer. When offering anything that we have, it is not the size of the offering that's important. It's the intention. So often in life, individuals will not contribute what they could, because they think, "I don't have anything of worth. Those other people could give more. They're wiser and richer. What do I have in comparison? I'm just a nobody." This is not true. Yes, there are people who, when they give something, can give big gifts, and everybody else then says, "Well, if they've given, why should we? We can't compare ourselves to them."

Take an international perspective. Go to any place in Japan, India, or Indonesia, where there are lots of poor peasants, and every time you go past a Buddhist shrine you'll see poor people giving things that were of value to them. They'll give food when they are hungry, so they can be more Buddha-like. The size of the gift is not as significant as the intention.

IF YOU WERE PRESENTED WITH A UNIQUE OPPORTUNITY, WOULD YOU BE PREPARED TO TAKE ADVANTAGE OF IT?

Have you had times when opportunity presented itself to you, but you weren't prepared to accept it, so you let it go?

You can't change the past, but you can prepare yourself to accept opportunities that may arise in the future. You can even create your own opportunities. The more prepared and open you are, the more things will come your way. Conversely, the fears you harbor will prevent you from engaging in opportunity. Then, you will sit on the sidelines of life and become the passive spectator who looks at others who engage in life. You will be filled with regret and longing.

To prevent that, we must prepare ourselves emotionally, spiritually, physically, intellectually, and creatively. We must take every part of our life that needs to be sharpened and start the sharpening process. We need to focus on what we want and unclutter our lives. Then when opportunity's there, we'll be ready to go and meet it, embrace it, engage it. We'll even be ready to create it.

IF YOU'RE BORED, IS IT BECAUSE SOMETHING IS BORING, OR IS IT YOU?

Most people are looking for someone to entertain them. If someone isn't paying attention to them in meaningless conversation, they get bored. But my view is that you should never be bored—not if you're engaged with life.

Down on my ranch I have a lemur. This lemur plays with everything. It never gets bored. It's always doing something. Then you look at the turtle, and the turtle looks a little bored. The turtle doesn't do a whole lot, but the active little animals like the lemur are always looking for something to do. The moment you go near the lemur, it will jump on you and go through your hair. It will look in your ears and every place it can. It's got to explore everything because it's fun to do so. The lemur is excited by life. It doesn't need mindless gossip, or TV, or movies, or dining out instead of cooking in, because it's not in a rut.

Are you more like the lemur or the turtle? Actually, the latter species has its good points too—its cautious, observant nature, its tortoise-like ability to win the race in the long run—but if you are like the turtle and finding it a little boring, don't despair. Unlike the real animal, you're not trapped in your turtledom. Any day, you can wake up and decide to be lemur-like. Try it! Think of ways you can figuratively jump through the trees. Think of new things you can explore, and new tempos you can use as you move through a day.

How much of our time do we use trying to change others versus doing something for ourselves?

Do you ever try to change other people? What right do you have to do that? None. The energy that you put into another person would be better spent on yourself. If someone asks you for help, you may have a moral obligation to help that person. But more often than not, people are not asking for your help. You're insisting that they take it. You have no right to insist. Take the energy that you're giving out, and bring it back to yourself. You have to be responsible for you.

If moments are all that we possess, how do we select what to do with the moment?

In any moment, we can focus on what's important, or we can distract ourselves with the unimportant. How much of your time is spent on the unimportant? If you are like most people, the answer is, most of it.

Throughout this book, we've talked about the virtues of living *right now*. Living in the moment allows us to immortalize the pleasure of another's company and the enduring emotions and energy that are being shared. These are brief interludes, and they must be enjoyed while they are happening. No two moments are ever the same. Soon we will miss the moment we've shared. We may try to recreate a moment, but we can't. So when we think, "That was a great time I had. I want to recreate the embrace, the kiss, the feel of the air, the sunset," we cannot. No special moment can ever be recreated, ever. So don't try.

By allowing yourself to be open to the moment, you allow another one to take its place, and the next moment could be equally as special as the last. At some point in life, when you're quiet, you'll realize that moments are not meant to be recaptured, but to be replaced. The ideal mode of living is to be open and vulnerable and prepared for the next moment. What we can do is enjoy something—something that touches us, something that resonates with our essential self, something that manifests in bliss—and we can say, "This is good." It is, but it goes.

In a sense, though, it is with you permanently: the energy you shared and the memory of that energy will be with you for eternity. The key is not to stay focused on trying to replay it; in doing so you close yourself off to engaging in another equally unique and wonderful experience. You must be prepared for the next experience, and to do so you must surrender the moment you're in. In short, you don't want to be living in the past—not in your past pain, nor suffering, nor joy, nor bliss. You want to be living in your present. The present allows you to have another blissful moment, or another painful moment, but at least another moment, and that too will pass. Everything, including time, is in motion.

I believe the ideal is to be living in motion. You're not stagnant. You're not fixed. You're not seeking other people's approval. You're not fearing failure. You're not distracting yourself with nonessential tasks or too many goals. Everything is in balance, and when that happens, the moment resonates and you feel it. You wake up ready for it.

Most people are never ready for their life. Maybe early on they are led to believe that they can be anything, feel anything, or do anything. But after high school or college graduation they hear, "Oh, that was just because you were a kid. Now get serious, because now you've got to get your membership in the circle of the known." Then you take a place in the hierarchical structure, and that's where you stay for life.

You've got to get out of that. You've got to break the structure, break the need to be in that structure to create the autonomous self. Of course when we have that kind of freedom, we understand our emotions and attitudes will cause people to notice us. The world always notices a happy person. There are a lot of sad people, depressed people, and melancholy people. There are so many that we no longer even notice them. But happy people are noticed. Positive people are noticed. People engaged in life, who are in fact the architects of their own life, are noticed, because their energy is so different.

Are you one of those people? You can be if you simply use the freedom that is already yours.

Don't Be Afraid to Create Who You Really Are

THINK ABOUT THE way you define who you are. Do you define your reality by what you do and have? For instance, do you define yourself by your job, your home, your children, your relationship with a loved one, or your physical appearance? Most people in our society have a need to keep up a certain image. In fact, for a lot of people, that's the only way they know who they are.

In Manhattan, a lot of people work after regular working hours. The question is why. What have they not achieved in a normal workday that keeps them working overtime? And what are they missing from the rest of their life? They must be missing out on something essential because they've made work so important. They've made what they do who they are. Think of the people you read about in newspapers and magazines who want you to know that what they do and look like deserves your attention. Their whole idea of who they are comes from that image. But what happens when they can no longer achieve the image? You can be certain that most of these people become depressed and frustrated. When something that you need to do to feel good about yourself no longer works, you no longer feel good about yourself.

We are an achievement-oriented society. In the past thirty years, there have been over five million baby boomer millionaires. There are almost a million new baby boomer millionaires right now. Their whole emphasis is on "the more I have, the more I own, the more I accomplish, the more I achieve, the more people will respect me." We add up how many accomplishments we have, and whoever has the most is the person we believe should be deferred to as someone of responsibility. The person who starts work early, leaves late, always gets his or her work done before everyone else does, and does exemplary work, is considered the most responsible. This is the person who is always willing to go out of his or her way to help you, not because he's truly humanitarian but because he knows he's going to get some respect from you. The moment you respond, "Bob, you're the best," or "Jane, that was terrific," you are contributing to that person's good feeling about who he is. Somebody likes him. But it's for something he's done, not for who he is. That's what happens when we are externally driven.

Why not have a philosophy of being that lets you just be? Such a philosophy says that through being—being present, being alive, being aware of who I am—I'm enough. I don't have to do anything for anyone to appreciate the uniqueness of my existence. Such is the philosophy of the East, where people follow thousands of years of tradition developing themselves internally rather than focusing on the external. So if you don't accomplish much in a day you're no less of a person as long as you honor inner, spiritual principles. Generally, those inner principles are spiritually connected. Spirit is complete. Hence, the being that gains a sense of identity from internal processes feels more whole.

Unfortunately, this philosophy does not fare well in our society. We look critically at internally motivated people and think, "I'm working two shifts to make ends meet; why aren't you?" "It's two o'clock in the afternoon; why are you meditating on life?" "Why are you wasting your time at retreats? What are you searching for?" If there is no material gain in sight, we don't understand and have little tolerance for such deviations from the norm.

In truth, we can have a great standard of living and yet be unfulfilled if we are not connected to who we are. It's not that having a great standard of living is wrong. The problem stems from giving up some important part of yourself to live life the way you think you should. You may earn a lot of money, but the price you pay may be so high as to not be worth it.

It's better to build on what you love. My standard of living comes from the joy and passion I get from my work. Nothing I do takes away from who I am. I don't have to own anything to feel complete. That's the difference between focusing on an internal process of being and concentrating on external achievements. One connects you to your true self; the other takes you away from that.

Our impermanence scares us. We want everything good to last, and so we delude ourselves into believing that we are fixed in time, like a cherished photograph. When I was growing up in a small town in West Virginia, virtually everyone I knew believed in keeping life the same. You were born and buried in the community. You worked there, and you married someone from the area. Life was rather predictable, as no one wanted change. Anyone who relocated from the outside was always suspect; it took years to gain people's confidence.

A sense of security accompanies permanency, but there's also a need for identification with others who are like you. That can breed fear of strangers. Frequently, a point of identity is nationalism, something that excludes all other ideologies, and disallows change.

Consider the cancer specialist who is trained to diagnose and treat in specific ways and always recommends the same treatments, regardless of the individual involved. The specialist makes the problem fit into his or her capacity for diagnosis and treatment with the tools that he or she was given. So that doctor will advise chemotherapy, surgery, or radiation, but never hyperbaric oxygen, vitamin C drips, herbs, or colonics, because those are not a part of the repertoire taught in school. And as valid as these other therapies might be, the doctor, if he or she has even heard of them, has no interest in recommending them. In the doctor's mind, they are useless, and anyone promoting such ideas is a charlatan. We have to look very carefully at our beliefs, inspecting where they come from, and questioning our need for permanence.

On a larger scale, we have belief systems whose roots go back thousands of years. These ideas keep nations stagnant and continually at war with neighboring countries or factions within a population. How realistic is it to expect all that to change? You often get the sense that the people involved simply want a sense of having things remain as they always were, regardless of the costs of violence. When permanency is your focus, reason is lost.

Think of the things in life that you want to be the same forever. You want your children to stay young forever. You want your puppies and kittens to remain cute and cuddly. When we hold on to those ideas that have nothing to do with the natural order of things, we start to feel anxious, even desperate. Maybe we've missed our moment to do or be something.

Much anxiety arises from our anger about what we lose in the moment, because our energy is generally focused somewhere else. Usually, we become preoccupied with future gains and lose sight of the moment. We're working toward something and the present moment appears not to exist. If you're always looking forward, how can you be aware of where you actually are? One day the people who are working late will come home and realize that their kids are no longer three years old, but ten. They're going to think, boy, doesn't time fly? But it only seems that way when you don't pay attention to the present. Time is the same for everyone.

Life passes in the blink of an eye. One day you're at the Super Bowl; the next day it's over and gone. I've been in auditoriums speaking to 5000 people. The energy is intense and wonderful. I'm looking in people's eyes and making a connection. I'm sharing a common energy and communicating at a level that everybody understands. Twenty-five minutes later, the lecture is over, and everyone has left. I sit alone in my hotel room, and I think, "I had the moment."

All we have are moments, nothing else. Most people want more than that. They want to recapture memorable moments. But we can't. According to one Greek philosopher, you can never step twice into the same river. That's because no two seconds in a river's history are ever the same. It may take the same course, but every drop of flowing water is different. No two kisses are the same. No two meals are exactly the same, even if you follow the same recipe. Everything is unalike. We need to appreciate that every moment of every day is different.

We have to understand the consequence of keeping our view fixed. Assuming that beliefs are permanent will limit our growth. Surrender that; allow in the anxiety and crisis that follows, and your life will flow. If you want to grow, you have to surrender. My parents went to their death without ever having to change anything. That's the reason they died young.

I visited my hometown many years after having left. Everything had changed except for the older people I grew up with. Talking with them I could see their loneliness and frustration as they tried to relate to a world that refuses to stay the same. There's a real fear of doing anything that doesn't honor the old beliefs. It reminds me of when a Japanese person comes to live in America, takes on some of America's cultural input, and then returns home. He is now looked at as being tainted. People look at his hair, his clothes, and his manners, and wonder what happened. They want their countryman to return to the way he was. Although the person might now feel more progressive and happier, none of that matters to them. They have a need to maintain traditional values in order to keep up a false notion of permanency. So change is the enemy.

Besides permanence, another concept people seem to like is compromise. How much time and energy do you put into trying to compromise? Maybe you've been taught that it's a good idea, and compromise *is* necessary in certain situations, up to a point. Then one day we realize that almost everything we do in life is a compromise. We take classes in school that are not relevant to our life. We vote for politicians who lack ethics and morals. We give these people the highest positions of authority, but they do not live up to our ideals. That makes no sense. You wouldn't want a child molester to teach your children, but you don't mind voting someone into office who has committed all kinds of offenses and told all kinds of lies. We don't let that bother us because we figure these are compromises we have to make. After awhile you end up living your life in the gray area. If you don't know any better you think the gray is okay, and you adapt to it. You adapt to everything that happens to you.

However, one day you wake up thinking, "I don't have the ideal relationship; I don't have the ideal family; I don't have the ideal home; I don't have the ideal job; I don't have the ideal body; I don't have the ideal diet; I don't have the ideal environment; I don't have the ideal friends. I don't have anything that's really ideal. I've taken all my ideals and compromised them. I decided to be practical and learned to adapt. If I got fat, I got bigger clothes. If I was an alcoholic, I'd go to AA meetings where I would get up and say, 'I'm an alcoholic, too. Let's smoke four packs of cigarettes, drink sixteen cups of coffee, get angry at the world, but no longer drink.'" These are all different forms of adaptation.

My idea is that we forget adaptation and look instead to transformation. Transformative processes are those that take us from where we are to another level. It all begins with an identification of what we want to transform. We've got to think, "What do I really want? What do I need to do to honor who I am?" That means no more compromises, even if everyone around you is offended by your attitude and actions.

Look at the blacks and whites of life. We all have individual truths. One person's individual truth allows him to lie and steal and betray people. That person has adapted to his circumstances, and lying was part of the adaptive process. This is manifested every day in corporate America. We saw it with the makers of DES. We see it now with Ford and Firestone, and with the manufacturers of Ritalin. In each of these corporations people knew what was right, and they intentionally chose something else, because they were in the pressure cooker of adaptive behavior.

When you're adapting your behavior you're in the murk and mire of life. You're in such a quagmire you don't see anything. It's only in those rare moments when you're disconnected from superficial realities—when you're viewing a sunset, for instance, or when you are watching children play, or petting your dog or cat—that you are spiritually connected. In that moment, you've reached universal truth.

There are two types of truths—universal and subjective. Universal truth honors everyone. Subjective truth, on the other hand, justifies harmful actions. It justifies killing people, or it tells you not to hire someone who is not the "right" age, color, or gender. It keeps people out of our neighborhoods when they are not like us. Subjective truth justified the killing of 900 thousand people in Rwanda. People killed their neighbors, people they had lived with their whole lives. You don't slaughter people when you are attuned to the spiritual. No, you have to disconnect from the spiritual in yourself and in your fellow man first. That's what happens in the gray area. But sometimes we'd rather not look at that.

There is a story about a man who spends his whole life looking for God. One day, he cames upon a stranger who says he knows where God is.

"Really?" says the man.

"Yes, right over there. Knock on that door."

"I've been looking for God my whole life," the man says. "Thank you."

The man goes over and as he begins to knock on the door he thinks, "I'm finally going to meet God. What will I say? I don't know. What do I want? I don't know. What do you say to God? I don't know."

He walks away and thinks, "I'm going to continue the rest of my life looking for God. At least now I know where not to look."

Similarly, we have to go out of our way to know where not to look for knowledge. That's a choice we make.

Every time you do something, you've made a choice not to do its opposite. If I choose to eat the wrong food, for example, then I have also denied the choice that would have kept me at a higher level of health. We have to ask ourselves, why do we keep making choices that do not honor our greater knowledge?

We are an aggressive and violent society. We have a need to control, due to our insecurity over identity. Do you think we would be funding the military industrial complex, the pharmaceutical industrial complex, and the agricultural industrial complex, if people were secure? Do you think we'd have this massive urban sprawl? Do you think we'd have all these skyscrapers if people were secure? We need to show control and dominance because our identity comes from what we control and dominate. This is true too in relationships. One of the reasons relationships break up, or become hurtful, is because people need to dominate. So you end up with a bond that is not supported by a spiritual connection, but rather one based upon the insecurity of the individual. We also pride ourselves on our dominance over nature, although unfortunately we have not looked at the consequences of our actions. Every hamburger we eat requires that fifty-five square feet of rain forest be destroyed. We do not respect the fact that this year we will destroy 1000 species of animals and plants just so we can have room to raise cattle in the former rain forest. So we dominate, but at an enormous cost. We dominate everything. What if we no longer had the need for our own identity to be superior to others?

In your quest to be true to yourself, you need to evaluate your current philosophy and style of living. Here are some questions for you to consider. My thoughts, which follow, may spur further insights of your own.

DO YOU LISTEN TO THE VOICE WITHIN?

If you are living a life that is attuned to your inner voice you are probably happy. Unfortunately, most of us are guided by external values, the ones we adopt from people around us and that often compromise our inner values. Let's say you want peace of mind, but you work in New York City where everything is rush, rush, rush. You work hard; you have too many responsibilities; you don't have time for what's important to you. In short, you're stressed out. Your lifestyle is challenging your inner values, and that creates conflict. You have to make a choice between honoring your inner self and your external values.

Part of our sense of permanency comes from obeying the rules. When we obey the rules we expect to be rewarded. We did what we were supposed to do. We reach fifty, and we start to think, "I'll work for another fifteen years, till age sixty-five. That'll give me another ten years to take it easy in Florida, play golf, relax."

What if we challenged ourselves? What if we said, "This is not how I want to be? I don't want to be like everybody else who is doing that because (a) it's not going to change how I feel inside, and (b) everything I'm doing is really an extension of those beliefs that told me how I should live the first part of my life. It wasn't a great job I did on the first half. And now I'm told that the second half doesn't count. I've done my thing, so I can take it easy, live in a gated community, and watch everyone else shuffle around and complain about their illnesses."

What if you decided not to play by any of the rules anymore? If something does not honor a universal truth, you are not engaging in it. Remember, you cannot do anything until you engage in energy. It's that engagement of energy that creates crisis. Now you wake up, and you transform your crisis. That's the mindset to have: I'm going to transform this crisis.

"Transform" does not mean "adapt." Adaptation means I have to accept it; I cannot change it; I have to just tolerate it. But transformation means it is no longer going to be a crisis. I am not going to have to duplicate it ever again. I will learn something with the gift I was given—i.e., this crisis—and I will never have this crisis again. That's transformation.

Then we are free to renew our earlier ideals, ideals that, at some point in life, we decided to give up. What do we do with ideals that we no longer want? We modify or deny them. Or we say we've grown up. Now we're more mature. Those were kids' ideals, and there's no place for them in the real, adult world.

Take back every ideal that you once had and gave up. You can do it all over again. You can begin new adventures. Seek adventure. Don't wait for one to come knocking on your door. Go find the adventures of life. Unload the unnecessary responsibilities. Start over. You absolutely can. The best thing you can do is say, "I'm starting fresh today. I'm creating a whole new belief, a whole new dynamic concerning what's important. I'm the only one who's going to be in charge of it. I'm not going to compromise anymore."

Of course to do that, you have to trust your choices. Do we trust our choices? And if not, then why not? Fear keeps us from trusting ourselves. We have a fear of the unknown, a fear of failing, a fear of disappointing people. We have a fear of not being able to control the external circumstances of our lives, a fear that someone will judge us for making the wrong choices, because some time in our life we were judged harshly for our choices, and we didn't like how that felt. So we look to other people to make choices for us, although most of the time those people's choices are the wrong ones.

We may then take another route, deciding not to commit ourselves at all if our negative experience has become a permanent part of our psyche, and we can no longer trust anybody. As long as you don't trust anyone you can't be betrayed.

We have to regain a sense of trust in ourselves. As long as our choices come from our spiritual nature they can be trusted, as our spiritual nature is always right. It's just the circumstances you find yourself in that produce the confusion. After all, if you have an ideal, and everyone around you has compromised their ideals, then you're going to be the odd person out. You have to trust that you can feel good about yourself, even if you're the only person thinking or doing the right thing. That's the confidence of trust in yourself. Once you gain self-trust, you'll be willing to trust other people, and you'll select the people who by their actions reflect your own ideals.

Your choices tell me a lot. If you are out of touch with your ideals you may want happiness, but you connect to the wrong things, and you don't find it. You want health, but you eat the wrong foods, and you drink the wrong drinks. You do things piece-meal because you're afraid of the choices you need to make. Hence, you don't have a holistic paradigm by which to live. You do things in bits and pieces because you don't trust the whole. You live a frag-mented life because the whole of life is simply too overwhelming.

One of the reasons we join with others, whether it's in a rela-tionship or some organized belief system, is so that we don't feel alone and disconnected. Yet the very thing we need to do is to dis-connect. It's what I call constructive deconstruction and it allows us to see what we're really made of. You may think that the floor you're walking on is solid. But deconstruct it, and you will find that it's riddled with holes. Step on the floor with some pres-sure—a crisis you are having—and you will go right through. Hence, we fear crisis because that tests the mettle of our beliefs. We don't want to show the world how incomplete we are. So we narrow our focus and take in only the bits and pieces we feel we can control.

HOW DO YOU CREATE YOUR JOY?

Do you keep a joy journal? You should. A joy journal will let you know each day that something you thought or did or shared with someone brought you happiness. It's important that you see how much joy you're allowing into your life—"allowing" being the operative word because more often than not we don't allow joy. Part of our guilt is manifested in our feeling we don't deserve joy. We've been judged to be bad or unworthy in the past, and we let that affect us in the present.

We need to wake up and realize that we can find joy in who we are. We needn't redeem ourselves through excessive responsibilities to another. Your joy should come from just being able to experience or share in the moment something that gives you pleasure.

ARE YOU A SELF-ACTUALIZER?

Do you set high goals for yourself? If you do, how do you go about achieving them? What have you surrendered so you can exceed your limitations? If you're not an achiever, how are you ever going to grow?

You've *got* to be an achiever. Achieve a sense of the inner self rather than emphasizing externals. It's not what's out there that you achieve that matters. It's inside. But to achieve inside, you've got to surrender excessive responsibilities outside. There's nothing wrong with achieving things outside if they're a mirror of your inner harmony. As long as it's harmony that you're creating from, then your inner harmony and joy are allowing external creativity and achievement that are not based upon ego or artificial needs. That's healthy. That's vital.

DO YOU SEE ISSUES CLEARLY?

Do you seek the help of others who understand you in your complexity? If you see issues clearly, then you're not going to need the help of others. If you don't, and you're not willing to go deep enough in yourself, then look for the person who is happy and healthy, and who makes the right choices for him- or herself, and then ask that individual for some guidance.

DO YOU SERVE OTHERS WITH NEEDS GREATER THAN YOURS?

One of the things that connects us with our spiritual self is the realization that we live in a wonderful universe. We've been given the gift of life. To devote our life to helping others who suffer shows that we're honoring the connection of our spirit to others.

You don't have to go to India to do this. You can walk down the streets of any city in America to find people in need. How many times have you walked past people who were homeless and thought that you were so very different from them? You kept walking. You felt uncomfortable. That's exactly when you should stop, go over, say hello, and gain a sense of who that person is. Listen to his or her story. How did he get there? And what can you do in that moment to make his life seem more alive and right? You could buy a hungry person a meal. In the wintertime, you could take the person a sleeping bag (a lot of homeless people are going to sleep outside no matter what).

Do something that makes a difference because if you were in that person's shoes you'd want someone to care for you. We say we're a caring society, but it doesn't show—not when we have 36 million Americans going hungry each night, not when we have 60 million Americans who are barely making ends meet and working themselves to death to do it.

DO YOU MAKE YOUR GOALS HAPPEN?

We all have certain goals, and that's good. We want to get our bodies into shape, live in a healthy environment, etc. But if you make the wrong choice, if you say, for instance, "I'd really like a garden," but you move into an apartment, then you've limited your chance of attaining what you want. If you say that you like peace and quiet but move into a congested area near an airport you're not honoring the connection. If you say you like to be around people who are creative and you hang out with bankers, you are not going to reach your goal. If you say you want to be around people with positive energy yet you select people who are toxic, then you're undermining everything that you say you want. We have to make sure that we create a reality consistent with our goals.

Do you really want what you're striving for?

How many times in life are you out there working hard to get something, only to find that once you get it, it's not what you need? There's a difference between your conditioned wants and your essential needs. You should be clear as to what is essential.

How much time and how many resources do you give to others who shouldn't have them?

The only thing you really have that's your own is your time. When you give your time away, you give your energy away. Sometimes it's to someone who shouldn't have that energy; you ought to keep it for yourself to accomplish what is important to you. Make a list of things that you're taking time to do that you don't actually want to do.

DO YOU REALLY KNOW WHAT YOU LIKE?

How would you know what you like if you haven't opened yourself up to new experiences? You keep yourself limited because you were conditioned to believe you wouldn't like certain experiences. How many men never go to the ballet because they've been conditioned to believe that real men don't hang out watching men jump in tights? How many people stick to the same few types of restaurants when they go out to eat? If I said, "Let's try some Greek food," and you did, you might discover a delicious new cuisine. You might like some of the dishes but not others, or—worst-case scenario—you might end up saying, "Gary, I didn't like it, but at least I tried it." And what's so bad about that? The sad thing is that so many people don't even make the attempt, because of their conditioning. If I went back to my hometown I can promise you that 99 percent of the people that I went to school with will have done nothing new in the past thirty years because they've stuck within the patterns of the known. When you stay within the patterns of the known, how can anything new happen? All you do is reinforce what you've already done, thinking, "If I keep doing what I already know is okay, then I'm not going to be disappointed." But that precludes the adventure of trying things.

When is the last time you met a person from a different race, or even a different gender, and sat with that person without judgment, listening to him or her explain his beliefs and values? The idea is not to be there correcting or challenging that person, but simply to listen. When was the last time you went someplace no one ever figured you'd go? The average American goes to the Grand Canyon and looks at a whole mob of other people looking at the same rock hoping a squirrel jumps. How original. We have to become more adventurous and imaginative.

ARE YOUR GOALS VAGUE?

I believe that if you create a goal, you should be crystal-clear about it. There should be no confusion. Unfortunately, fear often enters the picture. We think, "What if I don't succeed?" "I'm not really good enough." "I'm incomplete." "I'm going to fail." "Others are going to judge me." "I won't be loved." "I can't afford to change." And then we take that goal, and we dilute it down into the compromised area so that it becomes so fuzzy we never complete it. We say, "Well, I'm not really sure. I want to, but it's been three years in my head." And that's where we keep it.

To understand that you can indeed achieve, you first must know who you are. How in the world can you achieve something if you don't know who you are? Honor your own uniqueness, and then watch how clear your goals become, especially if your ideals are attached to them.

DO YOU SEEK CONSTANT DISCOVERY OR JUST OCCASIONAL LIMITED INSIGHT?

It's interesting to see how few people really open themselves up to new things.

"Gary, I did that last year."

"It was interesting, but I don't want to do too much."

"How can I justify it?"

"I'll take it easy, go slow."

"In another year, maybe I'll go to another play."

No, I'm talking about being alive every day. Rediscover something every day. Learn a new word each day. Try a new cuisine. Try your old cuisine made differently. Try speaking with someone in a different way, on a different level. Try connecting with what's essential. Stop useless conversation at the superficial level, and get to the essential part of what someone is saying. Listen to someone with an uncritical mind and see how different that is from when you listen to that person with a judgmental mind. Stop being the critic and instead listen neutrally and ask yourself, what is the person really saying? Then you can see how vague people are in their communications. People hardly ever say what they want. And when they do, it scares us. We're all trying to have two conversations—the politically correct conversation and the real one we're afraid of. Have the real one—and, by the way—you can't have the real one unless you first have it with yourself.

DO YOU SPEND MORE TIME AND ENERGY SEEKING HAPPINESS OR AVOIDING SUFFERING?

Most people try to prevent suffering. Hence, they keep themselves insulated from being exposed to things, figuring that, "As long as I don't do too much, I won't suffer. If I don't take risks, I won't suffer. If I don't venture too far, I won't get lost in my own life's consciousness." So often we simply hold ourselves within the circle of the known. Because we don't want to suffer, everything becomes predictable. But by doing that we suffer in a different way. We accept unquestioningly that which we believe can offer us happiness, and we attack anything that we suspect will bring us unhappiness. And it's all usually based on old beliefs.

As an example, a person has a diet that's causing arthritis. You show that a simple plan of exercise and dietary change can improve the condition. They'll fight you. They'll resist it. Or you might show that eating a certain way causes cancer and eating a different way prevents it. Most people will go on eating the way that causes cancer if that's the way they have been conditioned to believe is right. So it doesn't matter what the laws of nature proclaim is right. It doesn't matter what the big truth is. I find it interesting that even among people coming to our health support groups, rare is the person who does everything he or she needs to do. They usually end up doing just enough so that they don't feel that they are betraying their former beliefs completely. Frequently this is on an unconscious level, because when somebody finally lets it rip and changes everything, you see all kinds of magnificent changes occur.

DOES OUR SEARCH FOR VALUE AND MEANING BEGIN FROM A NEUTRAL PLACE?

If you are coming from a place that's not neutral, if you're already coming from fear or uncertainty or negativity, all you're going to do is take that negativity with you into anything new that you're trying to explore. Hence, we'll have doctors say, "I read the vitamin C study, but it's not conclusive." Those are the same doctors who would have said, several years ago, "I read a hundred studies on smoking and cancer and didn't find anything conclusive." They'll never find anything conclusive that challenges them. But if you gave them no studies—none—about something that's already part of their belief system, they'll say they have all the proof they need.

Look at the McMartins. They were a family that ran a day school in California. They were accused by some of the parents who had heard about a counselor who had manipulated a child into saying she had been sexually assaulted. For seven years the most costly and longest case in California history was driven through the courts. The McMartins couldn't even get bail. The media had them all guilty. In the end they were all innocent. Every charge was false. But there were no apologies. They went bankrupt, their reputation destroyed. That's what happens when you start from not being neutral. You start off already judging something.

You'd better ask yourself, the next time you look at something, where you are starting from. What's your starting point—neutral or biased? If it's biased, it doesn't matter what you do. You're not going to be able to deal with the issue honestly and effectively.

WILL WE GIVE UP OUR FALSE BELIEFS?

How can we possibly grow until we're willing to acknowledge what we no longer should believe? That's when you know that you're really growing—when you can pull back and view all your false truths. Make a list of the things that you have unquestioningly accepted up this point that you can no longer accept. Until you do that you're still attached to them. And how can you attach to something that's more essential if what's nonessential is holding your energy? You can't have two attachments. You can't attach to a universal truth and to a false truth. It just doesn't work.

Sometimes we see truths and they terrify us, so we focus our search where we will never find answers. When people come to me and tell me they're sick and I ask them to change certain things, that terrifies them. They don't want to change. So what do they do? They push the essential into the background and distract themselves. They'll do something over there when what they really have to change is over here. You have to be in my shoes to appreciate how many times this happens.

Imagine your life as a house, with you spending your time in only a few carefully tended rooms. Any guests coming in and out see only what you want them to see. They only see that one little area. And then one day, through some crisis, or through some serendipitous moment of abandonment, you walk out of the house and you turn around and look up and think—whoa—look at that house! Those three rooms are pretty neat. If I take someone into those rooms they're going to think I'm one terrific person. But over here I see four other rooms that are on fire—a slow simmer, but clearly they're on fire. I can say *(a)* I'm just going to live in this part, *(b)* I can go shopping, *(c)* I can take a nap, *(d)* I can cut the grass, or *(e)* I can paint the house. I can do all these things to make it look like I'm doing something. But if I don't put out the fire, what's the point? Likewise, in your life, you can say, I'll go to a workshop to make it seem like I'm doing something good. I'll continue to work on my good parts, and as long as I'm continuing to achieve something with my good parts—making a good personality even better, making a good body better—no one will look at the house that's burning on one side. No one will look at my weaknesses or deficiencies, and I'm sure not going to invite anyone in there because if anyone sees the deep, dark, burning part of my nature, who's going to want to be around me? So we hide.

Imagine if, as painful as it might be, you went into every room and ripped out what was causing the fire. Now your house is wonderful and complete. People can go anywhere in your house and you will not be embarrassed no matter what door or cabinet is opened. You are complete and whole. Why are we so afraid of this?

DO YOU UNDERSTAND
THE IMPORTANCE OF NOW?

Joy or triumph lasts only a moment, so when you have those special experiences you should stay in the moment, be present for it, and allow it to be as complete as it can be. And then when you surrender the moment, and that moment's gone, it will be complete. Its memory will be in your cells. Its energy will be there forever. Then, open yourself up to the next moment. Once you start seeing how much joy you can create by being present, you can stop always looking to the future.

Look at now, right now. All your choices that count for creating joy are in this moment, not in the future. But we're always saying *when* and *if*—*when* I get enough of something, or *if* I get this, then I'll be able to have that good time. No, there are no whens or ifs. Now is it, not when or if. The world is filled with people who went to their graves without ever experiencing the joy that was within their grasp because they just kept thinking it was beyond their grasp, and finally they gave up. They let joy slip away because they weren't present.

We cannot have joy and fear at the same time. We cannot have joy and incompleteness at the same time. But we can choose, believe it or not, what we want to have in the moment. The idea is to embrace change, as opposed to fixed reference points. Stop looking to all the fixed reference points in your life. Stop looking at how you looked when you were younger. Stop looking at the relationship that you liked. Stop looking at the kiss that was wonderful, that food that you ate, or something that happened. When we look to all the fixed reference points, what we're basically saying is, "I'm going to step twice into this water and it will be the same." No, every step you take, every thought you have, every breath you breathe is new. Surrender the need for fixed points, and your life comes into the moment.